Ogier's Youth

Les Enfances Ogier

A THIRTEENTH-CENTURY EPIC BY ADENET LE ROI

Medieval and Renaissance Texts and Studies

Volume 549

Ogier's Youth

Les Enfances Ogier

A THIRTEENTH-CENTURY EPIC BY ADENET LE ROI

Translated by

Anna Moore Morton

Arizona Center
for Medieval &
Renaissance Studies

Tempe, Arizona
2020

Arizona Center
for Medieval &
Renaissance Studies

Published by ACMRS (Arizona Center for Medieval and Renaissance Studies)
Tempe, Arizona

Front Cover
The cover image, a form of which appears in manuscripts A, D, and T, is from the Bibliothèque Nationale de France: Francais 12467 - fol 1 and represents Ogier presented as hostage to Charlemagne. The translator thanks computer professional Allen Tallent for transporting the image to ACMRS.

∞
This book is made to last. It is set in Adobe Caslon Pro,
smyth-sewn and printed on acid-free paper to library specifications.
Printed in the United States of America

To Jerry

Table of Contents

Acknowledgments

The kind assistance of Paul Barrette has been indispensable in preparing this translation in every step from beginning to end. He has read the translation multiple times, making innumerable corrections for accuracy and readability and serving as a source of relevant literary information. Any remaining errors in this text are mine alone.

Introduction

Les Enfances Ogier, or *Ogier's Youth*, was written in Old French about 1275 by an author from Flanders named Adenet le Roi. An epic poem, it corresponds in title and in basic story line to the first part of a work of uncertain authorship written about 1200, *La Chevalerie Ogier de Danemarche* (*The Knighthood of Ogier of Denmark*). In the context of a crusade by Charlemagne to expel the the invading Muslims from Rome and restore the Pope to his holy place, *Les Enfances Ogier* recounts the early heroism of Ogier le Danois, a character who became an enduring symbol of knightly prowess. His name and legend are still celebrated today. It is Ogier who can save the city or nation from those who would harm or destroy it. Central to the story of *Les Enfances Ogier* are the respect and friendship that develop between Ogier and his Saracen opponent, Carahuel, as honor propels them into mutual aid and protection. Also important is Gloriande, Carahuel's faithful fiancée, a strong Saracen princess whose interventions protect both men. This prose translation of Adenet's poem follows the edition of the Old French work edited by the Belgian scholar Albert Henry, the principal authority on the life and writings of Adenet le Roi. Between 1951 and 1971, Henry edited Adenet's four long poems, *Beuvon de Conmarchis*, *Berte aus grans pies*, *Les Enfances Ogier* and *Cleomadés.* He also wrote a volume which deals in the first part with Adenet's biography and in the second with the manuscript traditions of the four poems.

Life of the Author

Adenet le Roi wrote his four poems, all of which contain several thousand lines, between 1270 and 1285. From information he gives in his works and from household records of his employer, Gui de Dampierre, count of Flanders, we know more about Adenet's life than that of many medieval authors. He tells us that in his early years he lived at the court of Duke Henri III of Brabant, a poet himself, who taught Adenet to be a minstrel.[1] In *Cleomadés,* Adenet speaks of his gratitude to Duke Henri and of his sorrow at his death (*Biographie*, 12–13). After

[1] Albert Henry, *Biographie d'Adenet; La Tradition manuscrite* (Geneva: Slatkine, 1996), 13.

the duke's death in 1261 (13), Adenet stayed on with Henri's sons for a while; but, by 1270, he was at the court of the duke of Flanders, Gui de Dampierre (17). Circumstances at these two courts help explain Adenet's considerable literary output and his use of a French very close to that of the Île de France.

Both courts spoke this type of French; both valued literary, musical and artistic production and desired to be centers for these activities. Literary work and patronage were a tradition in Gui's family: he was a relative of the poet Thibaut de Champagne and of several other members of French nobility who supported literary work (33). Gui's wife joined him in the patronage of minstrels; the two spouses were book lovers who spent freely on manuscript copiers and illuminators (33–34). Henry tells us that for about twenty years, between 1265 and 1285, Gui's court was one of Europe's most brilliant (33). Adenet's title "le Roi" (the king) may mean he was in charge of diversions; certainly he was in charge frequently of distributing wages to the other minstrels (56–57). He probably knew and performed a great deal of music and poetry (52).

Flanders itself was a center of intellectual and industrial activity in Adenet's time, and French, the language of prestige, was spoken more widely than in Brabant (34–35). In addition, ties between Flanders and France were especially strong because Flanders, unlike Brabant, was under the sovereignty of the kings of France (36). At the death of Gui's father, conflict between Gui and his half-brothers, the Avesnes, as to who would become duke had been settled in Gui's favor by Louis IX (36). Gui made frequent trips to Paris and took Adenet with him (43). Louis IX's son Philippe le Hardi, who succeeded him, was married to Marie de Brabant, the daughter of Adenet's first patron, Duke Henri III. Adenet had known Marie in Brabant and knew her again in Paris as queen. He gave her a copy of *Berte aus grans* piés and *Les Enfances Ogier;* later she and her sister-in-law, Blanche of Castille, asked Adenet to write *Cleomadés* (45).

In 1270 Gui de Dampierre went to the Mediterranean to join Louis IX on crusade. He took with him his wife and two sons and a large entourage, including minstrels, of whom one was Adenet (20). However, King Louis IX died of the plague at Tunis a few months after Gui arrived, and a truce of fifteen years was concluded. Gui and his entourage traveled back home by way of Sicily, Italy and the Alps, taking more than a year for the entire trip (21). Details of various stages of the journey down to the Mediterranean and back can be traced in the account records of Gui's clerk Makel. We learn about payments made to Adenet and other minstrels and about Gui's buying Adenet a horse for eighteen pounds (22). In *Les Enfances Ogier* Adenet uses names of towns near Rome and information about Rome and its environs. After this trip Adenet remained in Gui's service for thirty years. It was Gui who asked Adenet to write *Les Enfances Ogier,* perhaps partly on the stimulus of this trip (19), but Gui's son Robert de Béthune had also gone in 1265 on a crusade against Manfred.[2] Gui and his family were evidently intensely interested in crusading.

We know neither the date of Adenet's birth nor that of his death. Gui de Dampierre fell out of favor with Philippe le Bel, who succeeded Philippe le Hardi in 1285. In 1294 Gui and two of his sons were imprisoned in the tower of the Louvre for six months. After another imprisonment in 1304, Gui died in that year. We last hear of Adenet upon a visit of Edward I of England in 1297 (*Biographie*, 47).

Thematic and Artistic Aspects

Les Enfances Ogier depicts Ogier as the star warrior in Charlemagne's successful effort to expel the invading Saracens from Rome and restore the Pope to his holy throne. Lines 8215–8220 explain the work's purpose, already briefly stated in the opening lines: to ensure that Ogier's deeds are widely known and held in high esteem in order to teach good people the right path to earn honor and the love of God. Henry observes that the work "propose[s] an ethical model" (*Enfances*, 49). (The words in quotation marks are my translation of Henry's French, as are all other translations in this book of his work and that of other authors.) Ogier is an ethical model from the work's point of view for his service to God as a warrior, for his personal character and for his interaction with the Saracen Carahuel. Adenet's Ogier is a powerful warrior but a compassionate and generous friend and companion in arms and an altogether admirable human being.

The narrator never misses a chance to point up Ogier's heroism, contriving to do so in various ways. Not only does he show us Ogier's battlefield prowess: he rescues Charlemagne and Namles in the first battle and yet again in one of the final ones, a nice structural balance; but he also reveals it in the enemy's complaints about Ogier's effectiveness from the first battle onward. The point is made repeatedly that without Ogier the French would not fare nearly as well. In fact, reports of Ogier's superiority as a warrior prompt Carahuel to engage Ogier in the single combat that, ironically, leads to their friendship. Later, in mid-poem in formal single combat, Ogier defeats the Saracens' most formidable warrior, Brunamon, in a battle Ogier undertakes to save his and Carahuel's honor. Upon Brunamon's death, the Saracen chief calls Ogier "a devil from hell" (line 4191), not the only time Ogier earns such an appellation from the Saracens. We also encounter a number of foils to Ogier that point up his virtues: the cowardly Aloris, the treacherous Danemon, the slander-mongering Brunamon and Charles's son Charlot of the poor judgment and the inappropriate comments. The adulation and affection Ogier earns are repeatedly emphasized. Whenever Ogier is

[2] Adenet le Roi, *Les Enfances Ogier*, ed. Albert Henry (Bruges: Rijksuniversiteit Te Gent, 1956), 20.

absent and threatened, the principal authorities, Charlemagne and Namles, as well as the rank and file of the army, express their apprehension and admiration. At other times Charlemagne, Namles, and Duke Thierri openly praise Ogier. Charles takes opportunities to have Ogier sit next to him. At one point late in the narrative Charles cannot get enough of gazing at Ogier. Late in the poem Ogier commands such respect from the rank and file that he is able to stop a battle in order to further protect Carahuel. Near the end of the work, one evening Charles is sitting in his tent with his closest friends: Namles, Thierri, and Ogier. This relationship to Charles, a result of Ogier's heroism, is quite a leap for Ogier from his status at the start of the poem where, thanks to mistakes of his father, Ogier has recently been Charlemagne's hostage.

However, the Saracen Carahuel is also a valiant warrior of ideal ethical behavior. Carahuel actually initiates the series of noble interactions between Ogier and himself by saving Ogier's life in a situation of treachery. Carahuel continues to conduct himself according to standards of highest honor throughout the poem. Henry notes that Adenet's work emphasizes Carahuel's portrayal as an "exemplary hero" more than does the source narrative, *La Chevalerie Ogier de Danemarche* (49). The depiction of an ethical ideal also applies to Gloriande, Carahuel's faithful fiancée, who, as noted earlier, takes crucial action to protect both the warriors. In Gloriande, Adenet's *Enfances* depicts a strong, intelligent princess of high refinement and nobility. In her is no hint of the frequently encountered bold and brassy Saracen princess who, becoming the lover of a Christian knight, defects to the Christian side. She treats Ogier with respect and affection, and Ogier is ready to serve her in time of need. Upon the death of her father and brother, Adenet shows Gloriande intensely grieving yet able to acknowledge Ogier's services. Critics have noted Adenet's penchant for psychological sensitivity especially in his portrayal of women. In its portrayal of Gloriande, the apparent intent of Adenet's work to present an ethical model extends beyond just these three major characters. In its authority figures, the work favors honor and dignity. There was never a king of more integrity and generosity than Charlemagne, according to this story; his counselor Namles is unfailingly noble; and even Corsuble, the Saracen leader, is depicted as competent, a fine and (mostly) honest warrior. Most importantly, the friendship between Ogier and Carahuel concludes by proposing mercy and courtesy as a model of diplomacy, a road to peace superior to arms. First, Carahuel out of honor saves Ogier's life; then Ogier saves Carahuel, who is also well-treated by Namles and Charlemagne. After these experiences, Carahuel vows that never again will he take up arms against Charlemagne. It is clear in *Enfances* as in Adenet's other works that his narrators delight in depicting nobility and harmony in human relations. Adenet's works typically end with marriages or at least with long-lost spouses recovering one another. Marriage seems to be regarded as an ideal state; lovers are faithful.

In a work so concerned with war and religion, what attitudes toward these subjects are evident? First and obviously, war and religion are inextricable here: the entire work depends upon the principle instituted and encouraged by the medieval Popes to motivate all the crusades: that killing the "enemies of God" on the battlefield is as high a calling as can be found and is one's Christian duty. The narrator inserts a little lecture or sermon rebuking those of his day who do not bother to go on a crusade (7712–7725).

The narrator is interested in knightly prowess and heraldry. He does recognize the horrors of war and in the midst of battle lists body parts lying around, notes the dead and wounded on the battlefield, mentions heads cleaved by swords, points out horses dragging their riders or running with entrails trailing. Apparently, though, such carnage is not shown to discourage warring but to show necessary and noble sacrifice, which anyway in the case of humans will earn God's pardon for all sins. Since no important sympathetic characters are killed in *Enfances*, despite the gore the reader may remain emotionally intact.

As to conversion, a convention of the epic is the lament by both Christian and Saracen warriors that a particularly admired warrior on the other side is not of their religion. This type of complaint, which often goes something like, "If only he were Christian/Muslim," appears in the early (about 1130) epic fragment *Gormont et Isembard*. In *Enfances,* Charlemagne leads a strong but unsuccessful effort to convert Carahuel after the fighting has stopped. The illustrious Christian knights who have participated in this attempt truly grieve that Carahuel will not convert; their efforts to convert Carahuel appear to be sincerely motivated by their conviction that his soul will be lost rather than by an attempt at a power play. In early parts of the narrative, the narrator seems to regard the "if only he were" kinds of statements with a light irony, as if he recognizes the futility of such sentiments; however, the knight's grief at Carahuel's failure to convert may reflect his own for his character. At the end of the poem the narrator says certain ones have reported that Carahuel and Gloriande did convert but that he has no authoritative source for that information and just doesn't know. He fervently hopes, though, that God will be merciful to such fine people as they were. This attitude would seem to hint at an inclination toward a somewhat inclusive religious view.

To turn our discussion to style, Adenet's work is remarkable for its unity. The incidents occur in a logical progression. He avoids digressions; his characters are consistent. At the end of the narrative, he ties up loose ends from earlier in the story. For example, late in the narrative Ogier finds out about the death of his beloved, Mahaut, who had died shortly after Ogier joined Charlemagne's army. Charlemagne invites Mahaut's father, the *chatelain* who cared for Ogier while he was Charlemagne's hostage, to come to camp and renew his acquaintance with Ogier. Ogier's father, who was at odds with Charlemagne at the beginning of the poem, is invited to the court and at Charlemagne's suggestion marries Charlemagne's sister. William Calin remarks that unity is not a quality often found in a *chanson de geste*.[3] *Les Enfances Ogier* distinguishes itself in that respect. The ancient dramatists and Shakespeare as well as nineteenth- and twentieth-century novelists all like unity. Adenet should not be frowned upon as somehow unworthy because he, unlike most *chanson de geste* poets, favors unity and carries it out remarkably well.

Although it contains courtly elements in interactions with Gloriande (comments on an example are in the end note to lines 7482–7489), Adenet's *Les Enfances Ogier* is a *chanson de geste*, an epic poem, both in content and in form. It concerns a military exploit in which the fate of a nation and its values are at stake, and its 8,229 lines are written in the traditional metric of the Old French epic, the decasyllable, although Old French epics byAdenet's time were usually written in the twelve-syllable alexandrine. Instead of ending his lines in assonance, as in, for example, *La Chanson de Roland*, Adenet ends every line of a particular *laisse* (the French term for the epic stanza) with the same rhyme, changing the rhyme with every *laisse*. This repetition of sound for an extended period is reminiscent of the effect of assonance; verse, however, is more difficult to produce.

Adenet uses a number of other conventions characteristic of *chansons de geste*. Scholars have long observed that epic poetry, including the *chansons de geste*, is composed to a significant extent of formulaic elements in both content and language. The insights of Milman Parry and Albert Lord in studying the Homeric epic and the "living epics" still recited orally in Yugoslavia in the twentieth century heighten attention to these aspects. In his book on *La Chanson de Roland*, Joseph Duggan reviews Alfred Lord's description of how formulaic actions and formulaic language are used to tell the story, present speech, and to provide syllabic and sound requirements. These formulaic expressions consist of word groups which remain the same in meaning but can be varied in syntax and vocabulary to fit the needs of particular lines. The word groups and formulaic actions were the tools available to the jongleur for his oral recitations of *chansons de geste* which he had previously heard; the jongleur's recitations were simultaneous with his re-creation of the poem. Each recitation might present a slightly different version of content and would certainly provide a different arrangement of language.[4] Using a computer, Duggan quantifies formulaic language in *La Chanson de Roland* and several other *chansons de geste*. Duggan's studies convince him that the *chansons de geste* were oral compositions, even the magnificent *Chanson de Roland* (26). The Oxford version of La *Chanson de Roland* was, he believes, taken down in writing from the lips of the singer (60). William Calin argues that French epics use the style of traditional oral poems but were composed in writing. [5] After Calin's remarks about Duggan's theory, the latter modifies his position somewhat on the

[3] William C. Calin. *The Old French Epic of Revolt: Raoul de Cambrai, Renaut de Montauban, Gormond et Isembard* (Genève: Librairie E. Droz, 1962), 13.

[5] William Calin, "Littérature médiévale et hypothèse orale: une divergence de méthode et de philosophie," *Olifant* 8.3 (1981), 256–85.

writing down of *chansons de geste.*[6] However, Duggan finds that works known to be originally written instead of composed orally, such as Adenet's *chanson de geste, Beuvon de Conmarchis*, show fewer formulaic expressions than do the oral compositions (26), a logical result since the writer does not labor under the time constraints of the jongleur who recites. Adenet's *Enfances,* also a written composition as are all his works, still contains numerous formulaic expressions; for he certainly seems to intend his work to be a traditional *chanson de geste.* It is evident, Duggan states, that Adenet had heard many recitations of epic poems (215). This discussion will show Adenet's abundant use of epic technique in *Enfances.*

Remarking that the epic poets usually convey a line's essential meaning in its first half (205), Duggan studies several works to observe their use of epithets and certain stock expressions in the second hemistich of the decasyllabic line to provide for the remaining syllabic requirement and/or the assonance. Adenet's lines frequently reveal this practice in epithets such as "Charles of the white hair," "Danemon the powerful," "France the bountiful" or "Rome the lordly city" and in numerous stock phrases such as "I don't want to lie to you," "they did not want to wait," "they stayed there no longer," "you should know," and "who was so worthy."

In another characteristic of the *chanson de geste*, frequently the beginning lines of a *laisse* repeat the content of the ending lines of the previous *laisse*, a technique which Jean Rychner calls *enchainement*,[7] which in other epics has been observed to emphasize or dramatize the content. At times this repetition serves to remind the audience of an oral recitation of the poem what had happened before a break in the recitation. In Adenet's *Enfances,* this type of transition is used with great regularity, especially in battle scenes, as if to create a tightly woven effect in the narration. See, for example, lines 2172–2177, 4604–4607, 5913–5918.

Yet another element typical of the *chanson de geste* is the repetition of successive *laisses* that present the same event from a different perspective. *Ogier* lacks this element but retains one aspect of it: many *laisses* between number CLIII and CLXXIV, which recount the final battle, start with a line that remarks upon the violence of the combat. In addition, at the death of Danemon, four successive laisses (CLXXVI–CLXXX) comment in the course of the laisse on his father Corsuble's grief and/or upon that of his fellow warriors. Again, at Corsuble's death, three laisses (CLXXXI–CLXXXIII) remark upon the warriors' grief. These repetitions follow the typical epic pattern of the use of successive similar laisses in moments of great crisis.

---

[6] Joseph Duggan, ""La Théorie de la composition orale des chansons de geste: les faits et les interprétaions," *Olifant* 8.3 (1981), 252.

[7] Jean Rychner, *La Chanson de geste: essai sur l'art épique des jongleurs* (Geneva: Librairie E. Droz, 1955), 74.

The chiasme, used to great effect as opening lines of laisses in *La Chanson de Roland*, is also employed in *Les Enfances Ogier* in line 5847, "Beautiful was the day and the sun radiant." Martin de Riquer observes that *La Chanson de Roland* is sparing in its use of comparisons.[8] Adenet's poem uses them rather frequently, however, often employing a small object to indicate the ineffectiveness of a piece of armor just destroyed by a blow in battle or using a small animal and its prey to express one warrior's fear of another. Among Adenet's more distinguished comparisons is one that Henry says (*Enfances*, 366) contains the only known use of that adjective in Old French: line 6769 has the Saracens remark of the Christians that "They are people of steel" (". . .Ce sont gent acerees." *Acerees* is the word in question). In another effective, grisly figure of speech, line 5785 tell us that "He made the sword bathe in the brain." Line 5725 reads "For he was powerful and strong as a tower."

As Rychner points out *(La Chanson de geste*, 64), the creation of suspense in statements of ominous foreshadowing is a time-honored narrative technique in the *chanson de geste*. An example in *Les Enfances Ogier* occurs early in the story when Ogier and Carahuel have come to the island for single combat. Lines 2581–2582 warn us that ". . .before they ever came back, / The hearts of the French would be in great sorrow over it."

Examples of formulaic elements of epic content that Adenet adopts are passages that describe the knights arming themselves for battle (lines 2552–2557 of *Enfances* give a good example) and the presentation of the battles themselves as a series of single combats. Many single combats appear in Adenet's battle scenes, combined frequently within a single *laisse* with more general descriptions of the battle and information about the combatants, as in *laisses* CLXVII to CLLXXI for example. Jean Rychner outlines seven steps in single combat (from spurring the horse to knocking the adversary dead) (*La Chanson de Geste*, 141) found over and over again in the *chansons de geste*. These quite logical and natural movements are faithfully delineated, with occasional slight variations, in single combat descriptions in *Enfances.*

A particularly memorable convention of the *chanson de geste*, used to impressive effect in *laisses* seventy-nine to eighty-one in the *Chanson de Roland,* is the description of the approach of the massive Saracen army that fills the landscape, its innumerable golden helmets gleaming from afar. In *Les Enfances Ogier* the approaching Saracens overwhelm the mountains, valleys, and roads in line 4802. The narrator insists again upon the great numbers of the enemy coming from everywhere in the landscape in lines 4861–4865, 5178–5185 and 5617–5623.

Earlier we noted that *Enfances* contains elements traditionally seen as courtly and that concern the treatment of women. However, the presence and participation of Gloriande no more keeps *Enfances* from being an epic than does that

[8] Martín de Riquer, *Les Chansons de gestes françaises*, trans. Irénée Cluzel (Paris: Librairie Nizet, 1957), 102.

of Guibourg in the William cycle. Instead, in saving the lives of each of the two main male characters, Gloriande contributes vitally to the epic's fabric. The combination of epic and romance elements is part of an evolving tradition. Each piece of literature is unique and should not be judged solely by adherence to genre criteria. As interesting as comparisons may be, the insistence on rigid ideas of complete genre conformity can operate to deny a piece of literature full and just appreciation. In the case of *Enfances,* we have seen how carefully Adenet has used epic conventions for its form. However, what truly marks this work is its depiction of the humanitarian values of justice, brotherhood and mutual aid practiced by characters opposed to one another in religion and in armed conflict.

Sources and Influences

Adenet's *Les Enfances Ogier,* which contains 8229 lines, corresponds largely to the first 3166 lines of the first part of *La Chevalerie Ogier de Danemarche* (*Enfances*, 22). However, Henry notes that Adenet omits many episodes in *Chevalerie* and makes important changes in characters and events (22) to effect the consistency, unity and focus noted earlier. The initial and central events which set up the friendship between Ogier and Carahuel occur in the first part of *La Chevalerie Ogier* and are repeated in Adenet's *Enfances*. However, the *Chevalerie* narrative ends soon after a battle that follows immediately upon the conclusion of a combat between Ogier and the Saracen knight Brunamon (25, note) with no further development of the friendship between Ogier and Carahuel. Adenet's work, on the other hand, does not follow that single combat with an immediate battle. After line 3166, Adenet continues his poem for some 4000 lines with his own inventions, which expand upon the friendship beween Ogier and Carahuel.

The friendship that *La Chevalerie* initiates and that Adenet expands fully between two adversaries, one Christian and one Muslim, is perhaps more highly developed than any other between two such characters in medieval French literature. The chivalric code that is the basis of the friendship had already been expressed in French epics, however. In his impressive two-volume study, *Les Musulmans dans les chansons de geste du cycle du roi,* Paul Bancourt traces the development of the code of honor shared by Christian and Muslim knights in the epic poems involving Charlemagne from the twelfth to the early fourteenth centuries.[9] This code required strict observance of fairness in combat and led at times to exchanges of good deeds in crucial moments with accompanying cordiality and warmth. As especially important to the development of the chivalric code, Bancourt cites, from the twelfth century, *Fierabras*, *Aspremont* and *Otinel*; from the thirteenth century *La Chevalerie Ogier* and from the beginning of the four-

[9] Paul Bancourt, *Les Musulmans dans les chansons de geste du cycle du roi* (Aix-en-Provence: Publications Université de Provence, 1982), I: 306–26. 2 vols.

teenth century *L'Entrée d'Espagne* and *La Prise de Pamplune*. (Unfortunately and inexplicably, Bancourt does not include Adenet's *Les Enfances Ogier* in his study.) The examples Bancourt cites from the poems that precede *La Chevalerie Ogier* present somewhat isolated incidents. In *Aspremont*, for example, Naimes (another spelling of the name of the character called Namles in *Les Enfances Ogier*) tells the Saracen Balan, who has come into the Christian camp as a messenger, that he will protect him like a son. Later, on the battlefield, Balan, not knowing Naimes was present, says that if Naimes were there, he would protect him. Hearing this, Naimes tells Ogier not to harm Balan (316). In *Otinel,* the release of prisoners by the Christians prompts Clarel to keep his Saracen comrades from further harming Ogier, who is wounded and surrounded (317). When one of them protests, Clarel cuts off his head with his sword (p. 320). In *Fierabras*, Bancourt observes that in a combat between Olivier and Fierabras, each of the knights tries to outdo the other in fair and generous behavior (312). However, the first part of *La Chevalerie Ogier* and most especially Adenet's *Les Enfances Ogier* take fair play and generosity between two knights of opposing sides to greater heights. Adenet's version is as much about the friendship that develops between Ogier and his Saracen adversary Carahuel as it is about the glory of the young Ogier as a warrior.

As for direct sources of Adenet's *Enfances*, from a study of details in eight works preceding and following it, Henry believes that Adenet drew upon one or more other sources that are now lost. Henry concludes that a Franco-Italian *Enfances Ogier* (manuscript V XIII), written at the end of the twelfth century, shares details with Adenet's that may have come from this source. In addition, Henry points out that Adenet himself in lines 7638–7641 of *Enfances* refers to other sources that have gotten the story wrong. Henry does not believe that these particular protestations are just the conventional ones of the jongleur (*Enfances, 44*).

Knud Togeby also cites evidence for the existence of a lost *Enfances Ogier* that preceded that in *La Chevalerie*. A troubadour, Guilhem de Bergadon, who, Togeby reasons from the dates of documents signed by the troubadour and his brother, died by 1199, refers to Ogier ("Augier") and his combat with Carahuel.[10] Togeby also notes that Jean Bodel in his *Les Saines* (ca. 1197–1199) uses the names Corsuble and Brunamont, which he could have taken from some lost version of *Les Enfances Ogier* (39).

Scholars have spent much time and effort trying to track down historical and other references to Ogier to discover if and how an Ogier of history was transferred to an Ogier of epic poetry. The Ogier of French epic poetry first appears in *La Chanson de Roland* (ca. 1100, Oxford version) and reappears in many of the French epic poems written after *Roland* and before and after Adenet's *Enfances*. As for an historical Ogier, an Autcharius served King Pépin.

---

[10] Knud Togeby, *Ogier le Danois dans les littératures européennes* (Copenhagen: Munksgaard, 1969), 38.

According to the *Annales Maximiani* (beginning of the ninth century) Pépin chose Autcharius, who was a duke, to escort Pope Etienne II to France in 753. In 760, Pépin selected Autcharius to go to Italy and assist in a negotiation between Pope Paul I and the king of the Lombards, Didier. Pépin characterized Autcharius as "gloriosissimus dux" in a letter to the Pope.[11] Later Autcharius served King Carloman, Pépin's son (78), who with his brother Charles (Charlemagne) ruled his late father's kingdom. According to the *Vita Hadriani*, a part of the *Liber Pontificalis* written close to the time of the events it records, at Carloman's death in 772, Autcharius escorted Carloman's widow and two young sons to the court of the Lombard king, Didier, to protect them from Charlemagne (65). Didier, with an army, went toward Rome with Autcharius and the widow and children to persuade the Pope to recognize the rights of the two sons. However, Charlemagne, whom the Pope had called to protect himself, arrived with an army, which besieged Didier at Pavia. Charlemagne himself continued to Rome where he donated additional lands to the Pope. In 774 Pavia and Didier surrendered to Charlemagne.[12] According to the Monk of Saint-Gall's account (late ninth century), Charlemagne then imprisoned Autcharius in Italy and later put him in exile in France (Lejeune, 90). That Autcharius was in an adversarial position to Charlemagne is supported, Lejeune believes, by his preceding history as a powerful vassal in Carloman's court. Carloman had been at odds with his brother for refusing to intervene with him in a revolt in Charles's territory of Aquitaine, his refusal resulting from the advice of his counselors, of whom Autcharius was surely one (78).

So these accounts put Ogier in conflict with Charlemagne. However, Lejeune points out that the official Carolingian records make no mention of Autcharius's flight to Italy with Carloman's widow and children; nor do they discuss just how Charlemagne came into possession of his brother's territory. She believes these omissions are a deliberate cover-up to avoid situations not appearing favorable to Charlemagne (79).

Lejeune sees the account of the Monk of Saint-Gall in the *De Gestis Caroli Magni*, written between 883 and 887, a century after the events in Italy, as an important step in the development of Ogier's legend. The monk gives an account of Ogier and Didier watching for the approach of Charlemagne's army; when the army finally appears, Ogier is overcome, presumably with fear, and faints. This incident, according to Lejeune, helps to establish the idea of Charlemagne's might and Ogier's subservience to him (88). Lejeune says that the monk does honor Ogier as a powerful warrior, who although he fought Charles in Italy

---

[11] Rita Lejeune, *Recherches sur le theme: Les chansons de geste et l'histoire* (Paris: Société d'Édition Les Belles Lettres, 1948), 75.

[12] Henri Pirenne, *Mohammed and Charlemagne*, trans. Bernard Miall (United States: Barnes and Noble Import Division of Harper and Row) repr. of George Allen & Unwin. First published 1939, 228.

and had angered Charles by fleeing with Didier's family, still admired Charles. Ogier's fear of Charlemagne augments the impression of Charlemagne's might, of course (90).

Other writings add to the image of Ogier as a loyal knight of Charlemagne. The *Conversio Othgerii* (ca. 1080), presents Ogier as Charlemagne's outstanding warrior, who in his old age sees the vanity of the world and decides to retire to a monastery, that of Saint-Faron à Meaux. Ogier is extremely pious, and miracles occur on his tomb (57–58, note 1). The story follows a standard formula for saints' lives (58–59). By the twelfth century Ogier's tomb and that of his fellow monk, Benoît, were located within a newly built chapel at the monastery.[13] Another account, written about 1160 by Metellus of the monastery of Tergernsee (middle of twelfth century) tells of an Ogier (Otcarius or Occarius), Charlemagne's excellent, loyal knight, whose son is killed by Charlemagne's son after a chess game the two had played. Charlemagne asks Ogier and Ogier's brother what he should do about it. Ogier does not want him to take any action; but in his sorrow he becomes a monk and, with his brother, founds the monastery of Tergernsee (*Ogier le Danois dans les littératures européennes*, 29).

Various narratives about an actual Ogier seem to have their own agendas, and historians find it difficult to establish more than a few facts about him that are certain. As for Charlemagne's campaign in *Les Enfances Ogier* to retake Rome from the Saracens and restore the Pope to his rightful place, no such event took place. "Saracens" such as those depicted in *Enfances* (those threatening Lombards don't count) did not invade Rome in Charlemagne's day, and Charlemagne did therefore not have to expel them.

A discussion of the influence of Adenet's *Les Enfances Ogier* must inform the reader of the difference between the Ogier of Adenet's poem and the first part of *La Chevalerie Ogier* on the one hand and the Ogier of the second part of *La Chevalerie Ogier* on the other. In *Les Enfances* of Adenet and the first part of *La Chevalerie*, Ogier is as he was in his first appearance in literature in *La Chanson de Roland*, Charlemagne's valiant and loyal knight. In the second part of *La Chevalerie*, however, Ogier is in revolt against Charlemagne. The story recounts that Charlemagne's son, Charlot, kills Ogier's son in a dispute over a chess game. When Charlemagne refuses compensation for this act, Ogier goes to war against him. At length Charlemagne captures and imprisons him, but when a giant threatens to destroy France, Charlemagne knows that only Ogier can conquer the enemy. Released, Ogier slays the enemy, and he and Charlemagne are reconciled. It is this final idea of Ogier as the loyal hero who conquers the enemy and saves the nation that prevails in works afterward. Knud Togeby notes that in all the re-inventions of Ogier following *La Chevalerie*, Ogier is presented

[13] Joseph Bédier, *Les Légendes épiques: Recherches sur la formation des chansons de geste* (Paris: Librairie Ancienne H. Champion, Editeur, 1926), II: 310.4 vols.

as Charlemagne's loyal vassal, not as in revolt against him. Togeby points to one exception to that rule in *Huon de Bordeaux* (70–71).

Togeby in his *Ogier le Danois dans les littératures européennes* lists all the works that include Ogier from the twelfth century into the twentieth century, in their several languages, providing dates, information about authorship and publication, résumés of Ogier's roles and more. B. Munk Olsen in his review of Togeby's book says Togeby has included one hundred thirty works in this monumental study.[14] Olsen remarks that Adenet's *Les Enfances Ogier* had a great influence on the Ogier literature that followed and that several *chansons de geste* mention or use Adenet's work: *Girard d'Amiens*, *Doon de Mayence*, *Gaufrey* and *Les Enfances de Uçer du Codex Marcianus XIII*. Olsen notes as well that Adenet's poem is the French work on Ogier mentioned most frequently in library inventories of the thirteenth through the seventeenth centuries and probably did receive the most diffusion (218).

Ogier's story has indeed captured the imagination of authors in most centuries since the thirteenth and in nearly every Western European country. *Le Roman d'Ogier en décasyllbes* (ca. 1310) retells the two parts of the story and adds three new parts: Ogier's trip to the Orient, his stay with the fairy Morgan and his return to France (*Ogier le Danois dans les littératures européennes* 134–147). *Le Roman d'Ogier en alexandrins* (ca. 1335) combines *La Chevalerie* with fairy material throughout and introduces courtly incidents (148–155). A Belgian writer from Liège, Jean Outremeuse (1338–1400), devotes three major works and part of another to Ogier, attaching him to Liège (158–171). *Le Roman d'Ogier en prose* (1496), a prose rendering of the version in alexandrins but in a style that attempts to make it sound like history, had at least ten editions in the sixteenth century (221–223). The Scandinavian history of works on Ogier begins before Adenet with the *Karlamagnús Saga* (1240) in Norwegian and continues with many other works, including that of the great Danish humanist Christiern Pedersen (1478–1554) (225–240). Togeby says that through the immensely popular poems—usually set to music—of B. S. Ingemann (1789–1862), Ogier becomes a symbol of the Danish people (269). A story by Hans Christian Andersen based on the poetry of Ingemann celebrating Ogier has him return regularly throughout Danish history (278). During Denmark's nineteenth-century wars against Germany, Ingemann's poems set to music were patriotic songs. The Danish resistance in 1943–45 was called Holger Danske (Ogier the Dane) (292). Louis Aragon's 1965 novel *La Mise à Mort* contains a page on Ogier (293). Jacques Barrois reports that in the early twentieth century Ogier was still a figure frequently represented in parades and pageants in Flanders, that "at Ath, at Huy, etc., each

[14] B. Munk Olsen, "Review of *Ogier le Danois dans les littératures européennes* by Knud Togeby," *Revue Romane* 10 (1975), 215–23.

year, a family of giants parades with Ogier at the head, his lance in his fist." [15] In this connection, in Adenet's poem, line 6975, Thierri, in speaking of the blows Ogier gives in combat says, "They are much more like the blows of a giant/ Who overwhelms all he strikes." Togeby relates that in Catalonia Ogier has become a national symbol and has been assimilated to Hercules (*Ogier le Danois dans les littératures européennes*, 287). Emmanuelle Paulain-Gautret in a book published in 2005 states that Ogier still is seen in marionette shows in Liège and that she saw an Ogier puppet in a marionette performance in Sicily. [16] She refers to Ogier as "a hero who haunts popular French literature up to the beginning of the twentieth century and who has furthermore survived equally in Italy, Belgium, the Low Countries and, of course, in Denmark" (16). All this information attests to the immense popularity of the Ogier legend over centuries in Western Europe.

Manuscripts and Editions

Nine manuscripts contain Adenet le Roi's *Les Enfances Ogier.* They are designated as A, A[1], D, E, F, K, L, T, and V. They date from the thirteenth, fourteenth, and fifteenth centuries and are housed in libraries in Paris, Brussels, and London (*Enfances*, 57). Of these manuscripts, Henry does not use A[1], which is a copy of A and is not always correct (*La Tradition manuscrite*, 100), nor E, which is not complete (103). After careful study of all the manuscripts, Henry chooses to use T as the base manuscript with A as a control. However, in editing the text, Henry refers frequently to the remaining manuscripts when questions occur (195).

Henry finds that all the manuscripts seem to have a strong relationship with T (191), which dates from the last twenty years of the thirteenth century (114), a time close to the composition of the work. He notes that the text has been transcribed with care and reread for accuracy as revealed by marks of correction (114) and that the handwriting is big and clear and seems older than that of Manuscript A (113). It seems to Henry that the work has come down to us in its original form in Manuscript T (113). He states that another scholar believes that this manuscript may be the very one that Adenet gave to Marie de Brabant (114). Henry observes that Manuscript T has artwork done in a style characteristic of the Île de France, as do Manuscripts A and D, which are also excellent copies of the text dating from the end of the thirteenth century. The artwork in Manuscript T features big, blue initials alternating with gold ones and margins with lines of blue and red. Adenet is curled up composing his story in the first

---

[15] Raimbert de Paris, *La Chevalerie Ogier de Danemarche*, ed. Jacques Barrois (Paris: Techner, 1812) rept. University of Michigan Librairies collection, I: xii. 2 vols.

[16] Emmanuelle Poulain-Gautret, *La Tradition littéraire d'Ogier le Danois après le XIIIe siècle* (Paris: Honoré Champion, 2005), 16, n. 2.

illuminated letter; the borders are embellished with leaves, imaginary animals and vielle players. On the first page is a large miniature (110 millimeters wide and 70 millimeters long) showing Ogier being delivered to Charlemagne as a hostage (113–114).

Perhaps Adenet or another reader did perform this poem, and his others, in Gui de Dampierre's court and elsewhere. However, as to the nine manucripts that we have of the poem, Henry says they are deluxe editions that were not for the jongleur; many were part of prestigious collections of the wealthy, were intended for reading by aristocrats and were then put away in their libraries and seldom taken down from the shelf (176, note 1).

Albert Henry's edition of *Enfances,* published in 1956, is the third volume in the five volume series that Henry published between 1951 and 1971. Previous editions of Adenet's *Enfances* were done by August Scheler in 1874 and by U. T. Holmes in 1946.

Translation Principles

It behooves us to have great respect for exactly how an Old French text is written. Its modes of expression reveal the development of the language and of a type of poetic art to that point, precious to preserve. A translator is, however, always subject to the art of compromise. As an English prose translation of an Old French poem, this translation already violates the principle of preserving rhythm and rhyme. Effort at least then has been made to keep most of the lines in place and to adhere to the literal meaning of the words. Yet the need to strike a balance between literal meaning and readability asserts itself. Typically, the lines of a *chanson de geste* each comprise a syntactic unit that allows a pause at the end of a line, a technique known as end-stop; and the sentence structure in such poems is often simple as opposed to complex. Because these patterns create at times a tiresome choppiness, this translation resorts often to structures that relieve that effect, for which the Old French original's rhythm and rhyme must surely have compensated. The translation sometimes therefore makes simple sentences into compound ones and combines sentences through the use of compound verbs or participial phrases. It may condense by means of prepositional phrases and appositives. For smoother reading, clause positions are sometimes switched, inversions put back into regular order and passive voice changed to active. Sometimes lines must be reordered to make sense, although the regular numbering system is retained, as, for example, in line 5506 and following. Occasionally, one line must be expanded over two lines, in which case the second part of the line is indented. The consistent use of past tense replaces the irregular tense shifts characteristic of medieval French. Sometimes word groups are rendered by English idioms that might be used in similar situations but are not quite what the French says. Perhaps what most disturbs this translator, however, is the use of modern English words that have no equivalent in Old French. This practice occurs here most frequently in an attempt to vary the Old French *moult* and *forment*, which mean *much* and *greatly*. Examples are *effusively* (line 1322), *profusely* (3373), *intently* (2105). Examples of other words used in the translation but not yet available as equivalents in Old French include *slumpe*d (412), *chuckled* (1358), *rashness* (3175), *bloated* (3176), *sincere* (2291). Such vocabulary is interpretative rather than literal. Interpretative vocabulary and modern English idiom make for a livelier translation, but this translator has in general opted for a more literal rendering to correspond more closely to the Old French original.

I have chosen to keep the forms of proper names of individuals as they appear in the Old French text as a reminder of its original language and to retain that much of its medieval flavor. The forms can vary by case in the Old French; I have chosen one and tried to keep it throughout. The name of Charlemagne's closest and most trusted counselor, Namles (in the nominative form) is spelled Naimes, in, for example, *La Chanson de Roland.* I like to keep the form Adenet chose. It helps us remember that spelling was not standardized.

Additional information about various items in lines throughout the translation may be found in the Notes section at the end of the translation itself.

Select Bibliography

Primary Sources

Adenet le Roi. *Berte aus grans piés*. Ed. Albert Henry. Paris: Presses Universitaires de France, 1963. Vol. 4 of *Les Oeuvres d'Adenet le Roi*. 5 vols. 1950–1971.

———. *Beuvon de Conmarchis*. Ed. Albert Henry. Bruges: Rijksuniversiteit Te Gent, 1953. Vol. 2 of *Les Oeuvres d'Adenet le Roi*.

———. *Cléomadés*. Ed. Albert Henry. Brussels: Éditions de l'Université de Bruxelles, 1971. Vol. 5 (in 2 vols.) of *Les Oeuvres d'Adenet le Roi*.

———. *Les Enfances Ogier*. Ed. Albert Henry. Bruges: Rijksuniversiteit Te Gent, 1956. Vol. 3 of *Les Oeuvres d'Adenet le Roi*.

———. *Les Enfances Ogier*. Ed. U. T. Holmes. Chapel Hill: University of North Carolina Press, 1946.

———. *Les Enfances Ogier*. Ed. A. Scheler. Brussels: Closson, 1874.

La Chanson d'Aspremont. Tome 1, Vers 1–6154: chanson de geste du XIIe siècle: texte du manuscript de Wollaton Hall. Ed. Louis Brandin. Paris: Honoré Champion, 1923.

La Chanson d'Aspremont: Tome II, Verss 6155–11276, chanson de geste du XIIe siècle: texte du manuscript de Wollaton Hall. Ed. Louis Brandin. Paris: Honoré Champion, 1924.

La Chanson de Roland. Ed. Léon Gautier. Tours: A. Mame et fils, 1872.

La Chanson de Guillaume. Ed. Duncan McMillan. 2 vols. Paris: Éditions A. et J. Picard, 1949.

La Chanson de Roland. Trans. Pierre Jonin. Paris: Éditions Gallimard, 1979.

La Chevalerie Ogier de Danemarche: a critical edition. Ed. Judith Belam. University of Reading thesis, British Theses online, 1994.

La Chevalerie Ogier; Tome I: Enfances. Ed. Muriel Ott. Paris: Honoré Champion Éditeur, 2013.

Corneille, Pierre. *Le Cid*. Edition of L. Lejalle et J. Dubois. Classiques Larousse. Paris: Librairie Larousse, 1959.

Gormont et Isembart: Fragment de chanson de geste du XIIe siècle. Ed. Alphonse Bayot. Paris: Champion, 1931.

Raimbert de Paris. *La Chevalerie Ogier de Danemarche*. Repr. University of Michigan Libraries Collection. Vol 1. Ed. Joseph Barrois. Romans des Douze Pairs de France VIII. Paris: Techener, 1842. 2 vols.

Raoul de Cambrai. Ed. and trans. Sarah Kay. Oxford: Clarendon Press, 1992.

The Song of Aspremont (La Chanson d'Aspremont). Trans. Michael Newth. Garland Library of Medieval Literature. Ser. B, 61. New York: 1989.

Secondary Sources

Aebischer, Paul. *Des Annales carolingiennes à Doon de Mayence: nouveau recueil d'études sur l'épique française médiévale*. Publications romanes et françaises CXXIX. Genève: Librairie Droz, 1975.

Adnès, André. Adenès, *Dernier grand trouvère: recherches historiques et anthroponymiques*. Paris: Éditions A. et J. Picard, 1971.

Bancourt, Paul. *Les Musulmans dans les chansons de geste du cycle du roi*. 2 vols. Aix-en-Provence: Publications de l'Université de Provence, 1982.

Bédier, Joseph. *Les Légendes épiques: recherches sur la formation des chansons de geste*. 3rd ed. 4 vols. Paris: Librairie Ancienne H. Champion, Éditeur, 1926.

Brault, Gérard J. "Adenet le Roi et l'héraldique médiévale." *Olifant* 25. 1–2 (2005): 141–49.

———. "Adenet le Roi and the Coats of Arms of Charlemagne and his Twelve Peers in a Medieval Roll." *Contez me tout. Mélanges offerts à Herman Braet*. Paris: Peeters, 2006.

———. "*Les Enfances Ogier* d'Adenet le Roi et la liste de sultans et de rois maures dans l'armorial Vermandois." In *Si a parlé moult ruiste vertu. Mélanges de langue et littérature offerts à Jean Subrenat*, 91–101. Paris: Champion, 2000.

Brooke-Little, J. P, Reviser. *Boutell's Heraldry*. 1950. London: Frederick Warne, 1983.

Calbris, Geneviève. *The Semiotics of French Gestures*. Trans. Owen Doyle. Bloomington: University of Indiana Press, 1990.

Calin, William C. *The Epic Quest: Studies in Four Old French* Chansons de geste. Baltimore: The Johns Hopkins Press, 1966.

———. *The Old French Epic of Revolt: Raoul de Cambrai, Renaud de Montauban, Gormond et Isembard*. Genève: Librairie E. Droz, 1962.

———. "L'Épopée dite vivante: Réflections sur le prétendu caractère oral des chansons de geste." *Olifant* 8.3 (1981): 227–37.

Chocheyras, Jacques. "Les Légendes épiques du Danemark (VIIIe-Xe siècles) et les origines de la chanson de geste." *Olifant* 18.3–4 (1993): 290–302.

Collomp, D. "Le Doigt sur la dent (geste symbolique du serment sarrasin)," *Le Geste et les gestes au Moyen* Âge. *Senefiance* 41 (1998): 605–24.

De Riquer, Martín. *Les Chansons de geste françaises*. 2nd ed. Trans. Iréné Cluzel. Paris: Librairie Nizet, 1957.

DeVries, Kelly and Smith, Robert Douglas. *Medieval Military Technology*. 2nd ed. Toronto: University of Toronto Press, 2012.

Duggan, Joseph. J. "The Generation of the Episode of Baligant." *Romance Philology* 30 (1976): 59–82.

———, Ed. *Oral Literature*. New York: Harper and Row, 1975.

———. *The Song of Roland: Formulaic Style and Poetic Craft*. Berkeley: University of California Press, 1973.

———. "La Théorie de la composition orale des chansons de geste: les faits et les interprétations." *Olifant* 8.3 (1982): 238–65.

Eusebi, Mario. *La Chevalerie d'Ogier de Danemarche: canzone de gesta*. Paris: Champion, 2013.

Farmer, David Hugh. *The Oxford Dictionary of Saints*. Oxford: Oxford University Press, 1978.

Farrier, Susan. *The Medieval Charlemagne Legend: An Annotated Bibliography*. Garland Medieval Bibliographies 17. New York: Garland, 1993.

Gough, Henry and Parker, James. *A Glossary of Terms Used in Heraldry. A New Edition, With One Thousand Illustrations*. Originally published At Oxford and London by James Parker & Co, 1894. Republished by Gale Research Company, 1966.

Grisward, Joël H. *Archéologie de l'épopée médiévale: structures Trifonctionelles et mythes indo-européens dans le cycle des Narbonnais*. Paris: Payot, 1981.

Hassell, James Woodrow, Jr. *Middle French Proverbs, Sentences and Proverbial Phrases*. Toronto: Pontifical Institute of Mediaeval Studies, 1982.

Henry, Albert. *Biographie d'Adenet. La Tradition Manuscrite*. Geneva: Slatkine Reprints, 1996. Vol. 1 of *Les Oeuvres d'Adenet le Roi*. 5 vols. Paris: Presses Universitaires de France, 1951–1970.

Herbermann, Charles G., et al. Eds. *The Catholic Encyclopedia*. New York: The Encyclopedia Press, Inc., 1913.

Hoyer-Poulain, Emmanuelle. "Tradition/trahison? Scènes de bataille dans les Enfances Ogier d'Adenet le Roi." In *"Plaist vos oïr bone cançon vallant?" Mélanges offerts à François Suard*, 1: 435–44. 2 vol. Lille: Université Charles-de-Gaulle, 1999.

Jones, Catherine M. *An Introduction to the Chansons de Geste*. Gainesville: University of Florida Press, 2014.

Keller, Hans and Bakelaar, Bette Lou. "Changes in Old French Epic Poetry and Changes in the Tastes of its Audience." *Olifant* 1.4 (1974): 48–56.

Krauss, Henning. "Ritter und Burger, Feudalheer und Volksheer. Zum Problem der feigen Lombarden in der altfranzösischen und frankoitalienischen Epik," *Zeitschrift für romanische Philologie* 87 (1971): 209–22.

Le Gentil, Pierre. *La Littérature française du moyen* âge. 5th ed. Paris: Librairie Armand Colin, 1968.

Lejeune, Rita. *Recherches sur le thème: les chansons de geste et l'histoire*. Bibliothèque de la Faculté de Philosophie et Lettres de l'Université de Liège, Fascicule CVIII. Paris: Société d'Édition Les Belles Lettres, 1948.

Leverage, Paula. "The Reception of the *Chansons de Geste.*" *Olifant* 25.1–2 (2006): 299–312.

Lombard-Jourdan, Anne. *Fleur de lis et oriflamme: Signes célestes du royaume de France.* Paris: Presses du Centre National de la Recherche Scientifique, 1991.

Lorcin, Marie-Thérèse. *Les Recueils de proverbes français (1160–1490). Sagesse des nations et langue de bois.* Essais sur le Moyen Âge 50. Paris: Champion, 2011.

Lord, Albert B. *Epic Singers and Oral Tradition.* Ithaca, N.Y.: Cornell University Press, 1991.

———. *The Singer of Tales.* Harvard Studies in Comparative Literature 24. Cambridge: Harvard University Press, 1960.

Lot, Ferdinand. Études *sur les légendes épiques françaises.* Paris: Librairie Honoré Champion, 1958.

Menegaldo, Silvère. "Adenet le Roi tel qu'en ses prologues." *Cahiers de recherches médiévales* 18 (2009): 309–28.

Meot-Bourquin, Valerie. "Les Figures de pouvoir dans les Enfances Ogier d'Adenet le Roi." *L'Épopée romane au Moyen* Âge *et aux temps modernes.* 2 vols, 301–17. Napoli: Fridericiana Editrice Universitaria, 2001.

———. "Les Enfances Ogier ou la chanson de geste entre tradition et conception courtoise." *L'Epique: fins et confins*, 127–153. Besançon: Presses universitaires fanc-comtoises, 2000.

Morawski, Joseph. *Proverbes français antérieurs au XVe siècle.* Paris: Champion, 1925.

Nebbiai-Dalla Guarda, Donatella. *La Bibliothèque de l'Abbaye de Saint- Denis en France du IXe au XVIIIe siècle.* Documents, études, et répertoires publiés par l'institut de recherche et d'histoire des textes. Paris: Éditions du Centre National de la Recherche Scientifique, 1985.

Nicolle, David, Ed. *A Companion to Medieval Arms and Armor.* Woodbridge: The Boydell Press, 2002.

Noble, Peter. "Saracen Heroes in Adenet le Roi." In *Romance Epic: Essays on a Medieval Literary Genre*, Ed. Hans-Erich Keller, 189–201. Studies in Medieval Culture XXIV. Kalamazoo: Medieval Institute Publications, 1987.

Olsen, B. Munk. Review: "*Ogier le Danois dans les littératures européennes.*" *Revue Romane* 10 (1975): 215–23.

Parry, Milman. *The Making of Homeric Verse: The Collected Papers of Milman Parry.* Ed. Adam Parry. Oxford: Clarendon Press, 1971.

Pirenne, Henri. *Mohammed and Charle*magne. Trans. Bernard Miall from the 10th French edition. First published 1939. Rpt. United States: Harper and Row, Barnes and Noble Import Division. (date and city not given)

Pidal, Ramón Menéndez. *La Chanson de Roland et la tradition* épique *des Francs.* 2nd ed. Trans. Irénée-Marcel Cluzel. Paris: Éditions A. et J. Picard, 1960.

Poulain-Gautret, Emmanuelle. *La Tradition littéraire d'Ogier le Danois après le XIIIe siècle: permanence et renouvellement du genre* épique *médiévale*. Nouvelle Bibliothèque du Moyen Age 72. Paris: Honoré Champion, 2005.

Ruggieri, Ruggero M. "Les Lombards dans les chansons de geste." *Actes du Congrès International de la Société Rencesvals (Heidelburg, 28 août-2 septembre, 1967),* Heidelberg: Carl Winter; Universitätsverlag, 1969, 37–45.

Rychner, Jean. *La Chanson de geste: essai sur l'art épique des jongleurs*. Société de Publications Romanes et Françaises LIII. Genève: Librairie E. Droz, 1955.

Stäblein, Patricia Harris. "Patterns of Textual Shift and the Alien Hero: Ogier the Dane in the Europeanization of the Old French Epic." *Olifant* 11. 3–4 (1986), 47–61. This article is a review of an untitled three volume series on the Ogier legend of which Togeby's book cited below is volume two.

Togeby, Knud. *Ogier le Danois dans les littératures européennes*. Copenhagen: Munksgaard, 1969.

Uden, Grant. *A Dictionary of Chivalry*. Middlesex, England: Kestrel Books, 1968.

Wylie, Laurence. *Beaux Gestes: A Guide to French Body Talk*. Cambridge: The Undergraduate Press, 1977.

Ogier's Youth

We must all arrange our lives
So that we can use them for good works.
To give alms is to encourage good
As is to record the good deeds of the worthy,
For no one hears such without becoming better.
For this reason it pleases me to tell a story,
Certain and true, which offers much to love.
It is about Ogier, who did much to be praised,
He, who, to win the love of God
And exalt and heighten his faith,
Severed the soul from the body of many a pagan.
By his hand many a Turk and many an infidel died.
Those minstrels who did not know how to rhyme,
Who only cared to fill up time,
Have falsified the story in several places.
In what concerned love and arms and honor
They did not know how to proportion or order the material
Nor to seize upon the words
Proper to a noble style.
For whoever wants to put a story into rhyme
Must make the meaning agree with the measure
And with reason, without the least discord,
Or the work neither can nor should succeed.
King Adam no longer wants to tolerate
That the story of Ogier, the vassal baron,
Be corrupted. Because of that he wants to think about
How he can restore Ogier to his rightful situation.
The one that King Adam must not refuse,
Whose orders he does without refusal,
That is, Count Gui of Flanders on the sea,
Pleased to command King Adam to undertake this task.
Minstrels will certainly weep
When he dies, for they could go far
Without ever finding his equal.

But may God keep him alive for us for a long time!
At the very moment when winter ends,
That bushes begin to bud
And little blades of grass start to push up,
Adam went—he didn't want to wait any longer—
To Saint Denis in France to inquire
How he could work on this story
In a way that would base it on truth,
For he would want to add nothing but the truth to the story
And remove lies.
He will seek them out and eliminate them wherever they appear.
A courteous monk, may God honor him,
Whom I heard named Lord Nicolas of Rains
Revealed to him the story from beginning to end,
How Charles had Ogier led
As a prisoner to the town of Saint Omer.
This story of which you hear me speak
Is gracious to say and to sing.
I want from now on to enter into the material.
I do not want to restrain or stop myself any longer.
Now may God grant that I may finish it
In such a manner that I cannot be blamed for it.

II

It happened long ago, in a time far in the past,
That Charlemagne, who did many worthy deeds,
Was in Spain to make war upon the pagans.
As he was about to return,
Messengers came to him from Hungary.
"Lord," they said, "we have come to tell you
That the Danes do not care anything about you.
They have ravaged a large part of Hungary.
Duke Gaufroi is behaving outrageously
When he makes war on Constance of the loyal heart,
Your dear aunt, may God keep her from harm.
She asks that you come to help her,
For she has such great need of help
That she will have to leave her kingdom
Because of the forces arrayed against her and go begging
If you do not find the means to avenge her."
Charles heard the message; he was almost beside himself.
He swore to God, the just father,
That he would go punish the Danes.

Before he returned, they would have paid dearly for their misdeeds.
If God the ruler of all saved him,
He would have Duke Gaufroi's head cut off
Unless he came there first to beg for mercy.
Then the king, who was full of knowledge,
Had all his barons summoned without delay.
He wanted to counsel with them about this news,
For that person is not wise—I can testify to it—
Who wants to embrace great things without counsel.
He knew quite well how to tell them what was occurring.
When the baron knights had heard him,
They saw well that he desired
To undertake the battle without delay.
Everyone praised him, duke, count and prince,
For one could not reasonably fail to do so,
For a friend must protect his friend
And provide material support and be prepared to undergo hardship
Or he does not have a right heart within him.
This counsel made the king rejoice.
Going at once without any delay,
He directed his army toward Denmark.
When Duke Namles learned of this great disturbance,
You may well believe that he felt great chagrin,
For Gaufroi's wife was Namles's sister.
This Gaufroi of whom you hear me speak
Had only one son—his name was Ogier—
And a daughter so lovely, that in truth, you could
Not wish for one more beautiful.
Flandrine was her name; now I do not wish to speak further about this.

III

This lady of whom you have heard,
The sister of Namles, who was born in Bavaria,
Was the mother of Ogier, who was praised so much.
She did not live long, which was a great pity,
For she was very beautiful and full of goodness.
Duke Gaufroi was already remarried.
He had remarried a woman full of evil,
For she never praised, pursued,
Did, or recognized any good deed.
He had three sons by her. The eldest was named Corras,
The other Hues, and the third Giboués.
When Namles saw that Charles was angry,

A letter was quickly drawn up and sealed
And carried to Denmark to Gaufroi
On behalf of Namles, who was his confidant.
Charles's anger was not hidden from Gaufroi;
Rather, it was certainly related and reported to him.
When he heard that King Charlemagne was
Thus tormented and troubled about him,
He was greatly frightened.
From throughout his lands he called his barons
To seek counsel, and he was advised
That he should go at once to meet Charles.
He should deliver himself entirely to his mercy.
Gaufroi heard it; he equipped himself at once.
He went away toward Charles well prepared.
With him was his son Ogier, who was sensible,
Sweet-tempered and courteous and well-taught.
He went toward Charles; that is the truth.
They did not cease their travel toward Charles until the two met.
The king had already crossed the waters of the Rhine.
Namles and the barons rejoiced because of it
When they learned such news of Gaufroi.

IV

When Namles heard the news
That Gaufroi was coming, he rejoiced.
He went toward him with a private entourage.
He met him at the bottom of a valley.
Gaufroi saw him; he raised his head.
He was very happy, and his people were comforted
When they saw Namles of the wise countenance.
They turned away from their path just a little bit.
Right at the entrance to a leafy forest
They stopped rather close to a meadow.
The good Duke Namles blamed Gaufroi
For his foolishness; he did not hide it from him.
"Brother," said he, "it was a foolish thought
That you had to torment such a lady
As Queen Constance the wise,
The aunt of the flower of renowned kings,
While he was making war on the pagans.
The king has sworn upon his crown
That this thing will be paid for dearly."
Gaufroi heard it; he was not pleased

Because he saw well that he would not hold out
Against the people that Charles had brought.
"Namles," said he, "I do not know whether or not Charles
Wants to destroy all my land.
This would not be done without many sword blows.
It would be better if a way could be found
For peace to be restored.
I seek mercy; I do not know if it will be found,
But, by the one who made the sky and the dew,
If I do not have it, Charles will have paid for
My land dearly before he has conquered it.
Many a lance will be broken,
Many shields shattered, many coats of mail ripped open
Before he is able to reach it."
"Brother," said Namles, "abandon this caprice,
For, God and the honored Virgin willing,
I believe that I can accomplish so much before dusk
That the work will be so far along
That it will turn out all right."
Then they planned out everything,
How it would be explained to King Charles.
Then Namles went away; he did not stay there.
He went to Charles's tent without delay
And recounted the affair in full.
On behalf of Gaufroi he asked for mercy,
And Charles agreed and granted it.
The whole army was joyful about it,
For everyone greatly desired to return;
They preferred to do battle
Against people who were not Christian.

V

King Charlemagne was a very valiant man.
Gaufroi was led before him.
Namles, who was wise in all circumstances,
Spoke wisely and courteously.
Germans and Franks
And lords from Brabant, Flanders, and the Ardennes,
And from Hainaut, Burgundy, Champagne,
Normandy, Brittany, and Picardy, and England,
And from Beauvaisis, Artois, Boulogne
Recommended to the king that he show mercy to Gaufroi.
And the king granted it although it was against his will,

But he did it this time for Namles.
He swore to God, who was put on the cross,
That it was their misfortune to have disturbed the Hungarians.
Reparation would be made; the Danish should be informed of this.

VI

You have heard how the affair went,
How Gaufroi reconciled himself to Charles.
Charles himself arranged the reparation
In such a way as I will now tell you.
It was that Gaufroi would go to Hungary.
He would kneel before his aunt.
He would ask mercy for his misdeed,
And he would compensate for all the damage done.
And after this Charles would send word to him about
His intentions and tell him
What tribute he wanted of him,
And because of these things he would expect to have good hostages.
Gaufroi got up; he did not stay there any longer,
For he was very glad that he had escaped with so little punishment.
He kneeled before the king at once.
All these things he agreed to willingly.
He delivered Ogier his son as hostage,
But he wept a little upon handing him over.
People said to one another, "What a fine youth we see before us!
Unless we are wrong, his looks alone show that he will be outstanding.
May God who made the whole world protect him!"
Gaufroi made all the reparations
In Hungary that Charles demanded; he forgot nothing.
After these things the army left.
Each combattant returned to his own country,
And Charles went straight back to Aix,
Where he stayed a great while.
Upon leaving he went back to France.
He sent the youth Ogier, of whom everyone thought highly,
To prison at Saint-Omer.
The castellan honored Ogier greatly, and so
The youth never wore irons or chains.
Duke Namles arranged it with the castellan
And made a solemn pledge to him
That Ogier would not depart from him,
That he, Namles, would compensate him for any risks he took
From treating Ogier well. In such a prison Ogier stayed.

VII

Lords, hear a story of renown,
Of love and arms, of honor and reason,
With lines that are gracious and good.
It is about Ogier, who possessed great prowess
Developed over a period of time;
And whose other qualites were such that
In him everything was good.
The most valiant of Christians, it is said,
Who most harmed the pagans, as it has been witnessed,
Were William, the baron of Orange,
Who had a lion's heart, and Ogier.
They played the same song
With harps that were bucklers or coats of arms
And brands of steel that were the bows.
With these harps they played many a tune,
Painful to hear to the Saracens.
I believe that they are now companions
In paradise on the lap of God.
He who would retain the lesson of such a master
Would be able to receive forgiveness for his sins
And obtain absolution.
I will not make you any longer sermon of this.
You have heard the reason
Why Ogier was put in prison
At Saint Omer with the castellan Hues.
He was there three years; we know this for sure.
This castellan that I have mentioned to you
Had a daughter of noble upbringing,
Beautiful and courteous. She was called Mahaut.
She was often by Ogier's side in their house,
For he was handsome and of noble visage.
The power of love, which certainly causes people to make mistakes,
Their youth and foolhardiness also,
Created between them such harmony
That the young girl made him the gift of her love.
She became pregnant; why hide it?
She had a son named Baudouin.
The castellan was loyal and worthy.
He endured the situation in peace for the love of Namles
And knew well that such a story
Was not worth getting angry about.
Here we will leave Ogier,

And we will tell you about the noble King Charles.
He was in Paris; with him were many high barons.

VIII

Charles of the wise heart was in Paris,
And with him were many princes and many vassals.
He wished to send word to Gaufroi
That Gaufroi should make the amends that he promised,
For it seemed to Charles that Gaufroi delayed it too long,
And the barons there recommended that he do so.
Quite soon the messengers were made ready.
Charles told them his wishes.
Not wishing to tarry, they went away.
Afterwards they hastened, they travelled so much that
They entered the land of the Danes.
They did not find Gaufroi there at all, but
They found his wife, may God damn her.
She was the stepmother of the imprisoned Ogier.
Of Gaufroi she had three young sons.
As for her children, whom she greatly cherished,
It occurred to her through her great evil,
That if Ogier were killed,
They would have the inheritance
Of Denmark, the very great duchy.
She thought of doing a perverse thing.
Here is what she had arranged.
Of Charles's messengers she honored not a single one.
She had each one's beard shaved against his will
So that Charles, who was so proud,
Would thus have his heart so inflamed with anger
That he would neither protect nor pity Ogier.
When the messengers of Charles were treated this way
So that they saw themselves thus disfigured,
You can well believe that they were very unhappy.

IX

When the lady had done
All she wanted to the messengers,
Then she came before them at once
And said maliciously to them,
"Lords, for God's sake, go on back.
I do not advise you to stay any longer.
Tell Charles in the hearing of all his people

That Gaufroi does not fear him at all.
Gaufroi would not," she said, "do anything for Charles.
If it does not agree with Charles, let him take vengeance.
Tell him that Gaufroi, to whom Denmark belongs,
Greatly repents of the promise
He made, and he holds
His promise in very little esteem.
If he were here, know it truly,
You would be hanged and swinging in the wind.
For this reason I beseech you to go back
Very quickly, as I recommend."
Upon hearing this, they got ready and went away at once;
They did not linger after this.
It was not very long afterward
That Gaufroi came back with a sad heart
Because his wife had acted foolishly.
He criticized her greatly and reprimanded her and accused her.
He knew very well that Ogier would pay for it grievously.
Within his heart he had great sorrow, and
He did not know what to do; it could not be otherwise.
He saw that matters were developing dangerously,
For he would not go to Charles, in my opinion,
Who would give him the fief of Bonivent.
Thus he remained in grief and in torment.
And the messengers rode hard,
Making no delay until they reached Paris.
There they found Charles the noble,
The Duke Namles, and many others besides
Because the king was holding his parliament.

X

Furious, the messengers descended on foot.
They came before Charles.
With great reverence they saluted the king.
"Sire," they said, "evil has befallen us.
We were in Denmark for your tribute,
But in your service we met with misfortune.
We were badly received by Gaufroi's people.
He was not there, for which Jesus be thanked.
Instead, his wife was there, for we found out through her
That if he had been there, we would have been hanged
Or flayed or burned in a fire.
Merely being killed could not have been sufficient, she said.

Because of their scorn for you, we were so vilely treated
That we have come back without our beards.
We understood well that he did not care a bit
If our treatment disturbed you."
When Charles heard it, his heart was so troubled
That he barely said a word.
He swore to God and his holy power
That the Danes would be punished even more severely.
They and Gaufroi would pay very dearly.

XI

Charles of the fierce heart was greatly angered
When his messengers came back without their beards.
He had all his barons come before him.
The king himself recounted to them the outrage
That Gaufroi had done, and they considered it to be madness.
"Sire," they said, "he has done you great humiliation.
Without any delay, all now
Must be convened and sent for, both the simple minded and the wise,
The young and the old.
Under you there dwell people of many languages
Of which several hold their domains from you.
Let them know everywhere, both by land and by sea,
That they must not be held back by wind or by storm,
Nor for any obstacle except prison or illness.
Let them come to Laon to your principal residence
So that you can do Gaufroi great harm.
We will go look for him and his lineage.
By God who made us in his image,
He will remain neither in plain nor in woods
Nor in mountain, in valley nor on shore,
Neither in burg nor in town, nor in a strong tower or dwelling
Unless he flees like a wild animal.
For his misfortune he sent you such a tribute.
Instead of beards, which he has taken as payment,
He will lose his head; he will not put other guarantees on it.
We will take neither pawns nor hostages."
"Barons," said Charles, "your counsel consoles me.
I want urgently to make this journey."

XII

Charles the king, who did much to esteem,
Had his letters sent across the land

To his barons who must help him,
For he wanted to destroy all of Denmark.
He wanted to have everything knocked down to the ground.
For their misfortune they had brought this great harm upon him.
Gaufroi believed it would be paid for dearly.
Charlemagne sent to Saint Omer for Ogier
In order to hang him or flay him alive.
When Mahaut heard that spoken of Ogier,
She felt such grief that one could hardly believe it.
One could not imagine anything that
Could have touched her more deeply than this development.
For when she saw him tied up on the horse,
She slumped down in a faint on the grass.
For him she died of grief—I'm not lying—
Before two whole months had gone by.
They led Ogier away at once.
Straight to Paris they went without further delay.
Most began to pray to God to take him away
And let him return safe and sound
And turn him away from death and pain.
Many wept out of pity.
When Namles of Bavaria, whom this thing should trouble greatly,
Knew this news,
He went to the king and started speaking with him about it.
"Sire," said he, "by Saint Richier,
You want to do wrong—I don't deny it—
When you want to condemn Ogier to death
In this land. You would have a very cowardly heart,
But if you want to act in a worthy way,
You will have Ogier spared
So that we can approach Gaufroi.
If we can besiege him in his fortress,
Send your war machines and Ogier along with them.
You cannot anger Gaufroi more.
You could not cause more dismay to him or his people."
Namles said all this to cause delay,
For his nephew was very dear to his heart.
"Namles," said Charles, "it would be well to grant it.
One must certainly act by your counsel.
Your counsel is loyal and upright.
I have needed your advice in many hard circumstances.
Gaufroi had your sister as wife,
But he has angered me by his outrageous

And shameful deed, for which I must be very angry.
So I know well that you would allow
Your head to be cut off rather than counsel me
To do anything that could be reproached as harmful."

XIII

"Namles," said Charles, "do you know what I want you to do?
Take Ogier and guard him for me.
I put you in charge of him in exchange for all you own
And all you might do in the future."
"Sire," said Namles, "it will be as you have said."
When Duke Namles left the king, he was so happy
And his heart was so full of gladness
That he had not had such joy since the hour that he was born.
When the court and the assembled barons heard this,
That Ogier was spared from death,
They thanked God repeatedly.
Charles did not stay in Paris any longer.
He turned straight to Laon
Because he had summoned his barons there.
I couldn't name them all for you.
So many of them had come and assembled there,
Some here, some there, some on foot and others on horseback,
That there seemed to be around 200,000.
But before Charles could very go far,
Before he could harm Gaufroi,
He would hear news that would anger him greatly.
And here all of a sudden was a messenger climbing the steps.
He was at once brought before the king,
Who greeted him courteously.
He was a valiant and renowned knight
Whose name was Raimon; a wise and prudent man.
He was of Roman extraction and born in a Roman province.
Charles saw him and recognized him with certainty.
"Raimon," said he, "what news do you have?"
"Sire," said he, "now you will know it very soon."
Then he told him like a man of sound opinion:
"Righteous emperor," said he, "now hear me.
Upon you depends all Christianity, for
You are its support; it is the very truth.
But it is lost if you fail it now.
King Corsuble has entered Rome
With many infidels in his company.

He swears a great deal to his god Mohammed
That in this year he will be crowned at Paris;
But, if it please God, you will prevent it.
You certainly need to hasten
Because the Pope is thrown out of Rome
And the country is completely ravaged.
There are many dead and wounded
And many exiled and badly provisioned.
Puglia and Calabria have fallen into great poverty, for
The earth is burned and the countryside laid waste.
You understand, Sire, that the Pope
And all the others, as you have heard,
Beseech you through me to rescue them.
For God's sake, good king, take pity upon them.
If you do not set out soon, you will never arrive there in time."
With this word the messenger concluded.

XIV

When Charles had heard the messenger speak,
His color began to change violently.
He ground his teeth, began to shake his head,
And looked around him at his people.
He called Duke Namles
And Salemon the baron of Bretagne
And Manesier the count of Montcler,
Oedes de Lengres, Ghibert de Mont Wimer,
Hues de Troies and Sanson and Guimer
And Widelon, who never knew how to be false;
Hues dou Mans, who was a formidable person;
From Normandy Richars, whom one must praise.
He did not want to forget Joffrois d'Anjou,
Hoel de Nantes and Gaifrei de Valcler,
Duke Fagon and Guy de Saint Omer,
And many other great princes that he saw standing around him.
"Lords," said he, "Let me be clear.
It behooves us to get our journey underway.
I thought I would be shaming and humiliating Gaufroi,
But Saracens turn my thoughts elsewhere.
First of all, I want to go where I may serve God,
For we must love him above all
And for his faith put ourselves in harm's way.
God will have those who do this dwell
In Paradise and will crown them next to him.

But by Saint Peter, whom we adore,
Duke Gaufroi can be well assured,
If God allows me to return,
That I will exile and ruin him
And I will have all his members cut off.
For his humiliation I would have had
His son Ogier dragged and hanged and flayed alive.
Know in truth that he could not have escaped from it;
But for the sake of his uncle, Duke Namles,
Whom one must certainly honor, I will let him be now."
Everyone began to thank the king.
You would have seen many crying with joy
That their journey was now for such a worthy purpose.
"Sire," said they, "prepare to travel now,
For by the one who protects us all,
We can hardly wait to come to combat
And be able to fight Saracens.
We beg nothing of you but to hasten."
"May God rule over such a people," said Charles.
"One does not have to talk to them long.
The king must be glad who has such people to guide
In whom one can find such counsel."

XV

When Charlemagne listened to his barons
He was very joyous, for it seemed to him
That each one wanted very much to start the journey.
In his heart he greatly esteemed them, and
He thanked the Lord God for their goodness.
A thought occurred to the good Namles
That he would take his nephew Ogier with him.
He presented it so convincingly that the king gave his permission.
He granted it on condition that
When Charles wanted him back, Namles would always give him up.
The king prepared to go; he did not tarry.
Before the third day they left.
The king broke his army up into three groups.
May God who formed the whole world guide them.
I will not speak to you any further of their journey.
The army traveled so much and hastened so well
That at Viterbe all reassembled
And lodged together around the town.
The next day Charlemagne sent word to

All his barons, and each one went there
To learn the plans that he would make
And how he would order his battalions,
How one after the other would go.
The good king set up five great battalions
In the manner that Duke Namles presented it and planned it.
In the avant-garde he put Duke Fagon;
Joffrois d'Anjou led the other battalion.
Hoel de Nantes would have the third echelon,
And Duke Richars would conduct the fourth
While Charlemagne would be in the rear guard.

XVI

In such a manner as I have recounted to you
Were Charlemagne's troops arranged.
Saracens were in the city of Rome.
When they had learned the truth about Charles,
How he and his people had hastened,
They saw well that he was not willing
To let King Corsuble have his kingdom
Without delivering many violent blows.
Some were glad of it; others were frightened.
Corsuble sent for King Danemon,
Who was his son and very dear to him,
For he had prowess and assurance;
But his heart was so false
That he was loyal to no one.
He sent for King Brunamon and Caradé,
King Sadoine and King Clodué,
King Androine and King Bruncosté.
Many other kings were assembled there
That I will not name now.
King Corsuble spoke first.
"Lords," said he, "he did us a great kindness,
Mohammed our god, when he led to us
Charles and those of his kingdom.
The sovereigns of Christianity
Are in their army; that has certainly been reported to me.
And they told me the pure truth
In estimating the number of Charles's people.
According to what has been reported to me
We have three times as many as the Christians;
So we may rest assured

That now I will have what we have desired so ardently,
That is, that I will have a golden crown put on my head
Right in Paris, for thus I have vowed.
This we will indeed have accomplished
If it please Mohammed, within this summer.
When these first ones are overcome,
Which means they will be dead or imprisoned,
Then you will have no reason to fear the others.
The French are assembled around Viterbe.
You know very well that we have destroyed
This country far and wide.
They will not find,
Unless they have brought it,
Barley or oats or forage or wheat
Or anything else whatsoever.
For which I counsel, if you are willing,
That we not move out of Rome
Until they come and assemble here.
They will soon come to us; that is a certainty,
For they are vain and of great pride
And if they can be trapped here,
We can do as we wish with them.
For if we were moved from this spot
And then spread out over the fields,
If they knew our people's mettle
Never would they be so hardy or so daring
As not to flee—that is what I have feared."
This counsel was praised communally.
Great and small were not in disagreement about it.

XVII

The Saracens all rejoiced
Because Christians had come
Upon them in such numbers. They repeatedly thanked
Mohammed their God for it with much heartfelt gladness.
The good King Charles upon whom sweet France depended
Was at Viterbe, but he had no great wish
To stay there a long time.
He keenly desired in his heart
To see Saracens soon
Because he was in anguish
That they had so grievously tormented Christians.
You should know truly that

He stayed only two days in Viterbe,
And on the third day, without remaining any longer,
The army left quickly.
You have heard how,
The day before, Charles the king
Had wisely acquainted his people with
The entire order of his battle.
He had done this so well that he had omitted nothing.

XVIII

In the month of May, after dawn one morning,
Charles's army left Viterbe.
At the break of day the army heard the mass.
Before the mass, the standard of Saint Denis,
Whom Christians greatly loved and pagans feared,
Was carried to the altar,
Laid upon it and rested there
While the mass was sung at a deliberate pace.
Immediately afterward, without delay,
They attached the standard very firmly
To its handle, of which the blade was wide
And very sharp, for it was well steeled.
There you would have seen many coats of mail,
Many a brilliant helmet, many a golden shield
And many a vassal who was eager for deeds of prowess.
"Sire," said Namles, "to whom will be given
Your standard that we have prepared?
No one has yet been chosen."
Aloris, who had greatly desired it, heard this.
He came before the king at once.
"Sire," said he, "do let your standard
Be given to me, if you do not object.
I am Lombard, and I was born at Valpree.
My company is peopled with a thousand Lombards.
I married the Countess of Calabria,
But Saracens have destroyed the land.
I would avenge myself of it, if it comes to a battle.
By that Lord who made the sky and the dew,
The standard will be bloodied with pagan blood,
Or I will lie on my back bloody, with mouth wide open."
Charles saw his great size and form.
He was handsome and tall; he had a broad chest.
"Friend," said Charles, "your thinking is good.

You are of a good size to do a great day's fighting.
You will have the standard; it will not be refused you."
Charles gave it to him by the painted handle,
And he took it joyously.
It would have been better if it had been in the laundry.
Aloris positioned his corps of troops.
Then the army moved with ease,
Riding well like honored people
And who, concerning war, were experienced and circumspect.
Before evening that day they arrived at Sutri.
There the army stopped and took lodging.
Very soon many tents were set up.
The news went to the Saracens
That Charles's army had left Viterbe
And had come to Sutri and assembled there.
They rejoiced greatly.
"Mohammed," they said, "what luck
That you have led these people to us!"

XIX

Our French were camped at Sutri
Lodged together around the city.
The pagans had so destroyed the countryside
That they found nothing there unless they had provided it
Or had carried it with them.
The French saw it; it annoyed them greatly.
Many wept about it
And swore to God and his sweet pity
That before they returned, it would be put to rights.
Either they would die or it would be avenged.
It was told and announced to Charles
That he would have a painful sojourn
If he delayed a long time.
This same day the king decreed
And it was proclaimed among the army
That the next day, right at daybreak,
They should be ready and armed,
All of them, on horse and on foot.
The Christians were glad of this command.

XX

The next day at daybreak
The French armed themselves; they stayed there no longer.

Charles the king called to Namles.
"Namles," said he, "do you know what I intend to do?
I do not want our entire army
To move; this is my will.
I would like to go to the city of Rome
In two battalions; that is what I think,
And let the other people stay here.
No foot soldiers will go.
The Saracens have greatly devastated this country.
Because of this I would like to know how
Our people are disposed so as to guide them best."
"Sire," said Namles, "as you wish."
Thus what Charles commanded
Was quickly proclaimed on his behalf to the army.
It was done as I have recounted to you.
Charles and Namles, in whom there was so much goodness,
Left in two well-ordered battalions.
At the head of the first the Lombards were established.
Aloris held the standard with the golden hilt,
With the stiff rod and the steeled iron.
Charles, who had a wise heart, rode
Along with his richly equipped people.
You would have seen there many an impetuous steed,
Many a shining helmet, many a painted shield.
May God, the king of majesty, conduct them so
That before they have turned back
There will be many a saddle pad overturned,
Many a man dead, many captured and many wounded.
Charles wanted very much
For all the others to go with him before evening.

XXI

Here we will leave Charles of the proud face
And speak to you of Turks, Arabians
Persians, Achopars, and Lutis,
Of which there were such a great plenty in Rome
That a living man never before saw so many together.
Seven entire years had passed
Since they had planned these military expeditions.
Thenceforward they had certainly thought when all was said and done
That they would conquer Charlemagne
And that Corsuble would wear a golden crown
In Paris as they had intended.

This same day that I am telling you about
When Charlemagne had left Sutri,
Danemon had gone out quickly
From the city of Rome, I believe,
With thirty thousand armed men in his company.
He had vowed—this is what the source said—
Not to return if he saw the French;
Rather, they would be needed at Sutri.
The pagans rode on their costly steeds
Until they saw the standard of Saint Denis
That the Lombard Aloris held in his fist.
When Aloris saw the pagans, he was frightened out of his wits.
Every single Lombard was completely terrified.
Both columns, I guarantee it's the truth,
Stopped without permission.

XXII

When the pagans saw our French people
And the standard, which was unfurled in the wind,
Danemon said, "Let's ride quietly.
I see the Christians before us now;
One can certainly see this clearly
Because they do not act the way we do.
We will engage them very soon, I think,
For the French are people of great hardiness."
"Namles," said Charles, "tell me plainly right now
What you think of this thing.
You know very well what will happen.
We shall have battle; it cannot be otherwise."
"Sire," said Namles, "by Saint Vincent,
They are in order and are eager for battle.
Since they put themselves before us in this way,
I recommend that we attack them right away."
"Namles," said Charles, "I agree."
After this word there was no more hesitation.
They cried, "Monjoie," and rode off joyfully,
Charles himself the very first,
And then Duke Namles and Joffrois with him.
Hues de Troies and Symon de Meulent
And all the others spurred on their horses together.
The Saracens expected nothing,
So they fell back in tumult.
They had much distress and confusion in reassembling.

There was much great noise of shields and lances.
Many of them were slain and many were bleeding.
They had had grievous encounters with brands of steel.
You would have seen enormous slaughter there.
When Aloris saw this massacre,
Even the gold of Bénévent would not have made him want to be there.
He called Gillebert de Clarvent.
Who was his cousin and whom he regarded as a close relative.
"Fair nephew," he said, "for God's sake, let's leave.
To stay is not safe.
I would not stay here for a valley full of silver.
Once dead, always dead."
And that one answered, "You speak wisely."
Aloris turned in flight and his company likewise.
He fled shamefully, the standard in his fist.
Charles saw it; it touched him in his heart.
He called upon God, the omnipotent father.
"Ah, God," he said, "I have not often seen
My standard-bearer fleeing; it is a horrible sight."

XXIII

When Charles saw his standard-bearer retreating,
You can well believe it had to weigh upon him greatly,
And nevertheless he could not torment himself too much.
Now the Saracens were beginning to move.
The first ones were about to be thwarted
When Brunamon, may God damn him,
Came spurring his horse, wanting to fight,
With twenty thousand Turks, who were very formidable.
Charles saw them and went to show them to Namles.
"Sire," said Namles, "have your horn sounded
Quickly to reunite your people.
There is only one choice; I can't tell you anything else.
We must certainly be determined to fight.
May Aloris suffer a bad death
For undertaking to carry the standard this way.
Were it not so, in truth I can swear to you
They could not last against us."
"Namles," said Charles, "I tell you frankly,
If God allows me to return,
I will have him dishonored."
They sounded the horn to reassemble their people,
Those who should fight,

And here all of a sudden were many Turks and many pagans charging
With Brunamon, may God destroy him,
To start assembling around Charles.
There you would have seen many violent blows given,
Shields and bucklers broken and destroyed,
Coats of mail torn and helmets with their metal circlets broken,
Brains splattered and bowels trailing,
Noses and faces and feet and hands cut off.
Charles the king began to shout, "Montjoie!"
In his fist he held the good sword of bright steel.
No weapon could protect those it struck.
Whoever could have seen Namles spur his horse then
And come and go among pagans
To comfort Christians with his sword of steel
And kill and wound pagans
Would have esteemed him as a man of very fine prowess.
Engerrans of Montcler fought well,
As did Hues de Troies and Guy de Saint Omer
And many others, may Jesus save them!

XXIV

The noise of the fighting was fierce; the battle was great.
Brunamon was a proud and powerful king.
All those who knew him thought him
Full of prowess and valor and reliability.
He rode an iron gray battle horse,
Strong and swift and impetuous and very fast,
That they called Broiefort.
He charged rapidly among the ranks
And made the day sorrowful for many of our people.
Upon his way he met a German
Whom he gave such a blow with his sword as he passed by
That the brains spilled on the ground.
King Danemon rode all around the ranks.
Following behind him were the infidels
Who violently attacked our people.
So they greatly harmed them,
But the Christians showed quite obviously
That they had no desire to die.
The good King Charles went proclaiming, "Montjoie!"
Namles of Bavaria, the sharp sword in his fist,
Bloodied many a Saracen that day.
Hues de Troies shouted, "Bourgogne!"

Guy de Saint Omer was in the middle of the greatest mass of men.
You would have seen lying there among the ranks
Many a fist, many a foot, many a shining helmet,
Many a lance fragment and many a gleaming shield;
And you would have seen many a Christian eager
To serve God and desiring honor.
And it was apparent by their deeds,
For they exposed themselves so much to danger,
That it was clear they did not fear death at all.
But there were so many of the people of Tervagant
That if Jesus had not intervened
The Christians would have ridden too far ahead.

XXV

Great was the fracas; there was much to fear.
You would have seen the French charge violently,
But there were so many of the demonic enemy
That just seeing them would have made you tremble with fright.
And Aloris fled all along the rocky path.
All the Lombards followed behind him.
Outside Sutri beside an old monastery
Many admirable young men,
Many sons of counts, of dukes and of princes
Had come to pass the time of day as
They awaited news of Charles.
Among them was the Dane Ogier.
They were a large company, you may be sure,
To my knowledge more than four thousand.
They looked beyond a boulder
And saw the standard of Saint Denis waving, but when
Very soon they saw it retreating,
You may be sure that they felt nothing but dismay.
Many of them began to weep,
For they thought surely that the others
Whom they had left behind were in mortal danger.
Then they started to pray to God with joined hands
That he would help Charles, him and his people.
Ogier, who had all good qualities, spoke.
"Lords, "said he, "by Saint Richier,
We are young people; we will certainly need
To acquire honor and advance ourselves.
Those are Lombards; I have heard said
That they are not worth a cent in arms.

Let each one seize one of them without delay,
The one by the bridle, the other by the stirrup.
Defeated people do not have the power to help themselves,
I have heard, any more than children or shepherds.
We will certainly be able to frighten them easily
And drag them to the ground and unhorse them.
I want to challenge Aloris for the standard.
If I can get hold of it,
I believe I can certainly wrest it from his hands.
They will have neither arms nor horses left.
Now let's take them away from them without delay
And move on and get ourselves ready
To help Charles the just and
Duke Namles, my uncle the warrior.
I want to carry the standard at the head of the troops.
If God who judges everyone grants us
That we come to deliver violent blows in time,
We will thin out the ranks so much that
The pagans will certainly be astonished."
Said one to the other, "That is good advice.
May God bring grief,
To anyone who does not help him out."
There was not one who did not agree.

XXVI

It was in May when the dew is sparkling
That Aloris came to the bottom of a valley.
On this morning he came from a place
Where he had had a miserable day,
He and all his people born in Lombardy.
The hardiest among them had his mind
Much more on his spurs than on his sword.
Aloris held on its painted handle the noble standard
Of Saint Denis of France the praised,
But it was not carried
In the customary way.
It had often been shown
In the largest assembly of infidels.
It was much feared by the pagan people.
It had often been stained by their blood.
If it could have spoken, it would have soon told
The true reason that it was ill-fated
And that it had not been suitably given.

Aloris's face revealed his fear.
His coat of arms was vert with a bordure indented
Of gold, with bezants gules.
His troops were badly frightened.
They were filled with so much fear
That they had not returned by the path
That Charles's people had first taken.
They had avoided the way on the left
And had entered into a big cavern.
There their people had stopped, being very quiet,
Until they had caught their breath.
The cave was isolated and lacked all comfort.
The squires had not forgotten the situation,
The covenant that they had agreed to
As I have indicated to you previously.
They went right across a meadow
Straight to where they had seen the standard turn.
In the cavern they found the people,
Who were crammed together there in fear.
They were surrounded on all sides at once.

XXVII

When the Lombards saw that they were trapped
In the cavern that they had entered,
There was not a one of them who did not have his head bowed,
For they were greatly ashamed that they were found in such a way.
The youth Ogier spoke first
Because of his desire and will
To know the pure truth
About what had happened to the others.
"Lords," said he, "tell us; hide nothing.
Where is King Charles of the iron will
And my dear Uncle Namles of the wise heart
And the barons who are such good men?"
Said Aloris, "I will tell the truth about it.
My troops and I escaped,
But all the others—let there be no doubt—
Are dead and captured and all cut to pieces."
At this word many sighed
And wept and tenderly cried.
"Truly," said Ogier, "you are as good as dead
If your horses and arms
Are not immediately delivered to us.

We want to have them now
So that we can help Charles the praised."
And those who had hearts full
Of cowardice and of great evil
Answered, "Have pity on us.
Do not kill or wound us
And we will do all you want."
Then they dismounted without delay.
Their horses were seized from many sides
By those who greatly hastened to disarm them and
Who then put on the others' coats of mail.
Ogier's group were soon ready as best they could be.

XXVIII

The squires hastened greatly to arm themselves.
They treated the Lombards so roughly
That they left them no possessions,
And they had nothing with which to arm themselves.
Ogier seized Aloris by the stirrup.
"Master," said he, "I am going to have to be blunt with you.
You must let go of this standard.
If you do not do it at once, you will pay for it dearly."
When Aloris heard him speak this way,
When he heard himself threatened by Ogier,
Who he could see was tall and young and nimble,
He was greatly afraid, and he started trembling.
He dismounted at once from his swift steed
And began to take off his arms.
Ogier armed himself, not caring to delay,
And put the sword on his left side.
At that time only knights girded themselves in that way.
Then he mounted, not wanting to wait.
At his neck hung the quarterly shield.
Then he took the standard of sharpened steel
And held it firmly in his fist.
Both fists were equally agile
And could handle these arms with ease.
While they were arming
Themselves, of this you may be sure:
Two messengers left
Who went to announce to Charles's people
What they had heard the Lombards report,
That he had had mortal trouble.

When Charles's people heard this, they were beside themselves.
The chamberlains and the bailiffs ran to arms
As did the drink masters, the cooks and the bottlers
From the household of Charles of the loyal heart
And the people of Duke Namles of Bavaria.
Whoever had no horse mounted on a beast of burden.
They started going toward the standard,
All five thousand of them; they greatly desired
To approach the pagans in time.
They spurred the horses; they had no wish to delay.
Now may God give them a joyous return!

XXIX

Ogier rode, he and his companions,
Until they arrived at the battle.
They saw the Turks everywhere in great numbers
And saw the great destruction they had wrought on our forces.
They had already taken the good Duke Widelon,
Hues de Troies and his brother Sanson.
They had taken and tied up Namles.
They had put King Charles on foot.
The youth Ogier unfurled the banner
On the stiff rod with the sharp tip
And cried, "Denmark!" in a loud voice.
He and his companions spurred together with God's blessing
And entered into the great press, swinging their weapons.
Ogier struck Escorfaut de Valbron.
Who fell headfirst dead from his steed of Aragon.
Afterward Ogier came with such force
That he threw down dead many a heathen Saracen.
Charles saw him; he showed him to Guy
De Saint Omer, who was a very noble man.
"Let's get going," said he, "by Saint Symon,
Now that Aloris has come back like a man of prowess
And is conducting himself well, like a baron,
His help is in good time.
I will make him a lord of my kingdom."

XXX

When Charlemagne saw the standard,
His heart was joyous and astonished.
"Ah, God," said Charles, "who never lied,
I have wrongly blamed Aloris,

The noble count, and his army, too.
They have nobly turned around
And have brought back many with them.
They are certainly five times as many men as I first saw.
May God in his tender mercies keep them,
For they give pagans a severe reception."
Then Ogier attacked amid the flowery meadow.
In the sight of Charles, he slayed a pagan.
With his sword of steel he cut through another.
Whomever he attacked I'm sure was badly treated.
When Charles saw that Ogier was handling himself well,
He raised his hand, giving him God's blessing.
The youth Ogier turned to the left
As God willed and directed.
He found Namles, whom the pagans had seized,
And Widelon and his brother Thierri,
Hues de Troies, Sanson and Amauri.
Ogier saw Namles; his heart was distressed.
He called loudly to the Danes,
"Let us spur ahead, for God's sake, I pray you.
I see my Uncle Namles of the valiant heart,
Being led away prisoner by Persians and Arabians
And Hues de Troies and many others also."
At this word they spurred on their horses to attack again.
Had you been there, you would have seen many a coat of mail torn,
Many a strong, shiny shield broken
And many a sturdy helmet shattered.
What can I tell you? The squires conducted themselves
There so that the Saracens
Abandoned Namles and the others as well.
Ogier seized an Arabian steed
And gave it to Namles, who leapt onto it.
All the prisoners were rescued, I'm telling you.
The pagans saw it and were astonished.
Said one to the other, "These are the people of the Antichrist
That the devils have sent back to us here,
And yet this morning they fled.
Mohammed our god has certainly abandoned us
If things last like this for long."

XXI

At the rescue of Namles the bearded
And of Hues de Troies the praised

And of many others that I have not named,
Many great blows were exchanged and given.
Very soon the prisoners were mounted once again, and
Everywhere the French were reinvigorated.
Charles himself recovered his steed.
The Saracens fell back behind
A measured acre, I would estimate.
This day Ogier had not rested.
In his hand he held the engraved sword of steel, which
He had stained with the blood of pagans.
Whomever he attacked he soon delivered to death.
Before him came Namles of the wise heart.
"Vassal," he said, "do not hide from me.
Who are you—tell the truth—
Who shouted, "Denmark!" so much
And killed and sliced open so many pagans
And put me in possession of a saddled steed?"
And said Ogier, "Uncle, by the holy God,
Haven't you recognized me yet?
I am Ogier, by the God of majesty,
With whom Charles must do his will,
Who he has received with so much hate because of my father
That he does not fear the hour that he would have me hanged.
It is right, for much wrong has been committed against him."
Namles heard it and praised God.
Never had he had such joy in all his life.
He wept for sheer joy.
He went to Charles and told him about Ogier.
When Charles heard it, he thanked God fervently.
Then Charles spurred the impetuous steed.
With Namles beside him, the valiant and strong.
They found Ogier amid the Turks.
Charles saw him, and he addressed him thus:
"Ogier," said he, "it's a good thing you came to me.
Because of your prowess we have recovered everything.
You must be well rewarded for this.
So it will be; let there be no doubt about it.
My reasons for anger toward you are pardoned,
Toward you and your father, because of your goodness."
Charles moved on forward without delay.
He took the sword of steel from Ogier's fist
And attached it to his left side,
For the pagans had completely cut up the scabbard.

Charles presented the sword to Ogier again,
And Ogier, who had certainly put it to the proof, took it.
Then Charles raised his arm high and
Tapped Ogier on the back of the neck.
Thus he made him a regular knight
And promised him a substantial portion of his inheritance.
"Sire," said the youth, "May God be pleased by your actions."
Ogier bowed his head.
His helmet, that pagans had batterd in many places,
Was broken and torn up, pierced and ripped open.
"God," said Ogier, "what riches I receive
In reconciling my father to Charles."
He spurred his horse on,
Holding the sword of steel in his fist.
He struck the first Turk that he met so hard
That he killed him.
Namles wept with joy and pity.
He guided his horse to Ogier's side.
Whomever they attacked had a ruinous day.
Had you been there, you would have seen a fracas of great ferocity.
The youth Ogier wielded his sword again,
Giving King Danemon such a blow with it
That he threw him back on the rump of the horse.
Said the pagans, "May such blows
Be given to the devil.
By this traitor we are undone.
We will have suffered too badly today, for
These living devils brought him back to us."

XXXII

The day that good king Charles
Made a knight of Ogier
The battle was fierce and strong.
Around Charles were assembled his people
Whom the Saracens had greatly tormented,
But then Ogier and the company
That he had led came to this battle.
The pagan people were badly beaten back,
And our people were greatly reinvigorated.
Many of them recovered their lances.
"Charge," said Charles, "for the honored Virgin;
Their people seem frightened.
They are defeated; I see well what they are thinking."

They charged together, all of them shouting war cries.
They attacked the Turks with such great violence
That many lay bleeding with their mouths gaping.
You would have seen many a buckler broken,
Many a cuirass cut into pieces.
The field was strewn with the fallen.
"Montjoie" was cried loudly there
And "Denmark" and "Bavaria the Wide"
And "Saint Malo" and "Anjou" and "Valee,"
And many other rallying cries that I have not named.
Ogier restrained himself—it is the proven truth—
Or there would have been even greater piles of defeated pagans.
Many a Turk feared his prowess,
For he had taken many of their lives.
The pagan people retreated
More than a crossbow shot when he spurred on his horse.
They could see by this that it was not their day.
They fled; they did not wait any longer.
Charles saw it and pulled in his rein.
Immediately he had the return sounded, for
He did not want his people endangered foolishly.

XXXIII

When Charles saw the pagans defeated,
He thanked God, the king of paradise.
"Right away, now," said he, "sound my great horn,
For I do not want to pursue.
Reason is worth more than extremes, in my opinion."
Thus it was done as I have recounted it.
The standard of Saint Denis was brought to the rear.
But before Charles reassembled his people,
There were so many dead Turks and Arabians
And Coumains, Persians, and Lutis
That one would have been astonished to see them.
Everyone came back around Charles.
They looked for the dead through the fields and in the surrounding territory
And they put the wounded back on their horses.
Each one left his companions there with a heavy heart
For in a critical moment you can tell who your friends are.
And here were the French charging rapidly,
Riding from Sutri on their prized horses
In three battalions; each group was equipped well.
There was not a one of them who was not angry and sad,

For they believed that Charles was certainly destroyed
And all the others were chopped up and killed
Because of the news that Aloris had told them.
They found the dead, here six, there seven, there ten,
Many a discolored helmet, many a white and gray-brown shield,
Many a broken lance, many a buckler knocked asunder,
Many a steel sword that had lost its sheen,
For each one was stained and blackened with blood.
Said one to the other, "Here was a great battle."

XXXIV

When Charles saw his people
Coming rapidly in three battalions,
He spotted Duke Fagon first,
Hoel de Nantes and Ernaut de Clarvent
And Foucheré, and many others as well.
"Namles," said Charles, "by Saint Climent,
Friends of such people must surely be happy."
"Sire," said Namles, "I certainly know that, in fact,
They are sad and sorrowful for your sake.
There are many of them, you should know this in truth,
Who would have gladly given
Half of all they had
To have been at this massacre."
"Certainly" said Charles, "I surely believe
That it is so and that it is not anything but that.
They should not worry about it,
For if pleases the omnipotent father,
They could very well be in that spot in a short time
Where they will be able, if Jesus wills it,
To make up well for all the delay
That they have had so far."
Around Charles they came at once,
Those who loved him very loyally in their hearts.
When they found him safe, they repeatedly thanked
God and his mother and the saints humbly.
They saw few there whose equipment was not
Broken, cut up, and bloody.
Said one to the other, "By Saint Vincent,
It surely looks as if they had a furious battle here."
Charles told them how
All had been recovered by Ogier.
"He is a knight who has displayed such exemplary behavior

That he is completely back in my good graces,
He and his father and all his relatives.
I have gained so much by Ogier's work
That I can honorably receive them."
This news spread throughout the ranks.
More than one thousand seven hundred rejoiced.
They esteemed King Charles greatly because of it.
Together they returned with him gladly,
Not stopping until they reached Sutri.

XXXV

Our French had returned to Sutri.
They thanked and praised God repeatedly
Because they had handled themselves so well.
They spoke a great deal about Ogier throughout the army.
Everyone said in truth,
All those that had been in the battle,
That if it had not been for his strength and goodness
And his vigor and great reliability
That the day would have gone badly for them.
The good Duke Namles took him to his tent
And rejoiced with him with a heart full of friendship,
For he kissed him and hugged him effusively
Before anyone had taken off any piece of his armor.
It is no wonder that he cherished him so,
Given what he had done that day.
Charles had not forgotten Aloris,
For his heart was filled with anger toward him.
Immediately, the king commanded
That he be hanged, that there be no further delay.
When Ogier learned of it, it weighed upon him so heavily
That he went to Namles and told him about it in detail
And begged and entreated him to prevail
Upon Charles to have pity upon Aloris
And spare him from death.
"Certainly," said Namles, "your will
Will be done and I am grateful to you;
I will do my best to see that Charles does not carry out his first plan
And acts in such a way that causes neither shame nor grief."
Ogier heard him; he thanked him greatly for it.
When they were ready to go,
They went to Charles in his tent.

Everyone whom they met
Looked at the Dane in awe.

XXXVI

For the reason that you have heard me tell
Duke Namles came to talk to Charles
With his nephew at his side.
When Charles saw them enter his tent,
He rose toward them; he did not care to wait.
He came toward Ogier eagerly, for he did not want to fail to do this.
Immediately, he went to kiss him and throw his arms around him.
"Sire," said Namles, "my nephew Ogier whom you see here
Comes to ask a boon of you,
That you would pardon
The misdeed of Aloris, whom you plan to hang.
If he did something blameworthy,
It was because his courage failed him; he could not help it.
One can scarcely borrow courage from others."
Charles chuckled; then he looked at
Ogier and said that he could not refuse
Anything he wanted to ask,
For he had done well, and he must love him for it.
He would spare Aloris now for love of Ogier.
But about one thing he could well boast,
That if it were not for Ogier, by Saint Omer,
He would have him dishonored.
Ogier bowed to the king,
And he knew well how to thank him appropriately.
Ogier kept Aloris from being destroyed
In the way you have heard me recount.
They sounded the horn for water; then they went to wash.
Ogier sat beside the king at supper,
For Charles took great pains to honor Ogier well.
And all of a sudden here was Charlot, the son of Charles the baron,
Who was coming from Aix as fast as he could go
Towards his father, to win honor.
In his company were many young men
Who had been dubbed knight with him.
Duke Thierri, the one from Ardennes
Who did much to praise, had given him arms.
He was Charlot's master; for to teach him
There was none better to choose as advisor,
For he was the kind of man, I have heard said,

Who is considerd a valiant gentleman.
Those who are guided by such people
Must necessarily become better.
They went to greet the king appropriately.
Charles saw him and was very pleased.
At this point I'll stop talking about them, for
I want to talk to you again about King Corsuble.

XXXVII

The Saracens had come back to Rome
Chagrinned and sad and with furious hearts,
For they had lost an astonishing number of their people.
King Corsuble had received the accounts
That his people had fought Charles
And that pagans were dead, captured, and conquered.
With his heart filled with anger, he called for Danemon,
Who came to him without hesitation.
"Son," said the father, "how you have disappointed me
That without me you have attacked Charlemagne."
King Danemon acquainted him with the entire
Battle such as it had been,
How Charles was on foot in the grassy meadow
And the French were almost all conquered
When a mass of their people reappeared
In which there were men of very great strength.
"We were so much hindered by these people
That theirs were rescued.
Many of them were distinguished by their prowess.
Among the others we saw one of them
Named Ogier, as I heard it.
He killed many men today
And wounded many and beat many to the ground,
Broke many a helmet and tore many a coat of mail
And pierced many a buckler and many a shield.
If these people had not entered the battle at this point,
The French would have paid greatly for their loyalty to the king.
They all would have been killed or captured.
We would have put King Charles in your hands.
And this is how Ogier brought misfortune upon you."
Corsuble heard it; he completely lost heart.
He cursed his gods, Mohammed and Cahu.
He did not esteem them the worth of a straw.

XXXVIII

King Corsuble heard the news,
How his people were dead and destroyed.
His face was red with anger,
But he could not do anything about it this time.
And all of a sudden there appeared a messenger in the vaulted hall
Who came before Corsuble with his head raised
And greeted him according to the pagan custom.
"Sire," said he, "do not be dismayed.
Carahuel is coming, the son of the king of Orcanie.
He is bringing excellent knights with him.
He has 20,000 pagans in his company.
He will want to have Gloriande, your beautiful daughter,
The noble, the elegant, as his beloved.
With you he will go to France the well protected.
He will not return if the land is conquered.
I have come here—I do not know what more to tell you—
To take land for his retinue,
For he does not want to do any wrong toward anyone.
Order immediately that it be put in my control,
For our army is a league and a half away."
Corsuble heard it; he thanked Mohammed for it,
For his anger was much assuaged by it.
The messengers were given land for Carahuel's command
In which their people could be well lodged.
The king called all his barons
And asked them to greatly honor Carahuel,
For King Carahuel was a king of great nobility,
Of great lineage from the kingdom of Persia.
He had done his part well in many wars.
"Now the French could certainly go to their destruction,
For there is no one of more prowess from here to the mount of Aumarie.
My daughter will be married to him.
That is Gloriande; I gave her to him
A year before this army was called to assemble.
He had already pledged his troth and become her fiancé.
But she was too young; because of that I delayed the marriage.
Now I will give her, for I have brought her up to the point
That it is a good time for her to marry.
But before that, my barons and I will have
Entered France, which I have coveted for a long time."
Brunamon heard it; he was greatly distressed by this news,
For he had loved the young girl so much

Because of her great beauty and elegance.
He loved her with a love so mad
That it was astonishing that he was still alive.
Her beauty was so perfect
That to see her was like hearing a beautiful melody.
She was as white and smooth as a lily
With the blush of a blooming rose.
Nature had so put her mastery to work
That no one since was ever more beautiful.
She was well-behaved and courteous and well-taught
And had all the qualities and learning
That the faith of her people required.
When she was told that Carahuel was coming from the country of the Saracens
And was near Rome, the mighty, ancient city,
She praised her gods ardently.

XXXIX

When Carahuel was supposed to come to Rome,
He was very happy; I don't want to lie to you.
A Saracen feared by all, Sadoine by name,
The son of the king of Monmir—his lands
And those of Carahuel bordered one another—
Rode out to meet Carahuel, for he was eager to see him.
They esteemed one another highly and were very glad to see one another.
At his leisure, Sadoine told Carahuel in great detail about Ogier,
How he knew well how to handle himself in battle.
"Any man would have difficulty sustaining his blows.
When at full attack he sets upon an adversary,
No arms could prevent that foe
From dying an evil death.
Already his prowess has made us flee
And has made the soul of many of us part from its body.
Carahuel heard it; it angered him so much that
His face turned red with rage.
He swore by Mohammed that he greatly desired
To strike Ogier in battle.
He burst forth with so great an oath
That the whole night he could not sleep.
He stayed awake until the break of day,
At which time he wanted to attack the tents of the French.
And Sadoine said, "I agree to it,
By Mohammed whom I must obey,

And you may be able to see me at the very front of the army
If my horse Baiars de Monespir doesn't fail me."

XL

When Carahuel came to Rome,
King Corsuble received him with great honor
As did his daughter, who was his fiancée;
For he was very handsome and noble and well-developed,
Courteous and wise and of good qualities
According to his people's customs, which he honored.
Many loved and trusted him.
Carahuel greeted Gloriande.
"My beauty," said he, "I am overcome with love when I see you,
For there is nothing in the world I love more than you.
I am resolved and ready to go to France
Where there are people full of prowess,
But I will not find any there so well equipped with weapons
Or lances or javelins so sharp
That anyone will fail to capitulate to our religion.
Many of them will be flayed alive or hanged
If they do not believe in Mohammed or Cahu.
Now Corsuble need not be angry
Nor in harsh desperation about the French;
All over France before fires are set in the morning
Many a good coat of mail will be torn up
And many a castle knocked down and destroyed.
They will not get the upper hand in their endeavor.
For love of you I will show my shield
To those of France; no one will keep me from it,
Before the day appears tomorrow."
Gloriande rightly answered and
Gladly looked upon King Carahuel,
For she was wise by nature and by practice.

XLI

Many pagans were glad because of Carahuel's arrival
And thanked Mohammed for it.
When Carahuel and Sadoine had talked and discussed quite a bit
With the well-turned and gracious Gloriande,
Courteously he took leave of her,
He and Sadoine not delaying any longer
But both going back to their lodgings.
When they were rested and refreshed,

They armed themselves well and put on hauberks.
A little before it was completely dark,
They left Rome very well equipped.
There were 10,000 of them; not one of them was on foot.
There you would have seen many a shield on their arms
And many a buckler with leather-covered surfaces.
They were a threat to many Christians.
They had traveled and ridden so far together
That they were within two leagues of Sutri.
They had arranged themselves very well beside a group of small trees
Where they prayed to Mohammed, to whom they were devoted,
That before they returned they would test themselves against
Our people in battle, for they greatly desired to do so.
But before they saw good daylight
They would have come quite close to them.
That night Charlot kept watch;
In his company were many esteemed knights.

XLII

That night Charlot kept watch.
He took Duke Thierri of the Ardennes with him.
Duke Fagon went with him also
And so many others that there were 10,000 of them.
In his heart he greatly blamed himself
That he had not yet seen the enemy.
Seized with a desire to approach Rome,
Charlot called Duke Thierri aside
And told him that it behooved him to go to Rome
So stealthily that the army would not know it and that
Nothing or nobody would prevent him from doing it.
If he found pagans, he would fight them,
Whether he wanted to or not, in spite of himself.
Duke Thierri agreed to it; nevertheless he showed
Many aspects of the plan about which he had grave doubts,
As would his counselors also.
Charlot spoke urgently to Duke Fagon about it at such length
That he agreed to go with him,
For in his heart he was well aware
That he had not yet encountered the enemy,
Had had nothing to do with them, no more than Charlot had.
Charlot was insistent for this reason.
Duke Fagon put his people in good order, and
Rightly and appropriately he left the watch,

Telling them how each one should conduct himself.
Then they left with two thousand men.
May God, who made the whole world, guide them,
For before they return many of them
Will regret the undertaking.
A Saracen who was patrolling the roads
Heard the noise; he stopped for a moment.
He was there long enough to hear
Our people coming, so he left at once.
As soon as he could he went back.
He went to Carahuel and told him immediately,
Then hastened to tell all the others about it.
"Lords," he said to them, "let's decide
How each one will fit into the battle!
Here are the French whom you can see already;
I left them on that knoll back there."
The Saracens heard him; each one prepared himself,
And Carahuel put his shield on his arm.
He took hold of the lance with a very sharp blade
And unfurled the standard immediately.
He and Sadoine, each was very eager
To be the first to attack,
For their hearts commanded them boldly to do this
And gave them confidence in carrying it out.

XLIII

Shortly before dawn
The moon shone and cast a great light.
It was beautiful in truth,
For the moon had dispelled all darkness.
The French rode in ranks and close together
For a short distance, and then they stopped.
They could hear many a horse neighing.
The French said, "How fortunate that we
Have come across those we sought; we have found them."
Some of them re-buckled their horses' saddles.
You would have seen many a knight make ready
For the battle and look very eager for it.
Duke Thierri called Charlot.
"My lord," he said, "I have done your will.
Now act so that people speak highly of your conduct
And so that Charles will not criticize us
For having found any speck of cowardice in us."

And Charlot said," Have no fear:
I would rather have my head cut off
Than to have any evil found in me."
Before they had their ranks in order
Or could finish arranging the details of their plan,
The pagans appeared, spurring through the meadow.
A measured acre before the others
Came Carahuel, with bridle abandoned;
Next to him Sadoine was on his left.
Each one was greedy for the first blow;
Each one wanted to steal it from the other.
The French saw it; they showed it to one another.
From both sides they spurred their horses pell-mell.
Leading the attack first,
Charles's son did not stop.
He and Sadoine clashed so forcefully
That their horses were left without riders.
Carahuel jousted with Duke Fagon until
Their lances broke and they had ridden past one another.
Duke Thierri, with his lance held straight forward,
Had struck down a pagan so hard that
His armor was not worth a thimble.
He thrust the strong spear into his body
And knocked him down dead at the edge of a wheat field.
He struck another with the broken lance
So hard that he knocked him to the earth.
Many a Frank and many a pagan were felled there
And many a shield was struck with many a lance.
After using the lances they continued their fight with their swords,
Striking great blows in the rescue
Of the wise king's son and of Sadoine.
Each one got back on his horse with much difficulty.
The fighting in this battle was ferocious,
But the pagans fought so furiously
That the French were completely surrounded by them.
You would have seen there many a hauberk torn all to pieces,
Many a buckler and many a shield with holes in them,
And many a strong helmet broken and rent into quarters
That lay on shoulders, their circlets broken;
Many a steel sword stained and bloodied.
The newly dubbed knights fought well.
The youth Charlot, with the engraved sword in his fist,
So attacked many a Saracen with it

That they both feared and praised him for it.
He and his companions proved themselves very well.
But without the intervention of the king of majesty
They would have turned back too late,
For many pagans gathered around them.

XLIV

The battle was so great that the warriors were apprehensive.
Our baron knights defended themselves well,
Duke Thierri and Charlot of the proud face
And many others, for they certainly needed to.
Fagon looked around and saw Desiier,
A valiant vassal; he was from Montdidier.
He had been struck through the body by a lance
So that he had to lean upon the saddle-bow.
Duke Fagon began to talk to him about it.
"Friend," said he, "I pray to God that
You would want to help us in this need:
I pray that you would speed your courser along
By pricking him a little a little with your spurs
And go up to the guard to tell the news
That they should come to help us right now.
If you do this you would be doing a praiseworthy deed."
"Sire," said he, "I do not wish to refuse you this,
But, by the one who has all to judge,
If I can do more harm to the Saracens
I would not leave even if my head were to be chopped off.
Have someone besides me be messenger.
But I am wounded and in pain."
And Fagon said, "By Saint Richier,
You are not going away like a coward."
Then Desiier spurred the good, rapid warhorse.
He went speedily away past a boulder alongside the road.
He headed straight for the guard and
As loudly as he could he began shouting to them
To go help Charlot if they held him dear at all.
He showed them the right path,
And the guards quickly broke ranks.
Disiier, not wanting to delay, passed beyond them
And did not stop spurring until he got to Charles's tent.
Very quickly he told him of the deadly attack.
Charles heard it, and he was greatly troubled by this news.
He had both Namles and Ogier informed.

To arms ran Germans and Bavarians,
Flemings and men of Brabant and Hainaut
And several other valiant and warrior-like vassals.
They all hastened mightily to get ready, and,
When they were mounted, they left at once,
Not pausing until they reached the fracas.
There you would have seen many a lance firmly grasped
And many a shield proudly held.
But the Saracens were already pushed back
Because those of the guard had come first
And had dampened their shouts a great deal.
For the French had slain many of them, who lay dead on the grass.
Already many of our French were pursuing the Saracens energetically.

XLV

Great was the pursuit and savage was the battle.
Sadoine said to the pagan people:
"The French are coming upon us, in front us and all around us.
Let's get out of here; I don't see any other way,
For if we stay, we shall get the worst of it.
We have a fourth of the people they do
And can gain nothing by staying."
Then they turned away through a dark valley
While defending themselves without too great a clamor.
Our French troops followed them closely.
Carahuel was a man of great valor;
If only he had believed in God the creator!
In his hand he held the good sword of color.
Its name was Courtain, and it was sharper than a razor.
He and Sadoine, the lord of Valflour,
Sought no respite from defending themselves energetically.
Rather they conducted themselves like people of great vigor.
And here was Ogier, the noble horseman,
Very well armed on his fast charger.
He had a lance of ashwood and a buckler painted with flowers.
And Sadoine said, "By the gods that I adore,
Here is Ogier, who the other day made
Many of our Saracens die in great pain.
I recognize quite well that horse of great price."
Said Carahuel, "May I never have honor,
And may Gloriande take away her love;
May I, as a result, never have possessions or joy
If I do not have a battle with Ogier right away."

Sadoine heard it and was very much afraid
That this undertaking would end in disaster.

XLVI

Carahuel turned the horse's head.
All around him his people held fast.
Marados of Bronsal, who was a Saracen of Portuguese extraction,
Handed him a short lance.
Marados of Bronsal held the tower and castle of Luserne.
Then he caused Garin of Anseume great harm.
Carahuel took the strong battle lance.
He held the buckler with crystal stones.
And here was Ogier coming down the slope of a valley,
Holding his lance on its felt in the manner of a good vassal.
He had already done so much among the royal people
That everyone considered him valiant and loyal.
Carahuel spurred up the side of a little hill
On a horse better than Bucephalus.
Except for Broiefort no man had seen its equal.
It was Brunamon the emir's horse.
Then Ogier conquered him in cruel battle
When they fought in equal combat
Right within Rome the imperial city
Where the Saracens caused many a heart-felt sorrow.

XLVII

Ogier looked over the flowery meadows.
He saw Carahuel coming in a great hurry,
In his fist a lance with a solid, sharp blade,
Heading toward him like a worthy knight
As if they had always done these things.
They nobly attacked one another
With the blades of lances, right in the middle of their chests.
They broke the wood and the leather and the glaze of the bucklers.
The strong hauberks of interwoven mail withstood the blows.
Their two lances were cut into many a piece.
Each one struck the other and went beyond his adversary like an accomplished warrior.
On the return they drew their swords of burnished steel.
Each one came toward the other fiercely and forcefully.
Ogier struck him on the shining helmet,
Giving him such a blow through the front of the face
That Carahuel was completely stunned by it.

If it had not been for the rim encircling the helmet,
As far as I can tell, Carahuel would have been killed.
He turned toward Ogier fearlessly.
The two of them had already fought violently.
However, Carahuel did fear a surprise attack,
For the French were coming by the plains and by the heath.
And here was Sadoine, who had taken him by the bridle,
For he saw too many of the enemy around him.
Then Sadoine said to him, "Hurry up.
Let's get out of here, or we'll do worse,
For I see the mountains and the valleys are already taken over by the French,
And Ogier has struck you hard."
And Carahuel said, "This knight is handsome,
Full of prowess and brave, fierce, and well-prepared;
Would to Mohammed whom I obey
That he had converted to our religion
And that he shared half my land."
And Sadoine said, "Quit talking like that.
That's doing us no good now.
We must give our attention to other things.
I see our people harmed all around us."
Then they righted themselves again on their costly steeds,
Seized with boldness and ferocity.
With them reassembled Persians and Lutis
And Coumains and Amoravis.
They gathered behind them; of this you may be sure.
Each one vied with the others to be in the first rank,
For each one was a valiant and distinguished vassal.
They reassembled their people very skilfully
And welcomed them into their guardianship
As shepherds do their sheep for fear of wolves.
So they went away as I have described to you.
Charlot's horns had already sounded
To have the pursuit stopped.

XLVIII

The noise, the shouting, and the war cries were deafening
As the pagans fled through a valley.
They were sorely tested on this morning, for
The Franks pursued them with great impetuousness.
And here was Charlot on his horse charging through the meadow
In a great effort to reassemble his troops.

For in pursuit the group had scattered,
Which could have brought about a disaster.
He had often reacted in this way in similar situations.
He seized Ogier by the golden buckler.
"Ogier," said he, "draw in your rein.
For I have already had the return sounded.
Apparently you did not hear it
Because your thoughts were fixed on pursuit."
Said Ogier, "Sire, so be it as you please."
Charlot's troops stopped around him;
From all parts they came and assembled.
They turned back without delay,
Carrying many back who were dead and wounded.
They arrived at Sutri, the standard raised.
Their army came back in to camp; they had done a good day's fighting,
For which they thanked God and his honored mother.

XLIX

When Charlot came back into camp,
The king was very joyous and glad about it,
For his barons had been snatched from peril.
If the help of the guard had arrived too late,
Such misfortune could have come from it
That the result would have been much damage and sorrow.
Charles was very angry with Duke Fagon.
Immediately he ordered that he break camp.
For this reason Charlot was sent to get them right away.
And they came; not one of them delayed.
In their company came many young and old,
With noses cut off, with lacerated faces.
Each one came there who was able to.
Of those who had begun the battle,
Many of them could not go,
For they had been wounded by lances and spears.
Duke Fagon was spoken to first.
"Duke," said the king, "the guard was your responsibility.
You had the entire army in your keeping.
You abandoned the guard, which makes me extremely angry.
Never do that again, for such behavior would make you worthless to me.
Everyone must be strongly counseled
That he must not distance himself from his guard
Until the light of dawn appears."
"Sire, it is true," said Fagon the esteemed.

"Duke Thierri, you should know,
Told us as much;
But your son pleaded with me so desperately
That I could by no means ignore him."
"For this," said Charles," you are pardoned,
But don't forget it next time."
All the people thanked Charles greatly for this.
Each one went back to his lodgings.

L

Charles and his barons were at Sutri.
Fagon was acquitted of all wrongdoing,
As was Charlot, for what you have heard about
That caused the king torment.
Right after Charles had left
The battle and had turned around,
Carahuel had gone back into Rome,
He and Sadoine together side by side,
And many another, wounded and maimed.
They sent a messenger
To recount the situation to King Corsuble,
How Charlot had to be left.
"If the rescue had not been so rushed
He and a thousand others along with him would have been brought back to you.
I am telling you the truth, believe me,
For Carahuel is a tried and true vassal,
Fierce and bold and strong and hardened.
He and Sadoine, each one has so proven himself
That the least valiant should be honored by it.
For if they had not been there — it is the very truth —
Of all the others not a single one of them would have escaped.
The great prowess of both of them saved us."
When Gloriande heard these words,
Her heart leapt with joy; and
She wrapped her arms around the messenger.
She loved Carahuel much more than before.
And Corsuble said, "That was madness
When they fought the French without me."
Gloriande said, "Sire, you have spoken badly.
They are young people; you know it truly.
It is very wrong for you to blame them for this.
The newly knighted must seek honor

As you did, Sire, when you were that age:
You conquered honor; that's why you have it,
For if you had not done so, you would not have it.
If honor is not acquired in time,
One can hardly ever obtain it.
For this I pray you, Sire, if you love me this much,
If they have acted wrongly, that you pardon them;
And when they arrive, you greet them warmly.
Do not be angry with them."
"Indeed," said Corsuble, "You request this of me
Because much nobleness and goodness
And kindness and politeness dwell in you;
And I will do it since you want it."
"Sire," she said, "Mohammed be praised for it.
May you feel his gratitude and joy 500 times for it!"

LI

When Gloriande, the elegant young girl,
Had said to her father all that was on her mind,
She did not linger long;
For Carahuel dismounted in front of the tent,
He and Sadoine and many another as well.
They greeted King Corsuble at once.
And there was Gloriande, who took them by the hands
And sat down between the two right away.
Gloriande said, "You certainly look like people
Who have just come out of battle,
For your faces seem stained with ink;
A maiden must surely be very glad to see
People who come back like this from combat."
King Corsuble spoke courteously:
"Lords," said he, "don't concern yourselves about anything.
I have been told all about your adventure,
How you have lost in this beginning; but
So goes war, know it truly,
One time happily and another sadly;
And so one loses sometimes and wins sometimes.
Now, do not be in too great a torment about it,
For by Mohammed to whom my heart belongs,
Before a week has passed or even sooner
I believe I will take such cruel vengeance
That they will die by the thousands and hundreds.

Carahuel was happy when he heard the king,
For he greatly feared his anger.

LII

When Carahuel heard Corsuble,
His heart was transported with joy.
And here came Danemon and Brunamon.
They dismounted before the king's tent.
Within it entered the young and the white-haired.
They were furious about the damage they had suffered.
They greeted the king in the name of Mohammed.
"Sire," they said, "bad things have befallen us,
For already the French have defeated us twice
And have pushed us back into Rome by force of arms.
You have lost many Saracens there,
So let's go towards them; for we have waited too long.
Let us rush up to them at once.
If we had defeated the first ones
And if we had eliminated the leader of Charles's forces,
We would have gone to France, which was our ancestors'.
The land lies unprotected;
Nothing prevents us from setting it all ablaze
If they do not pledge their fealty to you."
And Corsuble said, "They will forthwith be destroyed,
The cities burned, the castles battered down.
Never before will those of France have seen so many shields,
So many bucklers, so many sharpened swords,
So many spears, nor so many strong, pointed helmets
As I will lead there, nor as many long-maned warhorses,
For we are well-equipped to do this.
But we will await them here
Until they have departed from Sutri."
Everyone agreed completely with these words.

LIII

King Corsuble was greatly to fear,
For he had so many people that one could not count them.
King Brunamon began to talk to him:
"Sire," said he, "I won't try to hide this from you:
It would be good if it were arranged
For one of your princes who is well-spoken
To go ask Charles on your behalf
If he would be willing to convert to our religion

So that he would not let his people be killed
Nor his kingdom be destroyed and ruined.
If he would come to beg you for mercy,
You could let him return safe and sound.
But let him give you such concessions,
That you could command him in his land.
If there is someone who could make this widely known,
It would be the best way to frighten their people."
And Corsuble said, "I would surely want this done,
But I do not know who would be able to go there.
I must deliberate upon this."
Carahuel arose and
Went to present himself to Corsuble
To inform him that in the morning at daybreak
He would go to take this message to Charles.
And Corsuble said, "Vassal, you are a very fine baron.
In this agreement I would like to stipulate
That whatever you say to King Charles
Will be something I consent to."
Carahuel said, "I would certainly accept this privilege,
And I would scarcely have dared ask for it.
The king began to tap his tooth
With his finger in order to better confirm his intention.
And Carahuel bowed down to him.
Persians, Saracens, and Slavs said,
"Everyone should love Carahuel."
Brunamon felt nothing but anger, for
He would have much preferred, to raise his prestige,
To have been named to take this message you have heard me recount
Than to have had any amount of money,
But it was something he could not change.

LIV

Corsuble had allowed Carahuel
To go straight to Charles the king.
Gloriande sighed a great deal about it in secret;
Her heart was greatly afraid for Carahuel,
For she loved him loyally according to her faith.
Sadoine took Carahuel by the finger.
They both took leave of Gloriande.
The maiden said, "Carahuel, I implore you
That you keep from speaking impetuously.
I offer you this counsel by the faith that I owe you,

For the French are people of a very great arrogance."
Carahuel said, "My beauty, look at me.
My heart of hearts laughs when I see you.
You tell me this for my benefit; so I believe it.
For your love I will speak with care.
I commend you to the god of our religion."
At their leave-taking Gloriande wept just a little;
As much as she could, she followed them with her eyes.
Carahuel took Danemon beside him.
All three of them went away to their lodgings.

LV

Carahuel went straight to his lodgings.
With him was Sadoine, who dearly loved him,
And Danemon. Both were talking to Carahuel
About the mission to Charles
With which Corsuble had charged him.
King Sadoine exhorted him at length
To remember his promise and speak directly to the point
As he should; he implored him urgently to do this.
And Carahuel answered their concerns
By saying that the message, which he felt sure
He understood, would be conveyed correctly
And would place no blame on Corsuble
And that he himself would maintain his honor in it
Entirely, or else he would die for it.
Such was the custom at this time
That a boy did not take an important message
Since the deed could provoke war
And war was started by royal people;
King, duke or count: they were the people who were involved in it,
And therefore each one armed himself quite well.
Those a messenger encountered could see
That he was a messenger because he carried
His lance with the blade turned toward him and held it firmly in his hand.
Such a position was assurance
That no one would be threatened.
The weapon then signified
That he would deliver his true and certain message;
And if anyone dared to say he was not telling the truth,
It was established that combat would ensue.
He who carried a message in this way
Would be treated with great honor.

LVI

The next day, when dawn had broken,
King Carahuel did not tarry.
He arrayed his body with rich arms,
Girding his sword Courtain on his left side before
Mounting his rested warhorse.
On his head he had a very beautiful helmet well ornamented with gold
And with many a stone of great price.
From his neck hung a strong, bordered shield
And in his fist a painted lance
With a firm shaft and a blade of steel,
Which was turned toward him.
Sadoine commended him to Mohammed,
And Carahuel went out of the city,
Not drawing in the rein until he reached Sutri.
Right through the army he went to the master tent.
Our French stared at him fixedly
When they saw him so nobly mounted
And so richly armed with his weapons.
"By God," they said, "the king of majesty,
This one seems to be of great nobility."
King Carahuel did not linger.
He descended on foot from his impetuous warhorse
And unlaced and removed his helmet,
Throwing it back over his shoulders.
The French led him before Charles,
For they greatly desired to know the true message
That King Corsuble had sent to Charles.
In Charles's tent were assembled
Many a duke, many a count, many a prince, many a vassal,
For they had planned among themselves
That they would go to Rome before three days had passed.

LVII

Carahuel was standing straight and proud
Before Charles, the rich, powerful king.
He was a very able Saracen.
Looking at him intently, the French and Germans said,
"Here is a fine-looking knight,
Of a good size, not too short or too tall.
It is a great pity that in such a fine body
There is not a heart that believes in God, for
By his manner it certainly appears

That great prowess must reside in him.
His military equipment is suitable for such a knight."
Carahuel moved slightly forward and
Greeted the king in a loud voice which all present heard:
"May the god in whom the Christians believe
Save Charlemagne and all the rest!
I am a messenger from Corsuble the valiant,
The best king known to be living.
He is the crowned king of Syria.
All Nubia belongs to him;
Under him is all of Boucidant.
King, I have come to you by his command.
He sends me to you; listen to his message."
"Friend," said Charlemagne, "speak your mind."

LVIII

Carahuel said to Charles of the proud face,
"Corsuble has me sent to you
To let you know through me—let me be frank—
That you should have the hands of your people bound,
That they should surrender to him without shooting arrows
Or throwing lances, and you who have them to a commnd
Should go kneel before him
To implore of him this mercy
Because you dare to come and lodge here.
You will have your land to govern by his leave,
By a tribute imposed of fine, pure gold;
And you will agree immediately
To deny your religion,
And worship and pray to Mohammed.
If you do not do this, you may be sure
He will have all who are here cut to pieces
And he will have you flayed alive.
Afterward he will want to ride back into France,
For he is the one who should be king of it and whose right
It is to govern it because his ancestors were to inherit it.
If he finds someone who doesn't want to grant this,
He will cause this person to be destroyed and ruined,
Cities battered down and castles broken to pieces.
Neither chapel nor monastery will remain there
Which will not tumble down to earth.
You would be better off to choose to bow
Before Corsuble and make peace

Than have your kingdom undergo such destruction.
Now answer as to what you seek.
Do not increase your damage.
It is good to let go of a foolish undertaking."
"Friend," said Charles, "may God help me;
I do not feel very much like doing this.
You can certainly go back
To King Corsuble and tell him that
Before he gets a single little coin in France
I think I can show him many a noble warrior,
Shield around the neck, armed on the warhorse,
Who would not want to advise me
To subject myself to this thing.
Tell Corsuble I want to be straightforward,
That, by God, if he had had his men set up camp in the fields,
Or even if he tries to threaten me yet again
Before the sun has set tomorrow,
He would find me very close.
Instead, he has had his men go hide themselves in Rome;
And if he does not have his people leave Rome soon,
I will shortly go to put them under siege."
When Carahuel heard him speak thus,
In his heart he began to admire him greatly.
This king, he thought, does not have a cowardly heart.

LIX

When Carahuel heard Charles speak,
Within his heart he began to praise him.
At his response his face reddened,
And he spoke loudly so that he could be clearly heard.
"Charles," he said, "I'd like to go back now.
I see well that you do not want to submit
To Corsuble, nor worship his god, but
I would like to speak to you of another affair.
I have a sweetheart of whom I can certainly boast,
There is not one so beautiful on this side of the sea nor beyond it.
She is the daughter of Corsuble, who is to be feared.
She is called Gloriande; I do not seek to conceal her name.
For her love I would like to test myself
Against one of your men, if I can find one,
The very best that you can choose
And one who best knows how to use weapons.
In the early morning, right after dawn,

I will have my sweetheart brought to an island
This side of Rome that is called Valcler.
By whatever agreement you wish me to make
Understand that the one who goes there to joust with me
Need not be concerned that I will have him assailed
By anyone except myself; this I wish you to believe.
And if he can conquer me by arms,
He can take my sweetheart away with him.
He will not find one who will prevent him from it.
And if I can conquer him,
He will agree to abandon his religion completely
And serve and honor Mohammed,
But if he wants to scorn our religion,
I will have his head cut off at once."
Ogier heard this; he got to his feet.
He came to stand directly in front of Carahuel.
"Pagan," he said, "by the faith that I owe Saint Omer,
You cannot accuse the French
Of wanting to refuse you such a request.
By the faith that I have in Duke Namles,
My own dear uncle that I greatly love,
Upon this island that I heard you indicate,
You will be able to meet me early tomorrow
If I can get there."
When Carahuel heard him, he looked at him and
Called upon his gods with joy.
The French began to nudge one another.
They said that in Ogier they had a worthy vassal.

LX

When Ogier had thus made his covenant
For the fight of which I have briefly told you,
Charles's son, he of the noble physique,
Rose at once nimbly to his feet.
"Ogier," said he, "you speak entirely out of turn
By putting yourself ahead of me at this moment
For this fight; I am greatly offended by it.
Seek another; you will certainly not have this one.
I will have it myself, and rightly so.
You know well that the task belongs
To the king my father most certainly.
Do not be so bold.
It wouldn't take much, by Saint Vincent,

For me to require satisfaction for it."
Ogier heard it; he was so angry about it
And so ashamed that it pierced his heart,
But for Charles's sake he calmed himself discreetly.
When Carahuel heard this,
That it was Ogier who the very first
Had proudly answered him,
Neither gold nor silver would have made him so happy.
He said to Charlot in the hearing of all the people,
"Vassal, it is plain that the one who would speak to Ogier
So foolishly has an outrageous lack of sense.
The king does badly to allow you to do so.
By Mohammed whom I serve loyally,
The French surely can brag,
But if it weren't for Ogier, you may be sure,
Things would not go nearly so well for them.
I am looking forward to the fight with Ogier.
Therefore, you won't have any fight with me.
But if you really feel like fighting,
Fight you will have, this I promise you.
Tomorrow morning, you can count on it,
I will lead Sadoine of Clarvent into the island.
He is the son of the king of Boucident.
He will be well and richly armed.
If you go there, I implore you emphatically
That you kill him if he does not defend himself."
When Charlot heard this, at once he came gladly
To Carahuel, took him by the hand and
Promised the fight immediately
And that more than one thousand seven hundred would see it.

LXI

When Charlemagne heard it said
How his son had undertaken the battle,
You may be sure that in his heart he was proud of him for it.
But it bothered him greatly
That he had spoken to Ogier so foolishly,
And he thought that he would certainly have amends made for that
In such a way that would please Ogier.
It weighed heavily upon Duke Thierri, and
In his heart he thought that he would reprove
Charlot as soon as he left there.
He did so; he did not forget it at all.

Carahuel said to the king: "Listen here:
This battle will be tomorrow morning.
Your son will fight against Sadoine,
And I will meet Ogier whom I see right over there.
Do not fear any betrayal,
For know well that there will not be any
From King Corsuble nor from those on our side."
He raised his finger and struck his tooth with it.
This signified that he would loyally keep to
The agreement that he had made with them.
He would die, he said, rather than betray it.

LXII

Carahuel had promised the fight, and
He swore upon his faith repeatedly
That he would do as he said.
In such a situation was the battle arranged,
And Charles granted it and agreed to it.
Some praised the plan while others criticized it.
Fouchiers de Pierre Lee spoke to the king.
It was right that he be listened to,
For he had spent many a long day
On those who had forgotten the true religion.
"Sire," said he, "it greatly disturbs me
That such a combat is left to two young fighters;
Your army could be greatly saddened by the outcome."
"Fouchier," said Charles, "so help me God,
This Ogier is not a youth in the handling of a sword.
If it please God that he have a long life,
He will be a knight of hardened prowess.
His prowess is seen and proven,
And as for my son, by the honored virgin,
I would prefer that my head be cut off
Than cowardice be attributed to him;
For a young man who desires prowess,
Who wants to spend his life in arms,
Must seek honor until he has found it.
He must risk his life often,
For it cannot be otherwise. It is a fact that
Without danger there can be no honor in arms.
Fouchier heard it; he shook his head.
In his heart he thought a king in whom there is
Such an idea must be of great renown.

LXIII

Carahuel said, "Sire king, listen.
I will go back, for I have stayed too long,
And I see very well that you intend to do nothing
That Corsuble has proposed, nor do you desire to do anything."
"Certainly, "said Charles, "that is the very truth."
When Carahuel heard these words,
He took leave of the king; then he turned
Toward Ogier; he spoke with him in a loud enough voice
So that the barons could hear what he was saying.
"Ogier," said he, "you will come tomorrow morning,
You and Charlot, as you have promised,
To find Sadoine and me on the island,
Mounted, you may be sure, on horses.
You will see a standard deployed,
By which signal you will recognize us."
And Ogier said, "Never fear,
For if I can do it, you will have us there quite early.
But be sure that you do not forget
To bring Gloriande with you,
Your sweetheart that you have praised so much to us.
If she is as beautiful as you describe to us,
Your heart must overflow with joy."
Said Carahuel, "Yes, and much more.
And you may be assured of this,
That she will come and that you will take her away
If you can conquer us by arms."
Then Carahuel took leave of him like a prudent person.
He mounted his horse; when he went out of the tents,
Everyone looked upon him with great wonder;
For he was richly and handsomely equipped.
"Ah, God, "they said, "true king of majesty,
How very wise this pagan is
And very courteous and well educated!
If only he were baptized and raised!"

LXIV

Carahuel spurred the good, long-maned warhorse,
Not reining in until he reached Rome.
Many a Saracen who had waited for him
Outside of Rome came to meet him
And many greeted him in the name of Mohammed.
And Sadoine said, "What has happened to you?

How did the Christians receive you?
Will they let their country be put to the torch,
Or will they surrender to Corsuble
And pay him tribute according to his will
And believe in Mohammed and Cahu?"
Carahuel said, "That is not what I heard at all.
They have charged me with another task.
I spoke to Charles of the white hair,
A king who certainly seems ferocious and powerful.
You should know that from the king himself I have learned well
That they do not value us the price of a straw.
They would have run over us in no time, he said,
If our people had come out of Rome,
And our tents had been pitched in the fields.
Corsuble's message did not seem to be of great concern to them.
In answering, Charles presented himself well."
Hearing this, the pagans were silent and mute, for
Most of them were quite troubled.

LXV

Carahuel said, "Sadoine, you do not know
How things have turned out for us this time.
For the love of my sweetheart, Gloriande,
The blonde, the elegant, I have undertaken battle
Against Ogier, whose warcry is "Denmark,"
The one whom our pagan people complained so much about;
And also I have promised that you would do battle
With the son of the king of France the bountiful.
Good and early in the morning, after the dawn has broken,
We will boat down the stream through the middle
Of the prairie straight to the island of Valcler,
For on it there is a big, wide, level place;
And Gloriande will come with us.
I have taken this vow in this way:
If they conquer us by their prowess,
That they will take Gloriande to their country.
Nobody will be left to keep them from it.
And if we win in the attack,
They will convert to our faith, or they will lose their lives."
Upon hearing this, Sadoine thanked Mohammed for it
And heartily thanked Carahuel for it.
All the gold of Syria would not have made him so happy.
They entered Rome, the lordly city,

And set out for Corsuble's tent.
When Gloriande heard the news
That Carahuel had come back, she was delighted.

LXVI

King Carahuel dismounted at the master tent.
He and Sadoine went inside
Where many a Saracen stood up before them.
Carahuel greeted Corsuble and
Then recounted the message to him
From beginning to end, hiding nothing about it from him.
He told him the message Charles had truly sent him,
That before he gave up his country to him,
Charles's opponents would confront many a vassal of prowess
With shield at his neck and helmet closed,
A lance in his fist and a sword at his side.
Many a saddle would be completely dislodged,
Many a man would be dead, many captured and many wounded
Before Corsuble would set foot in France.
Carahuel continued, saying, "And Charles swore on his Christianity
That he wanted to have combat with you
And would have already met you in battle
If we had not shut ourselves up inside Rome.
Their troops were sorry
That we had not camped right in the fields
Where they would not have had either ravines or ditches
To have hindered their fighting,
For they wanted very much to begin battling with you.
And King Charles swore on his God
That we would be besieged within this city
If he does not find us shortly in the open field.
He seemed to me eager to fight and to want
Our troops to engage in combat."
With this word he finished his message.
When Corsuble heard it, he shook his head.
And vowed angrily to Mohammed
That for his misfortune Charles had sent him such a message,
That shortly he would pay dearly.
Carahuel reported in full to the king
That he and Sadoine would go armed to the island
Early in the morning when dawn had broken,
Against Charlot and Ogier the illustrious.
He described the affair entirely to him,

How Gloriande would be with them in the meadow
And how he had promised them upon his religion
That if they were conquered and brought down,
He and Sadoine, or overcome by arms,
Their opponents could take his sweetheart away in safety
Into the French army; he would never stop them,
Nor would they ever be troubled about it by any man.
And if it came about that they were conquered,
They had also faithfully promised
Before Charles and before his barons,
That they would convert to our religion
Or that each one of them would have his head cut off."
And Corsuble said, "I certainly approve of that condition.
Now may your weapons be so successful
As to conquer this Ogier of whom I have
Heard so much praise. Then you will have succeeded well,
For he is a man, as young as he is,
Who has done our troops great harm
And it is certainly known and proven
That the Christians would be much aggrieved by his defeat."
Carahuel said, "Sire, have no doubt about it,
If Mohammed has not turned against us,
We will do so much that people will say wonderful things about us."
At this word they left the king's tent.
King Carahuel did not forget at all,
Neither he nor Sadoine, to go
To Gloriande, who had much beauty.
She praised Mohammed for Carahuel.
She felt such great joy when she saw that he had returned
That she came and embraced him for joy.
At that place they removed Carahuel's armor.

LXVII

When Carahuel had gone back
And announced his messages to Corsuble,
Many a Saracen was very angry
That Charles had so scorned them.
They swore by Mohammed that this message would be avenged.
"Charles will be sorry he replied like this, for
The French are as good as dead; none will escape.
May Mohammed confound anyone who takes pity on them!"
Thus the pagans threatened Charles.
One planned for him to be drowned,

Another hanged and a third flayed alive,
A fourth boiled, and a fifth cut in pieces.
Thus was he condemned from all sides
By Saracens young and old.
The story will now leave them, for
Now I am turning my attention to Charlemagne.
The noble, esteemed king was at Sutri.
This same day the king took counsel
About how he could harm the pagans,
For he greatly desired to start a battle with them.

LXVIII

At Sutri were the French and Burgundians,
And Champagnards and Flemings and Frisians,
And those from Germany, Lorraine, Brabant,
And Artois, Hainaut, Hesbaye,
And Touraine, Anjou, and Bretagne.
People were there from many a region.
Many were afraid for Charlot,
For he was too young for such an undertaking.
They were not greatly worried about Ogier,
For they well knew his strength and renown
And his power, of which he had such a great abundance
That hardly any man could have more.
Duke Thierri took Charlot aside
To talk with him and Namles.
"Sire," said they, "be a man of such prowess
That in all courts one can speak of you
In such a manner that you are highly esteemed
And one can say that you are the son of Charlemagne."
And Charlot said, "By Saint Symon,
I will do so well, if it please God and his name,
That nothing but good can be said of me."
"Sire," said Namles, "May God grant you this gift!"

LXIX

When Duke Namles and Thierri the able
Had told Charlot what was on their mind,
Namles returned straight to his tent,
For he wanted to see that Ogier was equipped.
Speaking to him courteously and frankly, he said,
"Fair nephew, remember now
That a young man, when he is coming into his own,

Since he is eager to conquer honor
Must fear neither pain nor great effort.
He must be prepared for any eventuality in feats of arms.
You have undertaken battle with these unbelievers,
You and Charlot, but be looking out, now,
If you can, to help him
If you see that he has need of it.
If your arms grow weary from striking,
And inside your helmet you are sweating somewhat,
And you are laboring and out of breath from fighting,
Pay no attention to this discomfort
Nor in your heart be dismayed at all.
If you are at the point that I am describing.
You should think that those against whom you are fighting
Are in twice as bad a condition."
Ogier said, "Uncle, never doubt it;
I shall remember it well if it please God."
"Fair nephew," said Namles, "tomorrow you will carry
My true arms, for I order you to."
And Ogier said, "This gives me great joy.
I am very grateful to you for this.
When a man of such character seeks to lend me his arms,
I will not let them go as long as I remain alive;
For I do not know of any arms so ornamental
As arms which are of gleaming gold
With a sable lion rampant.
There is yet something else about them that is very appealing:
The border indented with flaming red.
The indented border will never stay like that, for
I will have red on the entire border at all times.
Now may God give them to me to wear and serve him."

LXX

The next day at dawn
The two youths arose and
Heard mass without delay.
After the mass, they armed themselves promptly.
Each one had arms to his liking
And a rapid and impetuous horse,
One that was strong and light-footed, eager and quite swift.
The young knights mounted at once.
Each one had a handsome helmet that suited him well.
They took their shields gleaming with fine gold

And their lances with blades of sharp steel.
Each one had a flamboyant banner.
When they were mounted, they were very handsome.
Ogiers set off, riding in two-point or jumping position.
He rode with his helmeted head held high.
Proudly he went, gripping his lance
And clutching his shield toward his chest.
He spurred his horse a little;
He was keenly aware of the horse's strength and power beneath him.
He thanked God, the radiant father, for it.
The French, Bavarians, and Germans said,
"Ogier is a very pleasing knight,
Of good qualities, courteous, and understanding.
And Charlot is also an attractive youth.
May God keep them both in his protection!"
Thereupon they left, staying no longer.
Charles lifted his hand in blessing at their departure.
Namles's heart sighed for them.
No man went following after them,
For this is what they had agreed to do;
Nor on the other hand did Saracens or Persians
Follow Carahuel either.
But before they ever came back,
The hearts of the French would be in great sorrow over it.

LXXI

Ogier, who was so worthy, rode along on his horse,
He and Charlot, the son of Charles the valiant.
I shall take you away from them for a little while, for
I want to talk to you again about Carahuel.
Good and early, right after daybreak,
He and Sadoine dressed themselves in their armor
So richly—I swear to you it's true—
That one who would want to describe it
Would need to study well what they wore.
They had already gone out to the island
Along with Gloriande of the fair face, and
They had a tent put up there
Where the young lady could pass the time agreeably,
Take shelter from the heat, amuse herself
And see and observe the battle.
They put up a banner
Showing their arms in quarter sections

That would designate them to Ogier and Charles.
No one can protect himself from treachery.
A Saracen, whom may God give evil,
King Danemon by name,
Was the son of the formidable King Corsuble.
With him he had thirty armed pagans.
They went to ensconce themselves in a place of hiding
Right near a ford by which they could go
Straight onto the island to hinder Ogier
And to dishonor and shame Charlot
If their comrades were having the worst of the combat.
Thus Danemon had it ordered.
He had it well hidden from Carahuel,
And he did not want a word of it said to Sadoine.
So they knew that it must not be revealed
That King Danemon had arranged such a thing, and
They would not have consented to do so even if their limbs had been cut off.

LXXII

One Sunday, you may be sure,
Carahuel went onto the island,
He and Sadoine, armed most nobly.
With them was the elegant young woman
Gloriande, who was in her first youth.
The whole place was resplendent with her beauty.
Her raiment was very costly.
And here was Ogier going down a slope to a valley.
He and Charlot were riding quite merrily.
The first thing they saw was
The banner that was on the tent; then they knew at once
That they would in no way fail to do battle, and
They unfurled their banners to the wind.
King Carahuel, who had great courage,
Saw them coming; then he said immediately
To King Sadoine: "Let us mount quickly;
Here are Ogier and Charlot also,
Who in Charles's tent yesterday promised me
What they have surely and in good faith done."
They mounted their horses quickly and nimbly;
They attached their helmets; each one took his shield
By the straps and hung it around his neck;
And Gloriande gave each one his lance

With its banner glittering and gleaming
After which she commended them to Mohammed for his protection.
Each of the two of them bore down on the stirrups,
Heading straight for the ford at a spirited pace
Because they wanted to show Ogier
That they could pass across confidently,
He and Charlot, with their directions;
For they had crossed there repeatedly that day.
They did not stay there long
When on the riverbank each one saw what the situation promised.
I will not talk to you about this long.
They crossed over by their directions.
What arms Carahuel had, truly
I will describe to you very briefly:
He carried a vermilion shield, fretty argent.
King Sadoine, to whom Persia belongs,
Bore a gold shield with a black serpent;
Those were their arms, you may be sure.

LXXIII

When they, both Charlot and Ogier the Dane,
Had passed the ford through the gravel,
When they were beyond it, they did not want to delay.
Each one prepared himself with a sure and fiery heart,
For he could put arms to good use.
They gripped their strong lance handles
And grasped their shields firmly.
Each one nobly sat upright on his warhorse.
Carahuel rode toward them.
In his hand he held his lance by the iron.
Courteously he called to them;
"Ogier," he said, "I come to announce to you
That I have brought all that
I promised you yesterday, you may be sure.
Here is Sadoine, the son of King Manesier,
Who is the adversary of Charlot, the son of Charles the warrior;
And in this tent, beside this meadow,
Is Gloriande, who is worthy of admiration,
The daughter of Corsuble, the good, just king,
She whose beauty is beyond price.
What could I tell you? You should know that to judge justly
No one could wish for one more beautiful;
Nature would have too much to study

To start making her again, if she were to do it.
Beside the tent I have had attached
A beautiful and costly walking horse
With an embroidered bridle and a saddle of pure gold
On which you can have the young girl sit.
If you can conquer us with the steel sword,
She will depart with you without danger;
For I have had her agree to it.
You will never have anyone interfere in it."
"We have come to claim her," said Ogier,
"But you make us wait too long."
Said Carahuel, "Stop threatening me;
For, by Mohammed who has all to govern,
Before the day draws toward evening,
We will be so successful fighting over her
That at the end of the day you will not feel like wooing her,
Or I will be lying dead, bleeding on the grass.
And said Ogier, "God can truly help us.
Go on back; leave off your talk.
How about letting us get on with the work,
For time is passing; what we want
Is to be able to get ahold of your sweetheart,
For there is no one in existence who would not want to
See and get acquainted with such a young lady.
God give me the grace that I may kiss her."
Carahuel heard it; he seemed to be on the point of rage.
His color changed with anger;
He wheeled his combat charger about
And said to Sadoine, "Let's turn our thoughts to conquering them;
Let's run upon them confidently without any delay."

LXXIV

On the island were all four of the warriors.
And Ogier said, "Charlot, be valiant!
In your heart say to yourself often
That you are the son of the very good King Charles,
The best king that ever any man saw."
And Charlot said, "By Saint Symon,
Let's spur first if that seems good to you."
And Ogier said, "May God be blessed!"
From both sides the companions spurred.
Carahuel attacked on his steed from Aragon,
Striking Ogier on the shield with the lion,

And Ogier attacked him in such a way
That each one broke off many a chunk with his lance.
They rode beyond one another joined thus like falcons.
Their thought was on their steel blades.
Sadoine spurred toward Charlot freely
And he toward him, with banner lowered.
With strong lances tipped with sharp, iron blades,
They struck with such great force
That the coats of arms of both were broken.
The blows made the shining hauberks resound.
Each of the two vassals had vacated the saddle and landed
On the hindquarters of his Gascon steed.
Next, each one fell next to a bush.
They jumped up again without a long delay.
Their horses were of such quality
And of such behavior and training
That they did not move an inch
Until each one heard the command.
They remounted quickly, for it was certainly time.

LXXV

When Charlot had recovered his horse
And Sadoine and he were remounted,
Each one drew the good steel sword.
They encountered one another hardily;
Each one gave the other many a rough blow.
In his fist Carahuel held the engraved sword
Courtain the beautiful, which shone brilliantly.
Ogier and he had not rested.
Rather they had attacked one another so much
That their shields were broken
And their strong helmets were dented in many a place.
Ogier looked; he saw Charlot boxed in;
Sadoine had seized him by the helmet and
Forced him to bend down in front of him in a dangerous way.
When Ogier saw it, his heart was angered.
He turned his steed around toward that part of the field
And spurred him on a little; then he raised his arm.
Full of fury and savagery, he held up his sword
And struck Sadoine with such force
That he threw him onto the rump of his horse
So that all the bands of his helmet fell off.
Sadoine was so terribly stunned

That he could not remember if it were winter or summer.
With this blow Ogier delivered Charlot.
Carahuel came right beside Ogier
And drew Courtain, the good sharp sword.
Aiming his blow at the left side,
He struck Ogier on the golden helmet
With a blow so great and so beyond measure
That a big piece of it was knocked down onto the meadow.
The hauberk was strong; he did not break the links.
"God," said Ogier, "father of majesty,
The devils have forged such a sword."
Said Carahuel, "I have found you again;
I have struck you well with this blow;
For your misfortune have you struck Sadoine so ferociously here.
By Mohammed, whom I hold as lord,
Before you have kissed my beautiful sweetheart
Or she has embraced you,
If I can, I will have made you pay dearly for it."
And said Ogier, "You have talked a lot about it.
Because you took this tiny thing from my helmet,
Do you think for all that that you have harmed me?
I assure you by my loyalty
Soon, if I can do it, you will be well rewarded."

LXXVI

Ogier turned around with a marvelous violence
With his fearful sword in his fist;
One could not incite a falcon more
To take a heron, I'm not lying to you,
Than he himself was incited in trying to attack Carahuel.
He brandished the sword again, full of fury and desire,
Thinking he could not fail with this blow.
He knew very well to aim for the top of the helmet.
He gave it such a blow that he made sparks fly from it,
But the blade slipped to the left
And knocked off the nose piece.
Then blows raining on his shield
Caused his hauberk to break off,
But he himself was not touched by the sword,
For his adversary could not reach it with an unobstructed blow.
Whatever piece of armor he hit fell to the ground.
These blows dazed Carahuel a great deal
And frightened and astonished him greatly.

Thought he: "Well, when this man makes a promise,
He certainly keeps it."

LXXVII

Carahuel saw his cuirass torn apart,
His helmet broken and his buckler marred;
He was very much tormented for the love of his sweetheart
Because the Dane had the mastery of him to such an extent.
In his heart he swore vehemently and promised
That before vespers or the hour of compline
Either his blood would be spilt on the grass
Or the battle would be otherwise concluded.
The son of Charles held the polished sword,
Which he had often tested by trying to strike Sadoine with it.
His buckler was very much broken apart from the effort.
He struck Sadoine on the helmet from Syria;
The circlet was strong; it neither broke nor bent, but
The sword was broken in two halves.
Sadoine saw it; he thanked Mohamed for it,
Thinking he would soon win
His part of the battle with Charlot.
Then he rushed upon him; he attacked him most violently,
Giving him such a blow beside the ear with his sword
That he nearly fell off the saddle.
When Ogier saw it, he turned red with anger.
"God help us," he said, "Saint Mary,
For this pagan has very roughly dealt with
The son of Charles of the bold face!"
He turned his rein right toward that place
Because he wanted to encourage and reinforce him,
To help the son of Charles,
Ogier raised his sword, which he had grasped firmly,
And struck Sadoine with such great force
That with this blow he would need a doctor;
He raised the sword again; concentrating intently,
He gave him a great blow; but the sword slid.
Thus it happened that this time with this blow
He cut off the head of the good horse.
Sadoine fell on the grass, which was turning green;
Upon falling, he broke his thigh in such a way
That in that year it was not healed enough
That he could bear arms.
So rudely he fell on the prairie

That his sword slid out of his fist
And the chain to which it was attached
Was completely broken and disjointed.
It was sunk nearly a foot into the earth.
Charlot bent down and seized it at once.
All the gold in Pavia would not have made him happier
Than the sword he had won.

LXXVIII

When Carahuel saw Sadoine fallen,
His heart was sad and furious;
And his behavior reflected his concern.
He swore to Tervagant, Mohammed, and Cahu
That before he died his defeat would be avenged at a high cost.
He spurred the good, long-maned warhorse toward Ogier
And gave him such a blow on his pointed helmet
That a great piece of it fell down to the ground.
The blow came down so violently
That it broke off a good quarter of the shield.
The good hauberk held the blow back.
If it had not, Ogier would have suffered great misfortune.
In my opinion, he would have been completely cut open,
For Carahuel had struck him that blow
As if he were aflame with prowess.
Ogier lifted the good sharp sword up again
And spurred the warhorse at once,
Striking Carahuel a blow in response
So ferociously and with such great force
That Carahuel did not know what had happened to him.
He knocked him off the horse flat onto the ground.
Said Gloriande, "Mohammed, what are you doing?
So wretched and sad am I! What has happened to me
When I have lost Carahuel the noble
Who is my sweetheart and my darling!
And for Sadoine my heart is moved
Because both were distinguished knights.
Now these infidel French will lead me off
Into Charles's army, alas! Now I have lived too long
When sure calamity has overwhelmed me."
Crying, she sat down on the grassy meadow,
For her heart was very sad and desperate.
When Danemon saw this situation,
He said to his people, "We have waited too long.

We have seen their misfortune well.
Let's go to their rescue, or they are done for.
By Mohammed, to whom my heart belongs,
We will now give Ogier a cruel greeting;
For he has killed and conquered our people,
But I think we can make him pay for it dearly."

LXXIX

When Gloriande, who was so beautiful,
Saw Carahuel, who had been thrown to the ground,
And saw Sadoine, who was wounded and injured,
Her heart was sad and pained about it.
She was in anguish for each one of them.
Beside Sadoine was the illustrious Charlot,
Who had stopped beside him to kill him.
And Carahuel had gotten back up on his feet,
Holding the engraved sword in his fist.
Embracing what was left of his shield
Like a valiant warrior,
He turned savagely toward Ogier,
Preferring to be cut to pieces
Than to have ever been accused of any ignoble ruse.
Ogier would have already killed Sadoine and Carahuel
When Danemon came spurring through the meadows.
The son of Corsuble, he was the king of Balesgués.
In his company were thirty armed pagans.
Ogier saw them all coming rapidly.
"Ah, God, father of majesty,
How badly Carahuel has behaved toward us
Who has thus betrayed and deceived us!
He has forsworn himself outrageously toward us,
But by the one who was hanged on the cross,
Before I die, my steel sword
Will be well tested on their bejeweled helmets."
And Ogier said to Charlot, with his arms raised,
"For the love of God, set your mind to attacking well!
Before you die, make them pay dearly.
If the Saracens have bought us at great cost,
At the very least Charles and Namles and the other barons
Will be more feared because of it.
Better that a man be dead and called brave and worthy
Than remain alive and dishonored."
And said Charlot, "It is the very truth."

Ogier bore down on his golden stirrups.
Each warrior was ready to defend himself.
Carahuel had managed to get back up
On his horse; he was greatly tormented
By what he saw, sad, and furious.
He guided his horse up beside Ogier.
"Ogier," said he, "do not suspect me:
Because I did not plan these false turns,
For I would prefer to be dismembered
Than to do such falsities.
By Mohammed, to whom I am sworn,
You will find me beside you like an upright brother."
And Ogier said, "You have said enough,
But I do not know how you will do it."
Said Carahuel, "Loyally. This you will see."
Danemon called out provocatively to Ogier,
"Vassal," said he, "now you are gone;
This time you should know that Gloriande will not be going with you,
For you will not take her away,
My beautiful sister who has so many charms."

LXXX

King Carahuel was extremely angry.
"Mohammed," said he, "how I am undone now!
From now on I will be considered a traitor!"
And here were pagans amid the grassy meadows.
Ogier had stopped opposite them,
If he had had a lance, he would have run toward them.
He and Charlot held their swords completely unsheathed.
From the pagans they received many a great blow,
And they also struck them many a great blow in return.
They defended themselves well—let no one doubt it—
But their defense wasn't worth two straws,
For Ogier's horse had fallen dead
Because he was struck in the attack by so many lances
That the blood ran from him in ten places.
Carahuel was so much beside himself about it
That he took Charlot by the bridle, thus drawing him aside.
He saved him; he went out of the press.
"Leave!" he said, "don't stay any longer!
You are Charles's son: if you are captured,
To spite him you will be hanged very soon."
Charlot heard it; he was entirely silent and mute.

"Ah, God," thought he, "true father of King Jesus,
Since Ogier is dead, I am lost.
We have been deceived by these false infidels.
Alas! Why did my father the king
Put so much faith in Carahuel? He was deceived too much."
Overcome by grief he entered into the ford.
The good, long-maned warhorse carried him to the other side.
He was so well defended by Carahuel
That he was not pursued by the pagans,
And so he went away like the saddest knight in the world
While Carahuel turned around and rode swiftly back.
He went to Ogier to help him,
Riding toward the Saracens who were running upon Ogier.
If he is going to be saved, it will be by Carahuel if he can do it.
And Ogier had conducted himself like a worthy warrior.
His shield was already all cut up
And his hauberk was torn in many a place,
But unless God above intervenes,
It will be too late when the French see him again.

LXXXI

When Carahuel saw Ogier on foot,
The sword in his fist and hugging the shield
That the pagans had split and broken in pieces
And his horse beside him cut up,
You should know that in his heart he had anger and pity
And he had much sincere esteem for him.
He spurred his horse
And did his best to help him.
He insulted the Saracens emphatically,
But the Saracens did not stop harassing Ogier for a moment.
Ten Saracens rushed into him
And forced him to his knees on the ground
Where they caught him and restrained and bound him.
They sent him to King Corsuble, who was in Rome.
They carried off Sadoine, much wounded and injured,
Having laid him on a shield.
With a joyous and glad heart King Danemon,
Who had sought this, took away his sister,
Gloriande, the noble and elegant.
Charlot went away with great anger in his heart,
Suffering grief beyond limits.
"Alas! What will they say," said he," the esteemed French,

When they see me come back without Ogier,
Whom the wretched infidels have killed?
Now may God through his sweet love have his soul!"
He sighed; tears poured from his eyes.
He did not delay until he arrived at Sutri.
The French said, "We have been deceived.
Ogier is dead; we have fared badly.
Here is Charlot alone, without him. Ogier has paid dearly.
We must take that into consideration."
There this day was many an aggrieved heart.
Many were wringing their hands and pulling their hair.
They were experiencing great grief for Ogier.

LXXXII

The son of Charles, Charlot the noble,
Came back into the French army with a sorrowful heart
Because he did not bring Ogier back with him.
He dismounted quickly at his father's tent
And went in as many others did also.
The French saw that all his equipment
Was cut into many little pieces.
His battered helmet hung over his shoulders,
For it was coming apart.
His face was black and blue and bleeding.
Said the French, "By Saint Vincent,
It certainly looks as if he came from an extremely hard battle, but
He would not return at all shamefully
If Ogier were present with him."
Charlot came before Charles promptly and
Told him all his adventure,
The end and the beginning of the battle.
And he certainly told them everything in this way,
How Carahuel had put him in safety,
Having him cross the ford speedily, for
If he had not, he would have been dead.
Before he left there
He saw Ogier on foot surrounded.
They had killed his young horse.
One in a hundred could not escape from them.
When Duke Namles heard these words,
He was so sorrowful that his heart nearly broke.
The duke grieved for Ogier most humbly,
In thanking God from his heart in good faith.

"Ah, God," said Charles, "true king omnipotent,
They have killed Ogier; I know it truly.
May God save my soul,
For never have I seen one of his youth with such prowess,
Nor so powerful nor so bold.
And he was so full of good qualities
That one would not know how to devise improvements."
Then Charles got up because of his anger,
Weeping bitter tears.
As this news spread all through the army,
The French wept piteously for Ogier,
Grieving greatly for him everywhere.

LXXXIII

When Charlot had recounted the whole situation
Before his father and before the barons,
Most of them were greatly saddened by it.
In the army the men heaved many a great sigh.
They led the son of Charles to his tent
Where the French disarmed him while weeping.
Duke Namles grieved very much for Ogier.
"Ah, God, "said he, "king full of humility,
Did ever before live a man of that age,
So handsome, so full of prowess, so full of confidence,
So very courteous or so thoughtful?
In him was nothing except goodness.
When I remember that the pagans have killed him,
It wouldn't take much for my heart to break."
Duke Thierri comforted Namles,
Like a wise, brave man who is full of loyalty,
As did Charles with a heart full of pity.
"Namles," said he, "it is the will of God.
Since it pleases him, now may all be according to his will.
The Saracens have dismembered many a vassal of mine
And in battle killed and injured them
And wounded me myself in many places;
But by Jesus, the king of majesty,
I have not before this had my heart so enraged
As I have for him, if God give me health!
It's no wonder if I came to love him.
When I knew him right by me at my side,
Shield on his neck and helmet attached
And in his fist the good steel sword,

I would not have sought other support."
Here we will leave Charles the illustrious
And the sweet Duke Namles, in whom there was no falseness,
And the French, who were greatly tormented.
The story will speak to you again of King Corsuble
And of the pagans, whom may God damn,
Who have led Ogier into Rome
Where some wanted to cut off his head.
The others said he should be dragged
And to spite Charlemagne hanged.
But Gloriande, the noble and elegant,
Spoke and told so much to her father
That he gave and delivered Ogier to her.
She led him away without delay
Straight to her tent; there they imprisoned him.
Certainly in her heart she hoped
That he would never be harmed by any man born.
They disarmed him and arranged things quite well around him
And washed his face with clear water.
The young girl honored him as much as she knew how,
For she knew that he had distinguished himself well in arms.
She greatly desired that he would convert
To the worship of Mohammed
And deny Christianity,
But he would never have done it for a valley crammed full of gold.

LXXXIV

Right at this point, you should know without a doubt,
When Gloriande had Ogier taken
Into her tent to imprison him,
Carahuel came to talk to Corsuble,
Right at the moment that he came from battle,
For he had done nothng to have his armor removed.
As he came before him, he began to express his dismay.
"My lord," said he, "let me be heard!
You had me take your message
To Charlemagne, which
I did without making any change in it.
When I saw, Sire, that they would not change
To our religion and worship Mohammed,
I undertook a battle, the more to honor you,
Against Charlot and against Ogier the valiant.
There it behooved me to swear on my faith

That they could return safe and sound
If they could best me and Sadoine
And that they could take Gloriande away.
I'm telling you the truth; I have no desire to hide it.
When I came back from delivering the message,
At the moment you heard me recount it,
You wanted to grant and agree to it.
But Danemon wanted to act
So falsely that one could accuse him of
Treason, which is blamable in the extreme.
And it should weigh so much on your heart
That you ought never to claim him as your son,
For no man should love a traitor.
Rather, one should punish and shun him.
If you want to make amends for this fact,
Have Ogier delivered to me right away.
I want to take him into Charles's army.
And I myself, to prove my faith,
Will go with him, for no one should think me treacherous.
And Corsuble said, "Let all this be!
I intend to have Ogier hanged and dragged
Or I will have all his limbs cut off
Or, to spite Charles, I will have him shamed."
Carahuel heard it; he thought he would lose his mind.
He thought he would certainly go crazy with fury.
He mounted his horse; he had nothing within him but anger.
He left Rome as quickly as he could go,
Calling no companion or no peer there.
He did not want to pull on his rein until he reached Sutri.
He knew quite well how to arrive at Charles's tent, and
When he arrived, he got down; but he did not want to stop there.
Thus he entered into the tent at once.
The French made way for him and let him pass.
He took his sword of bright steel by the point and
Went to present it to Charles on his knees.

LXXXV

Carahuel was before Charles the king.
He spoke wisely and properly,
In a loud voice; for he did not want to speak in secret.
Said Carahuel, "Charles, hear me.
Never say that I went back on my word.
I surrender myself to you, as I should do,

And I will certainly tell you the reason why.
The people of our religion have taken Ogier
Away wrongly and perfidiously.
King Danemon, whose rashness terrifies me,
Would kill him soon, to the best of my belief,
For he is bloated with pride and arrogance.
By Mohammed to whom I bow,
If my soul could go over there
So that the devils did not do their will with him,
Then there would be no treachery while I lived.
Fair lord king, because I see
That Ogier is in danger of harm,
I surrender myself to you, just as I swore
When I struck my tooth with my finger
In your tent, which more than three saw.
Have me quietly put in your prison,
And if they do evil or harm to Ogier
Do the same to me, by love I pray you;
If I am a traitor, my opinion is that I have gone insane.
To remove myself from so unseemly a situation
I give myself up, good king, before you.

LXXXVI

When Charlemagne heard Carahuel,
Who for Ogier presented himself like this,
In his heart he esteemed him greatly for it.
The noble king rose up before him
And commanded him to get up from his knees.
The king himself helped him to rise.
Very gently the king asked him
About what touched his heart most closely:
"Friend," said Charles, "listen to me!
Is Ogier dead? Do not hide it from me."
"Sire, no, but King Corsuble has him
In his prison and I do not know what he will do with him."
Charles heard and wept with joy, for
His heart told him that he would have Ogier again.
The French looked at the arms that King Carahuel
Who spoke to Charlemagne carried.
Said one to another: "The one who cut up those
Arms like this battled most ferociously!
That was Ogier! May God who created all things
Bring him back here to us safe and sound!"

Right at this point Namles came in.
When he had heard the news of Ogier
And why Carahuel had come there,
He praised God and his mother and the saints.
He put his arms around Carahuel
And almost kissed him,
But because of his religion he refrained from kissing him.
An idea occurred to Charles the king
That Namles should have Carahuel in his keeping,
For he knew well what he would think of him.
He gave him into Namles's care with his right hand.
Duke Namles took him to his lodging, and
Right on his bed there he removed his arms.
He promised him assuredly that he would have no other prison,
That he would lie beside him in his tent.
Next to his bed he would put his own bed.
And Carahuel thanked him most gratefully.

LXXXVII

The good Duke Namles, I tell you truthfully,
Honored Carahuel greatly and treated him with great warmth.
The Franks rejoiced with his news.
I will leave off talking to you of them here,
And I will tell you how the Turks and Arabians
In Rome were frightened for Carahuel.
There's a little something I forgot
That I will tell you; I will not wait any longer.
When Carahuel went out of Rome,
He confessed to a Saracen what he was going to do,
That he was going to Sutri to put himself at the mercy of Charles
Because the pagans had betrayed Ogier.
He asked the Saracen when he had left
To go to King Corsuble without delay
And tell it to him just like that,
And that he did; he did not lie about it.
It caused the Saracens great consternation,
And King Sadoine was greatly afflicted by it
As was Gloriande, the noble and gracious.
Ogier knew it; it pleased him very much.
Corsuble did not sleep that night.
His heart was sorrowful for Carahuel.
He feared greatly that they would mistreat him
And because of Ogier shame and dishonor him.

He would have liked to give Ogier back
So that he might have his friend Carahuel back.

LXXXVIII

The next day after dawn had broken
The pagans assembled,
Turks and Coumains and those of Barbary,
In the tent of Corsuble, who was king of Syria.
Brunamon, who was full of perfidy,
Was the first to speak.
He was king of the realm of Aumarie.
He was greatly envious of Carahuel
And hated him with very great evil intent,
For he loved Gloriande, Carahuel's sweetheart.
He was tall and strong and ferociously violent
And had proved himself in great feats of chivalry.
He got to his feet before the barons.
His voice was heard well in loud words.
"Sire," said he, "I will not lie to you about it.
Carahuel has done outrage and folly
And falsity and very great deceit
And injustice and great lack of good sense.
Never before has a pagan king done such deviltry
As to go toward Charles's side.
I say that he has relinquished our religion
And betrayed the pagan army to Charles.
Certainly he has forfeited his land.
He has lost everything—you should know it—this time,
Body and possessions, honor and dominion.
Here is what I propose; if there is anyone who contradicts it,
I take this challenge against all men."
Most agreed with what he said.

LXXXIX

When Brunamon had thus spoken
And no one challenged him or his word,
Rather most had gone along with it,
His heart was extremely joyous and glad,
For he thought he had certainly gained everything.
A pagan told Gloriande about it.
Her heart was greatly chagrinned
And very sorrowful and very anxious.
She herself told Ogier, and

When Ogier heard it, he felt sadness and pity.
He saw the maiden, who had wept
So that her sweet face was wet with tears, and
He knew that it had greatly touched her
That they had talked thus about Carahuel.
"My beauty," said he, "do not have an angry heart.
For if I had myself equipped
And had a good horse and sword and lance
And a strong shield and well-barred helmet,
I would undo all the reasons why
They have condemned Carahuel.
I pray you, my beauty, in very great friendship,
That no other than I be granted this privilege."
With joined hands Ogier begged this of her.
When the elegant young girl
Heard Ogier, she thanked him profusely.
And she esteemed him greatly in her heart.
Her heart was completely filled with joy.

XC

Said Gloriande: "Ogier, since you want
To have this battle, you shall have it.
You will come with me before the king my father
Right now, without delay
Before the group has disbanded.
With me I will take one hundred armed Saracens
By whom you will be well guided and guarded.
Said Ogier, "My beauty, for God's sake, make haste."
Thus it was done as you have heard.
Ogier was led from there to the tent of Corsuble
Where the pagans looked at him with astonishment.
Said one to another, "This man who is so young
And renowned was born
At a propitious hour—if only he were not Christian.
Many of our people fear him."
Gloriande was at Ogier's right side.
She stopped directly in front of the king.
Said Gloriande, "Lord Father, hear me.
Carahuel is to be married to me.
You yourself gave him to me as a gift.
I must not tolerate that he be dishonored
Nor that his land be forfeited or taken away.
If I did not love him much more than another

It would not be the right loyalty
Since he is my lord and my sweetheart.
Brunamon has declared his wishes.
He has sworn to you
That Carahuel has turned against you
And has gone to Charles to betray you.
I contradict him in that and, as you can see,
Here is Ogier, who is my defender;
And he has presented himself here for Carahuel.
Receive the challenge to Brunamon,
And when you please, arrange their encounter,
And, fair Sire, treat Carahuel justly,
For you have few such as he in your court."
Upon hearing this word, Ogier passed forward.
He spoke to the king like a thoughtful man.
"Sire," said he, "the words Gloriande has spoken
Are all the truth.
Carahuel is a proven, loyal man
Who should be honored for it in all courts.
I will prove this with Brunamon
So that you will see it, and if I am conquered,
It will certainly be right to hang me on a gibbet."
And said Corsuble, "You shall have the battle
Since you make this challenge
And it is the desire of King Brunamon.
Come back before me next Wednesday
Equipped and ready with all weapons."
At this word, each one left there.
Said the pagans, "Ogier is a demon
Who was made and created to destroy us.
May he be turned over to the living devils.
Corsuble does badly when he does not deliver him to death."

XCI

King Brunamon, who did many a fearsome deed,
Was tall and broad and had a savage face.
In the pagan army there was no greater knight.
Known to be strong and agile,
He could not find a horse so large
That he could not jump on it without putting his foot in the stirrup.
As he headed off to his lodging,
He thanked Mohammed profusely
That he had this battle with Ogier.

He would not have been so happy for one thousand pounds of pure gold,
For he believed he would avenge all the others with it.
Not wanting to tarry there,
Gloriande went straight back to her tent
And did all she could to make sure that Ogier was well cared for.
She did not treat him as if he were a prisoner
But made him quite comfortable according to his wishes.
For his prowess he was extremely dear to her heart.
"Ogier," said she, "if you see fit
To send word to King Charles,
I would have a good messenger made ready for you
Who would go beg Charles
Not to harm Carahuel for your sake."
Said Ogier, "My beauty, I have no desire to refuse.
Instead, I will do what you suggest without reservation."
And Gloriande thanked him.
Then the beauty, wanting to delay no longer,
Had the messenger prepared at once.
Ogier wanted to give him a message
For Duke Namles, his uncle the Bavarian,
Which would make Namles welcome Carahuel in Charles's army
And embrace and celebrate him wholeheartedly.

XCII

When the messenger heard Ogier,
He wasted no time in preparing himself.
He had made his preparations so completely
That the next day, at daybreak,
He mounted his horse as soon as he was ready.
When he was mounted, he took his shield;
He took his solid, sharp lance by the iron.
He spurred his horse, which ran rapidly,
And did not hold back the rein until he arrived at Charles's army.
The French people knew at once
That he was a messenger when they saw him.
Before the tent of Charles the redoubtable king
The messenger dismounted from his long-maned warhorse.
He entered and saw Charles
With his barons and his close friends around him.
The Saracen gave them a noble greeting.
Charles, whose heart was much aggrieved
Because he thought he had lost Ogier,
Received the greeting very correctly.

XCIII

The messenger spoke to the king quite wisely:
"Sire," said he, "I will tell you briefly
Why I am before you at present.
Which one is Namles to whom Bavaria belongs?
Ogier his nephew sends me to you
And also to him." And when Namles heard it,
He at once took the messenger by the hand.
Then he hugged his neck and embraced him tightly.
"Friend," said he, "tell quickly:
Is Ogier alive, by God omnipotent?"
"Yes, indeed, Sire, you may be sure.
He sends me to you and implores you earnestlly
That Carahuel not be put in any situation
In which he would be tortured."
Then the messenger told about the battle
Very thoughtfully, as with good knowledge of it,
All just in such a manner
As you have heard the first time,
And the motive and why and how.
"And the battle," said he, "certainly
Will be tomorrow, as it has been agreed."
This news came much to the liking
Of Charles and Namles and the other people,
Who in common accord said
That in Ogier prowess and strength
Had allied themselves in loyalty.
And they thanked God and his mother
And the saints over and over that he was alive.

XCIV

When the messenger had finished his message,
He took Namles and led him to one side.
"Do me, Sire," said he, "the great favor,
If you please and if you would,
To let me speak to Carahuel a little.
Quite briefly I will show him
The pure truth of this thing,
How Brunamon has wronged him
And how Ogier presented himself
To his challenge, just as I have told you.
Then I will go back, for I have stayed too long
When he has told me what he wants to."

"Friend," said Namles, "it will not be refused you.
Come with me to my tent,
For in that place I hold him imprisoned."
This one thanked him and bowed to him.
"Namles," said Charles, "what did the messenger say?"
Then Namles told him all that
He had implored and asked.
"I will go with you," said Charles, "in the name of God."
After this word they turned from there.
They went to Namles's tent; there they found
King Carahuel, in whom was such great goodness.

XCV

Charles of the proud face came to Namles's tent
And with him many a duke and many a prince
And many a baron, whom I am not going to name.
They found Carahuel the admirable.
He was playing chess with a knight
Whose name was Oedes de Mondidier.
And Carahuel, who always knew what to do,
Came at once to Charles
And greeted him; he wanted to draw back then,
But Charles had him come toward him,
Pulling him toward him by the coat;
For the loyalty he had shown toward Ogier
Made him love him and hold him dear.
When Carahuel recognized the messenger
That he saw beside Namles the Bavarian,
He knew him well, and he had a great desire
To know what he had come to tell.
Said the messenger, "I never before saw a prisoner
Who had less to fear of his prison."

XCVI

The messenger went at once toward Carahuel
And greeted him in accordance with the false religion
On behalf of Gloriande, the noble and gracious,
The daughter of King Corsuble.
Then he told him, in the hearing of all, about
The betrayal of which King Brunamon, the lord
Of Abilant, was accusing him
And how Ogier had laid down the gauntlet and accepted the challenge.
He recounted the entire agreement.

Carahuel heard it, and his feelings changed.
He gritted his teeth and shook his head.
One could see well by his appearance
That within him were wrath and great fury.

XCVII

When Carahuel heard the news,
That he had been accused of deceit and it was said
That he must have betrayed the pagan army,
Abandoned Mohammed and denied his religion,
His face reddened with anger.
In his heart he thought that if his honor
Were not saved and garanteed, he would die.
He spoke to the king; courteously he implored him
That he would release him this time
So that he could go to the pagan army.
"I will come back, Sire; do not doubt it at all,
If I am not dead; in truth I promise you.
King Brunamon accuses me of great villainy,
But I know well that this is motivated by jealousy
Because he loves my sweetheart Gloriande.
Never since the day that I became her fiancé
Has he been able to love either me or my kin.
He is a powerful king and of great nobility,
A worthy warrior, valiant, full of chivalry.
He has people with him of very great, unreasoning violence
Who would soon do Ogier perfidious harm
If the battle were going badly for him;
But I think I can be such a companion there
That Ogier will not be attacked.
Now therefore please allow me,
Sire, the trip; my opinion is that I am
Too much delayed in going." Charles granted it to him,
And Carahuel wisely thanked him.

XCVIII

Said Charlemagne: "Carahuel, listen.
About this trip that you request of me,
I pray you urgently that you hasten there right away.
You have proven yourself so loyal toward us
That you should be both believed and loved
And in all places henceforth always honored.
I give you a gift and want you to take it:

Go and come as much as you please
Without ever asking leave of me."
"Certainly," said Namles, "Sire, you are absolutely right,
For he will never behave falsely."
Then Duke Namles went to Carahuel.
"Ha! Sweet friend," said he, "if you love me this much,
Keep Ogier from being delivered to death.
If he can be delivered from this field
Alive, for the love of God, arrange it so
That he comes back, if ever you can,
And you remain for him in that place.
And if Corsuble does not want to agree
To this bargain and it is not his wish,
At the very least let him be re-imprisoned.
Whatever befalls him, save his life."
Said Carahuel: "Sire, never doubt it;
For he or I, if it is within my power, you will soon have again."
"I hope," said Namles, "that you will work it out as it should be."
Of this there was no further discussion.
At once his horse was led to him.
Ably and soon he equipped himself.
Then Carahuel the renowned took leave,
As did the messenger; then each one mounted,
And Carahuel parted from Charles's army.
The barons of France esteemed him highly.
"This Saracen," said they, "is very wise
And very courteous and intelligent.
It's a great shame that he is not Christian."

XCIX

When Carahuel left Charles's army,
He and the messenger, who was not a novice,
Often spoke of Charles of the proud face.
They esteemed him highly in deed and in word.
In his heart Carahuel was much chagrinned
Because of Brunamon, who had accused him
Of relinquishing Mohammed
And of betraying the Saracens.
Relentlessly and more and more it touched his heart.
He did not want Ogier the bold
To do for him what he had undertaken.
Rather he would do it; he himself had promised he would,
And he would abandon this project reluctantly.

Carahuel the noble hastened so much
That he soon came to Rome, the lordly city,
Where he was welcomed with gladness by his own.
Many a heart rejoiced at his coming,
And many were angered and afflicted about it.
The people of his country were very joyous about it.

C

King Carahuel, who was so worthy,
Did not want to stir one foot from where he was
Until he had seen the good Dane Ogier.
He had no need to delay
To arrange what must most concern him,
For already it was very close to nightfall.
He started to make his way toward Gloriande,
Not wanting to tarry until he got to her tents.
Gloriande had gone outside of her tents
To enjoy herself in taking
The evening air, which she liked very much.
With her were ladies and knights
And damsels, servants, and squires.
When she saw Carahuel returning
And noticed the messenger beside him,
Her heart leapt with joy,
For she loved Carahuel with her whole heart.

CI

When Carahuel saw the lovely young woman
Before her tents and with her people,
He got down from his horse quickly
And went to Gloriande at once.
He greeted her most courteously indeed,
And she received him gladly.
With her first words she asked him how
He came back, and he therefore
Told her about it from beginning to end,
How it was; he forgot nothing about it.
She, who was full of good intelligence,
Esteemed King Charles highly,
Him and Namles, and said that
They had acted nobly and loyally toward him.
They did not talk very long there
Because Carahuel had a great desire

To talk urgently to Ogier,
For boldness forbade him strongly
From having anyone fight Brunamon
Except himself, for his heart was set upon it.
If others than he defended his honor,
He saw clearly that he could
Be blamed for it slanderously.
Very near there was Ogier
In a tent, kept nobly with care,
And Carahuel went there at once
With Gloriande, who very courteously
Had often kept him company in his tent.
The news of Carahuel spread through
The pagan army; when Brunamon heard it,
He was not happy about his return;
For he preferred that it be otherwise.
King Corsuble did not have a sad heart.
Instead, he thanked Mohammed well for it.

CII

There where Ogier was as I have told you
Came Gloriande and Carahuel with her.
Ogier rose to meet them when he saw them.
Carahuel greeted him with heartfelt joy
As Ogier did him, no more nor less
Than necessary and appropriate.
Bold-hearted Ogier's lodging
Was quite fine, noble and attractive.
Neither sheet nor rug was lacking,
For Gloriande had commanded it thus.
All three agreed to sit down.
So Carahuel recounted everything,
How Charles and Namles had welcomed him
And all the others honored and served him.
Ogier was very glad when he heard it.
Said Carahuel, "Ogier, I thank you very much
That you have undertaken to do battle for me this way
Against Brunamon, whom I regard as an enemy,
For he has certainly deserved it
When he says that I have betrayed King Corsuble.
I myself, I thus swear to you,
Will prove to him that he has lied about this.
The battle will be mine since I am here.

Leave it to me; in the name of love I beg it of you;
For you know well, if I consented
To have another defend my honor
Instead of me, I would always be
Shamed and considered a failure."

CIII

When Ogier heard Carahuel say
That he himself would do the battle
Against Brunamon and that he thanked him
For having presented himself in court for him,
In his heart he esteemed him greatly for it.
He was right, it seemed to him,
To fight the battle since he was there.
He did not know what to do; reluctantly would he let him
And reluctantly would he refuse to allow him to do
What he requested, since his own honor was in play.
Then he thought that he would seek a way
By which, if he could, he would fight the battle
In such a manner as would be honorable
To Carahuel, or he would allow Carahuel to fight.
When Gloriande heard the words
That Carahuel spoke to Ogier
About the battle that he said he wanted to have
With Brunamon, she eagerly wanted
To hear what Ogier would answer,
For she knew Ogier well enough to believe
That he would make so courteous a response
That the honor of both would be saved.

CIV

And Ogier said, "Carahuel, listen.
About the battle that you have requested to have,
It seems to me that you ought to have it,
But I implore you to save my honor
In such a way as you will hear me say.
Since the challenge was delivered from me
First, as you know,
If I do not appear in court tomorrow
Equipped and ready for combat,
It is my opinion that I could be blamed for it.
Because of this I implore you, if you love me at all,
That tomorrow I be armed along with you,

That you will take me to the court before Corsuble.
Then I could not be criticized
When I would be represented like that.
Then you will request this battle
With Brunamon, if you can have it,
For you do not know if he intends
To fight you if you propose it.
Perhaps tomorrow his wishes will be such
That he will not want me to be released
So that I go onto the field against him.
And if it is thus, be assured
That if it is within my power I will be your man."
Said Carahuel, "You certainly speak well about it,
Like a loyal, bold and thoughtful man.
Your counsel will not be refused."
Said Gloriande, "Certainly you have the right to ask this.
In all courts one must be highly regarded
Who gives counsel like this."
Thus they agreed, and each one got up.
Carahuel and Gloriande left there, and Ogier stayed.
Gloriande honored him greatly, and
Upon parting she hugged him.
When Carahuel had taken her to his tents,
She lingered there very little,
Returning to Ogier at once.
By her command his bed was carried
To Carahuel's tent, and it remained there all night.
Carahuel spoke at length about Charlemagne
And Namles, how he was kept by him.
Carahuel told Ogier many things.
On the next day, when day had broken,
Each one of them, when it was time, got ready.
They armed themselves; then each one mounted his horse.
Both were equipped
Well and properly and with very handsome battle gear.
They went toward the court, as you hear me say.
The good Dane commended himself to God,
And Carahuel the esteemed commended himself to Mohammed.

CV

Carahuel sat armed on the charger
With Ogier, who was such a worthy knight, beside him.
Whoever saw them ride together

And bear down firmly on the stirrups
Could well say that they were noble and redoubtable,
That they certainly seemed to be knights
And that each one inspired fear.
And Gloriande, the beauty with the loyal heart,
Had come now to her father to announce
That Carahuel wanted to vindicate his honor
Against Brunamon and dispute him by combat
And to know if he would want to agree to it.
A messenger who had heard Gloriande speak
Went to inform Brunamon of this.
The messenger headed straight for the tent
Where Brunamon was getting ready and
Told him everything; he did not want to leave out anything
That he had heard said at the court.
Brunamon heard it; he became angry.
His color changed with fury.
"By Mohammed," said he, "whom I love,
For all the gold of Montpellier I will not change my mind
About fighting with Ogier.
There is no man for whom I would yield on this."

CVI

When Brunamon the bold was armed,
His Arabian warhorse was led to him.
It was Broiefort. There was in no country
At that time a horse of greater price.
His body was large, his flesh hard and massive
And deadset on pursuit, from the back to the chest,
Violent, powerful, strong and ardent.
Everything needed in a well-built horse
He had in him, I tell you briefly.
King Brunamon took hold of the saddle bow in front,
Jumping into the saddle without using a stirrup.
Said the pagans, "Whoever undertakes to do battle
With a man made like that surely must be stupified."
Brunamon swore to Mohammed to whom he was subject
That if he escaped from the battle alive
And could conquer Ogier,
Just as soon as he killed him
He would assail Carahuel immediately
And provoke him to battle.
He would accuse him again

Of being an evil traitor who had lied about his faith,
Disavowed and abandoned his gods
And betrayed King Corsuble.
He said it aloud so that it was well heard.
Then he seized his strong shield,
Which was gold with three small, gray-brown lions.
The lance handle, of which the iron was burnished, was solid
And the helmet rich, well painted with fleurs-de-lis.
He turned his path toward the court,
Afire and enthralled with love and arms.
The Capitol, I think they say,
Was the place where this field was established.
Long it was and wide, enclosed with stakes.
For a long time those who were involved in combat
Had always fought there.
Corsuble of the fierce countenance came there
And with him King Danemon, his son,
And Gloriande; this he allowed reluctantly.
On her head she had a crown of rubies.
The place was lit up with her beauty.
Often she prayed to Mohammed that he would help
Carahuel, who was to be her husband,
And Ogier, who was valiant and noble.
As to Brunamon, she prayed that he be dishonored,
For he had committed a crime against Carahuel.
There were plenty of Achopars, of Lutis
And of Coumains, of Turks, of Amoravis.
Places were occupied everywhere
So that people could see who turned out the worst.

CVII

Carahuel and Ogier came equipped
Into the park that I have described for you
Just as I have told and recounted to you previously.
They entered the park as if they knew what was ahead of them.
Of their duties they had forgotten nothing.
With Carahuel came plenty
Of Saracens who were knighted,
Very richly and nobly mounted,
Both of his staff and of his kin;
For Carahuel had commanded them
That no one have a heart so daring
As to do Ogier any harm;

And they had sworn upon Mohammed
That they would first have to be dismemebered,
Come what may; of that there should be no doubt.
Right at the entrance to the park they stopped.
When the wise Carahuel
And Ogier had entered into the park,
Everybody stared at them,
And many a pagan marvelled
That they were both armed.
Those who did not know why asked,
And when they learned the truth
Many attributed great worthiness
To King Carahuel and praised him highly for it.
They had not been there but a little
When Brunamon with the rapid warhorse
Entered the field like a man of great furor.
All three were led before Corsuble.
King Carahuel spoke first
When they had introduced themselves in such a way
As was the custom at that time.
"Corsuble, Sire," said he, "King Brunamon,
Who has accused me of falsity, has acted badly.
He has said that I have turned my back on Mohammed
And betrayed you and acted disloyally
And have turned to Christianity.
I say that he lied, and I myself
Will prove it to him; you see me here ready.
Release Ogier from the pledge that he gave.
He has accomplished so much and has conducted himself
In such a way that all good people must be grateful to him."
Brunamon heard it; he nearly went out of his mind.

CVIII

Brunamon felt only anger
When he heard Carahuel speak this way.
Very fiercely he raised up
On his stirrups and shook his head violently.
"Corsuble, Sire," said he, "I hear
King Carahuel here who
Asks for battle with me, and
By Mohammed whom we must adore
I really don't want to refuse him,
Not according to the plan he described to you,

But in such a form as I would like to show you.
It is that first I would like to fight Ogier,
And if I can outdo him by my weapons,
Have Carahuel brought back to me at once.
Thus he and I will fight peer to peer
Because no one could give me anything
That could make me want
To avoid battle with Ogier.
It's too bad for him that he ever came to present me his pledge
To remove ignominious blame from Carahuel.
I believe I will make him pay dearly.
Before the sun sets
I believe I will do much battle with each of them.
Have the place vacated and cleared out,
For you are making us wait too long.
I would not do otherwise for anything you could imagine."
Carahuel heard it; he began to sigh.
He was very sad that he could not find a way
That could lead Brunamon to fight him,
That he could not make him change his mind,
That he did not want to change this battle plan for anything.
He had made such an effort to do so — know this without a doubt —
That there is no man who could blame him about it.
But for many a man it is often better
To let be what cannot be changed.
He looked toward Brunamon.
Then he said to him — he could not help himself —
"King Brunamon," said he, "I have never seen
Anyone augment his value by boasting too much.
Now may Mohammed never allow you
To carry out your plans."

CIX

When Carahuel saw that
His battle plan would fail,
In his heart he was much sadder about it
Than he showed himself to be,
For he had a heart of such nobility and character
That he scorned all outrage and arrogance
And desired to do everything honorably.
When Ogier saw that he would have the battle,
In his heart he thanked God profusely
That Carahuel would take part in the battle

So that his honor would be kept entirely.
King Brunamon, who wanted very much
That the battle begin without delay,
Rode carefully by those assembled to see him.
He raised himself nobly on the stirrups
And proudly palmed his lance.
From time to time he gripped his shield.
Carahuel took Ogier, whom he liked so much,
And led him by the bridle to the rows on his right.
Then he said to him all that it seemed to him
Was reasonable and appropriate.
What would be the use of saying more about it?
He took leave of Ogier the way he should.
He left the lists, as was proper.
Then those there whose duty it was
Closed the gates again very tightly.
Then it was shouted that no one should be so bold
That he would move now because of anything that he heard
Or saw, and that anyone who did anything else
Would be struck and killed.

CX

When all those who had no reason
To be there had left the lists,
King Brunamon and Ogier waited
Until they were ordered
To do what they had come to do.
And when they had heard this command,
Then each one seized his shield,
Brandished his lance and struck his horse
With his spurs; and the long-maned warhorses
Bolted violently from their places.
So the distinguished vassals came together
And gave one another such great blows
With all their strength that the sharp lances
Were broken and shattered up to their fists.
Neither one nor the other gained
Or lost the worth of a straw at this blow.
They passed beyond one another; each one drew his bare sword.
King Brunamon was very angry
That he had not beaten Ogier with this strike
Since he had hit him with a full blow.
He saw plainly that something had gone wrong.

He cursed Mohammed and Cahut about it
So loudly that those around him heard it plainly.

CXI

King Brunamon's ferocity was very great.
He turned his face toward Ogier and
Struck his horse with the spurs.
Away he went toward him, his good sword ready to strike.
And the Dane, who was such a fine person,
Came back toward him, the reins released.
They gave one another great blows with their swords,
But Ogier struck him first.
He gave him such a blow on his bejeweled helmet
That flowers and precious stones were knocked to the ground.
Blows rained on his shield
So that a full quarter of it was removed.
And Brunamon in turn, with his engraved steel sword,
Struck back on the painted helmet
So violent a blow that he cut off
Nearly a half of the strong golden circlet.
Ogier raised his sword; he pursued forcefully.
He struck Brunamon again so hard
That he nearly threw him to the ground.
He had dented Brunamon's helmet so deeply
That his head was ringing in it.
This blow affected Brunamon so much
That he thought twice about continuing.
I have not yet told you
How Ogier coveted Broiefort.
As soon as he saw him when he entered the field
And saw how he was made,
He badly wanted him as a conquest.
He would not strike any blow
That he feared might injure or kill the horse,
For in his heart he had thought
That if it pleased the king of majesty
That he conquer the Saracen,
He would take possession of the impetuous warhorse.
Of this the story will speak no longer.
King Brunamon turned the horse
Right toward Ogier and shouted to him,
"Vassal," said he, "you have not outdone me.

Instead, you will end up paying dearly for what you have done."
Said Ogier, "God's will be done."

CXII

Brunamon came savagely toward Ogier
Like one so enraged that he wanted
To kill or maim him.
And the Dane, according to the customs of knighthood,
Came back toward him, his steel sword in his fist.
King Brunamon gave him a heavy and violent blow
On his helmet of pure gold,
So that the helmet was ruined.
He knocked a large piece of it onto the grass.
And the Dane struck him back once again
Such a great blow on his costly helmet
That its strong circlet broke into pieces.
If the sturdy hauberk's inner lining of mail had not been doubled,
He would have had his body severed
From his soul at this blow, you may be sure.
The heavy blow made him lean forward.
Then Ogier spurred his horse to approach him further.
He went to grab Brunamon around the neck,
Making the horse surge forward a little
And Brunamon bend forward.
Why should I speak to you further about it?
Neither bridle nor harness, saddle bow nor stirrup
Were worth a penny to him
Nor kept him from falling to the ground.
Brunamon felt only rage.
When he saw himself so roughly
Thrown from his horse to the ground,
He saw well he had no need of a warhorse,
He jumped back to his feet; he did not want to delay any longer,
For he was a strong, powerful and agile man.

CXIII

King Brunamon was back on his feet.
It's no wonder if he was tormented
When he was knocked to the ground like that.
He looked at Ogier, who was coming rapidly toward him
To do him harm, and then he decided
That if he could he would kill
Ogier's horse or make the horse go wild;

For if he did not manage to dismount him,
He saw clearly that he would be dead and conquered.
The Turk abandoned his shield,
Throwing it onto the field.
With both hands he held the engraved sword,
Which was sharper than sharpened razors.
He came toward Ogier aflame with great rage
And struck the horse on which he was mounted,
The blow fell right on his leg,
The one in front on the left side.
The blow was delivered with such great force
That the lower leg of the horse, was broken
Near the knee, right against it.
This blow made the horse swerve so
That he was thrown to the earth at once.
When Ogier saw that he was brought to this,
He wrested himself from the saddle bow so violently
That he was not encumbered by the horse.
Said Brunamon, "Master, jump over in my direction.
I have many more blows in my repertoire.
I have not yet used them all.
Very quickly, if I can do it, you will know it
If Mohammed has not forgotten me."
And Ogier said, "Vassal, do not boast,
For you will not conquer me by words."
At this remark each one brandished his sword again.
Each one came toward the other ready to strike.
They gave one another great blows on their bejeweled helmets
So that they were broken and their circlets came off.
Ogier's sword flew into pieces.
What was left was not even two feet long.
Ogier saw it; he was very angry about it.
And yet he did not seem frightened about it.
Boldly he went toward the Turk.
His heart was aflame with great violence.
He brandished what was left of his steel sword
Like a distinguished vassal.
He struck the pagan on his golden helmet
At the place where the helmet was most broken.
The blow fell with such force
That the helmet and the golden-mailed hauberk
Were not worth two peeled eggs to the Saracen.
The sword sliced right to his teeth,

And his brains splattered all around him.
Then he fell dead, and Ogier the wise
Praised God and all the saints greatly for it.
He very much regretted Brunamon's death.
"Indeed," said he, "it was a sorrow and a pity
That such a vassal as you was not Christian.
If in the pagan army there are some more like you,
Charles could certainly be grieved about it."

CXIV

When Ogier had accomplished all these deeds,
As you have heard, he then turned at once
Toward Broiefort, the horse he wanted so much to possess.
He took him by the silver bridle;
Nimbly he put his foot in the stirrup,
Mounting swiftly and ably.
His heart was glad when he felt the saddle-bow.
Ogier then had this horse for a long time,
As the story teaches and bears witness,
But I will not make a long speech about it now.
Many of the people were sad for Brunamon, and
Those who loved him were terribly tormented.
Said one to another, "By Mohammed, why is King Corsuble
Waiting to hang Ogier?
If he does not hang Ogier, he does not love Brunamon."
Many of them were talking together this way.
But Gloriande, the elegant young girl,
And Carahuel, they and their relatives
And their friends, of which there were many,
Thanked Mohammed very often
That the combat had turned out like this.
It was just, for Brunamon had
Acted wickedly toward them and falsely.
Ogier sat nobly on Broiefort
Completely still in the middle of the field;
In this place he awaited any command from Corsuble,
For he did not want to make any kind of error.

CXV

In such a manner as you have heard me recount
—Without telling a lie—was the battle
Between Brunamon and Ogier the valiant baron.
King Carahuel, who was so worthy,

Had the gates opened at once.
He entered the field without stopping;
He came up to Ogier the Dane and stood beside him
And asked him how he was.
Ogier said, "It is thanks to God that I am as you see me.
I would like to go back
To the French army; if you could arrange it,
I would love you for evermore."
Said Carahuel, "I should certainly strive
To do whatever you want
When, to honor me and save my life
You were willing to risk your life.
By Mohammed, whom I worship,
You will be in Charlemagne's army before evening,
Or I will go there to show my good faith.
And if Corsuble should not want
To hand you over
In order to keep me with him, you must have no doubt
That I will have you safely guarded
By people of my kingdom."

CXVI

King Corsuble's heart was very sad
When he saw Brunamon lying dead on the field,
And Danemon his son was greatly grieved by it
When he saw him dead, bleeding on the ground.
His heart moved him to sigh frequently.
On all sides people were lamening him greatly
For his great prowess.
They swore to Mohammed, in whom they believed,
That if their ruler Corsuble
And his capable son Danemon
Let Ogier, that evil tyrant, escape
So that he could very well come before them again,
It would be much too late to repent of it.
They continued saying such things in many places.
Carahuel came before Corsuble at once.
He spoke to him loudly so that everyone heard.
"Sire," said he, "tell me what your opinion is.
Ogier threw down the gauntlet to defend me.
Do you believe he has carried out his part fully?"
"Indeed," said Corsuble, "it appears so,
Whether it be horrible or pleasing."

But King Corsuble said these words while bowing deeply
And lowering his face,
For his heart was greatly touched
That he had lost so vailant a Saracen
As Brunamon, and one so powerful.

CXVII

Said Carahuel, "Corsuble, listen to me.
You are a powerful king, trusted and loved,
Of pagan kings the most dreaded,
And the richest and the most renowned.
And if you are all you heard me say you were,
You must certainly praise Mohammed.
And for love of him you should
Always behave in such a way that you are considered loyal.
In my whole life I have never heard said
Anything for which you could be proved blameworthy
Except about Ogier, whom you see here.
But toward him you have acted very badly
And toward me, when you detained him
Contrary to the agreement you made with me.
For I told you indeed, when I returned
From delivering that message for you,
How I was separated from King Charles.
You certainly approved all my reports.
And since you reneged on your promises,
Everyone who is loyal and thoughtful
Must be of the opinion that you did wrong.
Many a worthy and brave man is harmed by bad counsel, but
Perhaps you were blinded by it
As so many others have been; you are not alone in being deceived.
I implore you, Sire, if once I was your close friend,
If ever I did anything to please you,
And if you want to believe loyal counsel,
That you agree to give Ogier up.
I will take him back to King Charles's tents.
I will come back, if I am able,
Tomorrow, before the day is over."
Corsuble heard him; he hesitated a little
Before answering him; and when he had reflected,
"King Carahuel," said he, "come forward.
You are certainly right in what you have said to me.
If I had done in time what you have said,

Brunamon would still be alive;
I have been deceived by bad counsel.
Get Ogier and take him back
To the French army; may he go to
One hundred thousand devils and be commanded by them!
I do not believe that he is a mortal man.
He is an unchained devil from hell
In the guise and form of a man.
Get him out of my sight at once!"
Carahuel heard him; he bowed toward him
And thanked him greatly; then the king arose
As did all the others, some joyous, others angry.
Corsuble seemed indeed to be tormented.
And Carahuel went back toward Ogier.
He took him by the bridle and turned away from there;
They went out of the lists side by side.
This combat was over very early in the morning,
For it was far from even mid-day.

CXVIII

Carahuel left the field gladly.
At the entrance of the field were his people,
Who came toward him joyously.
They were very well and powerfully armed.
Great numbers of them gathered around Ogier
To guard him and to do his bidding.
Carahuel held the good Dane's horse
By the silver rein; he looked at Ogier very often,
For he loved him with his whole heart.
"Ogier, "said he, "you have acted
Very honorably and loyally toward me.
I succeeded so well with Corsuble
That before the sun sets
I can arrange for King Charlemagne to see you."
When Ogier heard this, he felt joy in his heart.
He thanked Carahuel happily and fervently
As a courteous man fully aware of the situation.
Carahuel went to his tents at once
Where he and Ogier dismounted.
And Gloriande came there quickly,
For she did not want to wait long.
She greeted Ogier very courteously
And the Dane, like a wise person,

Returned her greeting properly.
"By Mohammed," said the elegant beauty,
"All those who love Carahuel at all
Should take great care in serving you;
And his friends and relatives should obey you,
For you have nobly kept
All his honor and all his possessions
Like a worthy and brave vassal of great boldness."
And Ogier said, "My beauty, so help me God,
God has certainly done it for the sake of justice."

CXIX

King Carahuel had come to his tent.
He and the beautiful Gloridande
Welcomed and honored Ogier.
What was left of his helmet
The beautiful girl unlaced and removed
And then looked at him sweetly.
She saw his black and bloodied face.
As if she had vowed this one hundred thousand times,
Against his will she washed his face
With her very soft white hands,
Which were whiter than any flower of the meadow.
She wiped his face gently and tenderly with towels.
"God," said Ogier, "father of majesty,
May you increase your beneficence to this caring person."
They had him eat a little; but if he had had his way
He would have tasted no food there.
Ogier hurried through his meal
For he had a great desire and will
To see Charles and his barons again.
When he had eaten, King Carahuel then talked to him
And offered him
Most of his very large kingdom
If he would worship Mohammed
And renounce Christianity.
"Indeed," said Ogier, "it hadn't even occurred to me.
I would rather have my head cut off.
But it is very noble of you to say this to me.
I thank you greatly for your friendship.
If I could, you may be sure,
I would yet see to it that you were rewarded."
Carahuel thanked him for these words.

He saw well that he would never succeed
With the request that he had made.

CXX

When Carahuel heard Ogier,
He clearly saw that he would have his head
Cut off before he would renounce God.
He then no longer wanted to broach the subject at all,
For he saw that words were of no use.
"Ogier," said he, "from Brunamon the redoubtable
Whose soul you have emptied from his body,
You have conquered the very best warhorse,
The most powerful, the lightest of foot
And the most impetuous, as I dare say.
No man of arms who wants to advance himself
Could wish for more than to be rewarded with that kind of horse.
It seems to me that you are very experienced in that area
So that you would understand
How much that horse would mean in your hour of need.
With you two I would like to put
Such a jewel as will inspire dread:
Courtain, my sword, which is made of such steel
That no one has ever esteemed a sword more valuable than this one.
By Mohammed, who has all to govern,
I would not be able to put this sword to better use anywhere
Than with you; I do not say that to flatter you.
In my service your sword was broken
To save my honor from injustice.
Take mine; I beg this of you."
Then he took it off; he gave it to him at once.
"Indeed," said Ogier, "I do not want to refuse you.
I thank you very much for this gift,
For never, by Jesus the just father,
Have I ever seen anyone get a reward for his service
That I value as much as this one."
He took the sword by the ring of pure gold.
With keen joy he embraced it
Closely and began to kiss it.
Afterward he attached it to his right flank.
If someone had given him Montpellier,
He could not have had a happier heart.

CXXI

When the Dane had taken the sword,
Courtain, the beautiful, the very finely steeled,
Joy overtook him.
It was planted deeply in his heart,
For he had very much coveted the sword earlier
When the four knighs were at the combat
On the island in the valley below Rome
About which I have told you before.
He fastened the sword onto the golden swordbelt,
The sword from which those who denied the faith
Received many a heavy blow.
About this subject no more will be recounted.
King Carahuel called his people.
He told them to arm themselves without a moment's delay
And implored them urgently to hurry,
For he had been told in secret
That Danemon had assembled a great many people
Before his tents; it was hard to tell what their plan was.
It was something that displeased him greatly,
For King Danemon of the mountains of Valfondée
Had proven himself full of treachery.
Then King Carahuel's people were very soon in order.
There were ten thousand, each one helmeted.

CXXII

King Carahuel did not want to stay there any longer
When he had gotten his people into good order.
"Ogier," said he, "you should mount.
Take your leave; let's be gone."
Ogier heard him; he was pleased.
Ogier took leave of Gloriande, the young girl
With the fair face, without forgetting
Anything or the words that should be said.
"Ogier," said she, "may this God who can do anything
And can govern all save you."
Then Ogier mounted—he did not care to wait—
On Broiefort, the praiseworthy horse.
From there they left as you have heard me tell.
The pagans, Saracens, and Slavs said,
"If one can find plenty of warriors like Ogier
In France, we can indeed swear

To Mohammed without lying
That we'll be very delayed getting home."

CXXIII

King Carahuel, who had so much goodness,
Courtesy, honor, and loyalty,
Went out of Rome, the admirable city
With Ogier beside him on his left.
They rode right toward Sutri.
The story will speak to you again about Danemon,
Whose heart was very full of falsity,
Betrayal, and disloyalty.
He and his people had already rushed so much
That they were lying in wait south of Rome beside a meadow
In a thicket with few branches.
They were determined
To do Ogier harm if they could,
For Danemon had his heart aflame
And afire with great hatred for him.
He and his people had thought
That just as soon as they had captured him
That once they had him, there would not be a word said
Before they killed him: this is what they had planned.
For Brunamon's sake they had developed so much hatred
That was so bitter and so full of cruelty
That if they had cut him up in pieces
They would not have believed they had killed him
And would hardly have been satisfied.
In this ambush that I have told you about
There were not much more than a thousand knights.
And here was a Turk spurring toward them very rapidly
Who reported to Danemon and his people
That Carahuel and Ogier had left
Rome and had such a great number of people with them
That they could certainly be estimated at ten thousand.
Danemon heard it; he nearly went out of his mind.
He said to his people: "We've been tricked.
King Carahuel has rolled the dice for us.
By Mohammed to whom I have given my heart,
If I had known that he had planned
To take Ogier back with so many people
I would have thrown in so many of mine from Rome
That, if he had sworn it on Mohammed,

He would never have delivered Ogier
Back to Charles. My heart is sad and angry
That he is escaping us, for he has caused us great harm
And he will continue to harm us, of that there is no doubt,
If he remains alive and healthy very long."
The Saracens were stricken with sorrow
And shocked and sad and tormented.
For a little they would not have stayed there
When they saw Carahuel the renowned coming,
He and his people, nobly equipped.
They were coming grouped in two battalions.
They let them pass; and when they had passed,
They turned back pensive and dejected.
With sorrowful hearts they re-entered Rome.

CXXIV

King Danemon and also his people
Entered Rome very sorrowfully.
And Carahuel rode in gladness.
He would not have been as happy to have gold or silver
As he was, knowing,
As it seemed to him, that his promise would be kept
To King Charlemagne, to whom sweet France belonged.
I will not make you a long speech about this.
Handsomely and properly and in orderly fashion
They went so far that they saw truly
They could certainly be in safety.
Then Carahuel commanded all his people
To return except for just four
And they did so,
For there were none who had any desire
To go against his wishes.
He kept four of them, and the others at once
Went on back without delay.
Upon departing, they urgently implored
King Carahuel, whom they loved greatly,
To come back as quickly
As he could; and certainly he
Assured them that very shortly
He would come back, Mohammed willing.
Thus they left their lord.
They made no stops until they reached Rome.

CXXV

When Carahuel was separated from his people
And each one of them had turned back
Except for the four who had remained with him,
After that he hardly tarried.
He made his way straight toward Sutri,
He and Ogier riding side by side.
They made such good progress that soon they saw the tents
Where Charles and his noble barons were.
Said Carahuel: "Ogier, you can see
The place where many are eager to see you.
You must certainly praise your god
That though you are quite young, you are so valiant
That everyone loves you very much already."
Said Ogier, "Sire, you are so much inclined to love me
That it makes it seem to you that I am such;
If I were what you believe me to be,
I would be enriched five hundred-fold."
Said Carahuel: "So help me God,
It seems to me that this is the truth,
And there is far more in this than what I have said.
May Mohammed persuade you by his holy benevolence
To decide shortly
To give yourself to his service.
It is a great misfortune that you are Christian."
"Indeed," said Ogier, "rest assured
My feelings are such
That my heart could never relinguish it."
Said Carahuel, "I certainly hear what you are thinking;
You would rather be cut up in pieces
Than to abandon your god."
"Indeed," said Ogier, "that is true."
Speaking this way they went along one beside the other
Until they entered into the army of the native French.
They seemed to be messengers, for they
Turned their swords toward them.
Among the army they went as you have heard.
No one ever recognized
Ogier because he was armed
Like a pagan and mounted on a different horse
Than he had been at departure, and
His face was swollen in places and bruised.
It is no wonder his complexion was changed,

For he could very well have been discolored
From the blows he had taken and given
Since he had passed the violent fords of the Toivre
When they fought on the island in the meadow,
He and Charlot, as you know.
They headed straight for Charles's tent,
King Carahuel and Ogier the wise.
They both dismounted from their impetuous warhorses, and
Each one entered the tent.
As for the other four of whom you have heard
That Carahuel brought with him,
Each one of them stayed outside.
Charles had called his high barons.
Namles was there and Joffrois the renowned,
Duke Fagon and Guis the esteemed,
Thierri of the Ardennes, who was called valiant;
Hues de Troies, who was born in Burgundy.
I would never be able to name you all of them.
Carahuel observed this all attentively.
He greeted Charles very properly,
For he was extremely courteous and circumspect.
He took Ogier and said: "Sire, here,
I am returning Ogier to you; I have kept my word."
Charles at once rose opposite him.
He threw his arns around Ogier's neck.
Charles kissed and hugged him a great deal.
Joy seized him; he was afire with it;
He had not felt such joy since he was crowned.

CXXVI

Charles the redoubtable king felt great joy
When he saw Ogier, who had come back.
Namles was so moved with joy
That he could scarcely remain standing.
He could not speak for joy; rather he stayed silent;
And when he spoke, he said, "Ah, King Jesus,
May you be praised, true father on high."
What can I tell you? They hugged the Dane
And beheld him with great joy.
Among the army there arose such loud shouting and hooting,
A hue and cry as if fires had been set throughout the army.
Everyone came running there from all sides.
No one had ever heard of greater joy.

If God himself had come down among them,
I do not know how they could have made more noise.
Indeed the tree in Charles's army had grown so well
That it burst into flower and leaf with joy.

CXXVII

The French were wildly enthusiastic in their rejoicing.
They thanked God the father creator,
When Ogier, the noble warrior, in whom there was
Nothing except goodness and sweet temper, came back,
They looked at him front, back and all around.
Many of them were aastonished
That he was as cut up as he was all over.
"Here is a young man," said they, "of great valor.
It certainly looks as if he has not had a moment's rest
Since he left here the other day.
King Charles is right to love him so much.
It surely looks as if he has been in a battle
In which he had to give many a blow,
And thus he should be considered a fierce warrior."
They looked carefully at the warhorse of great price,
Which had belonged to Brunamon the emir.
The pagan people whose lord was Carahuel
Were holding the horse
In front of the emperor Charlemagne's tent.
This was Broiefort; never had anyone seen a better horse.
Said one to the other, "By the true savior,
One must certainly do honor to such a vassal
Who is such a true model of prowess."

CXXVIII

King Charles felt only elation
As did Namles, his loyal counselor.
What could I tell you that I have not said before?
Let me go straight to the point.
In Charles's army, whom may God keep from hindrance,
There was not a baron, a duke, a count or a prince,
Small or great, sergeant or knight,
Who did not thank God from his heart
That Ogier had been restored to them.
They started going back to their lodgings
Glad and joyous and in great desire
To encounter the Saracens soon.

Charles the king, in whom was only wisdom,
Knew how to thank Carahuel as he deserved
For he had found his deeds entirely upright.
The good Duke Namles, who was so worthy,
Had the four Turks in front of the tent
Escorted to his lodgings
And made very comfortable.

CXXIX

When Carahuel had spoken to Charles
To his satisfaction and much to his pleasure
And thanked him for the loyalty
That he found in him in such abundance—
And it was certainly right for him to be appreciative—
Then the king led him aside
By the right hand to one part of the tent.
He called Namles to this council,
Duke Thierri of Ardennes the bearded
And Widelon of the valiant heart,
Duke Fagon who held the city of Tours,
Hues de Troies and Sanson the renowned,
Joffrois d'Anjou of the wise heart.
All those had stayed there
And many of the others had gone away,
For it was already getting dark.
Ogier remained with the other barons.
King Charles asked Carahuel
About the battle, how it had been.
And so he told him all
About it; he did not hide anything.
"Sire," said he, "upon my word,
I do not believe that in Christendom
Or in pagan lands or in any other kingdom
Did any king have a knight greater or more illustrious
Or more powerful or of greater valiance
Than was Brunamon, whom Ogier has conquered."
The barons heard it; they slapped one another on the back.
They thanked God, the king of majesty, for it
In their hearts, and they praised him greatly for it.
Charles looked toward Ogier
With loving eyes that
Expressed his great affection.
Then they got up when he had recounted to them

What many heard with a glad heart.
Then Duke Namles went up to Carahuel.
He wanted to take him away, for he had stayed a long time.
He took his leave; he did not stay there any longer.
When he left, King Charles embraced him.
So did the others, and they greatly thanked him
For having conducted himself so well toward Ogier.
Courteously, they commended him to God.
Namles took him and Ogier away
Into his tent; there they took off their armor.
As for the four Turks, their armor
Had already been removed and put in safety.
All this was done through a desire
To honor Carahuel that much more.
When they had rested a little,
They went to supper, for it was prepared.
They sat down when they had washed.

CXXX

Carahuel and his Turks sat at supper
In the tent of Namles, the vassal baron.
Beside him was the praiseworthy Ogier.
It wasn't necessary to entreat or order
Duke Namles to have him think of them,
For he did so much for them, you may be sure,
That one could not reasonably improve upon it.
If I wanted to enumerate all the ways
That Duke Namles was able to honor them
And to repeat all they said,
I would make the account go on too long.
Because of that I want to pass over it rapidly.
When it was time, Namles, who understood things quickly,
Had them go to bed,
For Carahuel had said that
He wanted to get up before dawn.
Because of this they went to bed as soon as they could.
Namles had their arms brought back
Right at the hour that it was reasonable to put them on.
Then they got up when it was time to equip themselves.
They were ready; they only had to mount
Just at the hour when dawn was breaking.
There is no need to speak more about this;
Everything was done exactly on time with nothing forgotten.

CXXXI

The next day, at the break of dawn,
King Carahuel mounted his horse.
He and his men departed.
Ogier and Namles accompanied them
With a great number of their people, as reason dictated.
At his departure Carahuel commended
Namles to God and thanked him greatly
For the friendship he had shown him in his need
And for honoring him in such a heartfelt way.
"Certainly, "said Namles, "I do not know what will occur
In this war nor what will please God in it,
But rest assured that if it ever happens
That I can help you, your courtesy
Will be rewarded, whatever it takes."
King Carahuel bowed to Namles
Courteously, and then he turned
Toward Ogier; they hugged one another.
In parting each one of them wept.
Very softly the Dane begged him
To warmly greet Gloriande, whom he esteemed
Highly, as soon as he saw her.
Carahuel said he would not forget
But would do it willingly and from the heart.
In such a manner the one separated from the other.
Namles went back to Charles's army,
And Carahuel rode so much
That he was back in Rome very early in the morning.
The very first thing he went to talk to Gloriande,
And so as soon as he approached her,
He greeted her at once on behalf of Ogier.
This greeting pleased Gloriande very much,
For in her heart she held Ogier in high regard.
"May this God," said she, "who made the whole world
Grant him everlasting joy!"
King Carahuel then described to her
The honor that Charlemagne's people had bestowed upon him.
Above all he praised Namles,
For he honored him with his whole heart for Ogier's sake.

CXXXII

In the middle of Rome the lordly city
Was Carahuel, who was a powerful king.

He had greatly praised Charles of the proud face
And Namles and Ogier the marquis
To Gloriande, who was his sweetheart.
After that, he left that place.
He went back straightaway to his lodgings
Where his people gave him a heartfelt welcome.
I have forgotten to put in a little something
That it is very fitting I should tell you
Because this story is true and of great value.
I would hate to leave out
Something that was shown to me at Saint Denis.
The same day that King Brunamon, who was
Fierce and bold, was killed on the field,
He was buried in Rome very close
To the place where Ogier had conquered him.
He is still there, as the manuscript tells us.
About this no more will be told now.
Carahuel the noble came to the court, and
Many hearts were rejoiced by his coming.
King Corsuble took him by the right hand and
Seated him beside him then.
And thereupon King Danemon his son said to him:
"King Carahuel, you have created a bad situation for us
That Ogier has thus escaped us alive.
By Mohammed, to whom I am subject,
He has done us harm; he could do worse to us
Before my father seizes France
Or wears a crown at Paris.
If you had listened to me, I assure you,
He would never again mistreat a pagan."
Said Carahuel: "A false man should be disgraced!
And if he is, he is rightly barred
From fiefs on earth and in holy paradise."
Danemon was disconcerted by this word
And kept quiet; thus was he silenced,
For he knew very well that it was said for him.

CXXXIII

Danemon heard Carahuel,
But he did not want to answer him
About the matter that angered him.
He read his little speech elsewhere.
He held himself silent and mute

Before his father, for King Corsuble had known
Nothing of the recent ambush that
His son had set, he and his miscreants,
And perhaps he would not have consented.
When he spoke, he said, "Too long has my father
Lived, who has so much courage
And power that many have known,
Who has not run upon Charles for a long time
When he has with him so many elite pagans
Of perfect and developed prowess
And who have been of arms and heart so ardent
That never were people more violent when faced with combat.
They await only his command;
At once the French would all be conquered or dead.
The French could consider us cowards
Because we have not come out of Rome for a long time.
A few people have insinuated themselves here.
Let us run on them; we have waited too long.
It would have been done a long time ago, if I had been believed."
"Son," said Corsuble, "I have heard you well.
We have received damage,
But, by the faith I owe Mohammed and Cahu,
The Christians have suffering coming to them in abundance.
Before three days go by, they will give up great tribute;
For they will have fought with my people
If they do not flee back to where they came from."
Said Carahuel, "I have certainly seen enough of them
To know that many strong shields will be pierced
And many hauberks broken and divested of their mail
And many a vassal will be dead and knocked to the ground
Before they can be conquered by threats.
Let your barons and your friends be called soon
And be advised that from here
We move tomorrow right at daybreak
To go there where they have stopped."
This advice was retained to great good
By King Corsuble of the white hair.
He and his son held to it completely.

CXXXIV

King Corsuble called his barons,
The Achopars, the Turks, the Slavs.
He called the Africans and the Aragonese.

He had people there from many regions.
If I wanted to name all those by their names
Who were convoked to this council
The story would be too long because of it.
They were assembled in the tents
Of King Corsuble of the white moustache.
King Danemon spoke right at the outset
When it was time to talk.
"Lords," he said to them, "what will become of us?
It is my opinion that we are operating in cowardly fashion
When we stay safely inside of Rome
And we know that Christians are so close to us.
They could very well say that we are frightened of them so much
That we dare not leave here.
If you approve it, tomorrow we will ride out.
At daybreak we will be on our horses.
Because we have stayed here too long,
It is right that we hurry now that much more."
And they responded, "This is very good advice.
So be it. We agree to it.
There is nothing on Earth that we desire so much
As to fight hand to hand with them soon.
It is not right that we even hesitate,
For the number of our people is so great
That there are many more of them than we need.
With a single voice let us entreat King Corsuble
That we not refuse this advice."
Said Danemon, "He and I both grant it.
We want it wholeheartedly
So that we will not do it any other way
If Mohammed grants that we live that long."
Thereupon they got up without further delay.

CXXXV

Those of vile lineage rejoiced greatly
When they agreed that in the morning
They would come close to Charles, the son of Pépin.
There was great commotion in Rome that night
As the people of Apollo prepared to leave.
At daybreak, when the night was over,
Pagans and Saracens mounted.
There you would have seen many a purple banner
Attached to a pine shaft

Of which the points were sharp and steeled,
And many a swift, strong, select steed.
So many were there of Cain's lineage
That if the one who made wine from water did not intervene
They would come right upon
The French people and those from beyond the Rhine.
Many of them were so inclined to pride that they did not
Esteem Charles the worth of a Roman half-penny
Or all the others the tail of a mastiff.
The mountains, valleys, and roads were full of them.
One could certainly keep track of such a procession.

CXXXVI

When the Saracens had come to the field,
The whole countryside was resplendent
With standards and shining helmets
And with banners and waving pennants.
That morning the weather was very fine,
So gracious, mild, and pleasant
That there was no heart that was not rejoicing.
The pagans had eight very large battalions
So full of vile unbelievers
That one could certainly fear them.
All of them were commanded by a king.
The first had Danemon the powerful
And the second Carahuel the valiant,
The third Androines and the fourth Grohans,
Who had a black shield with three white lions.
Androines had arms with much ornamentation;
They were vert, semé of
Bezants of shining gold.
The fifth echelon had an African king
Whose name was Cardos of Bradigans.
He carried very well known arms
Of gold with a black griffon flying.
The sixth had a rich, powerful king
Of great prowess named Abilans.
He had blue arms with two white horns.
The seventh had his brother King Braimans.
The shield he carried was vermillion with three white tabs.

CXXXVII

I have correctly enumerated the echelons
And named those who commanded each one.
King Corsuble headed the eighth.
It was the largest, as was right.
He carried arms bendy or and sable,
And Danemon his son had the same
Except that his had a border gules which
Distinguished them and went very well with them.
He who would describe at some other time the arms
That Carahuel carried
Perhaps would make them seem like a jumble.
King Corsuble sat on his horse.
He bore down on the stirrups confidently.
One could very well say, because he went
So joyously and held himself
Very nobly and with a proud demeanor
That he looked like a powerful and valorous king.
And rightfully he should have looked like that,
For he advised his people wisely,
How each one that day would carry on,
And he exhorted them in timely fashion
About what was appropriate for armsbearers and those seeking honor;
For in his time there lived no pagan king
With more valor than he, just as everyone said.
Because he knew how close King Charles was to him
And that he was coming closer,
His heart leapt with joy.

CXXXVIII

Before all the Saracens who had slept there
Had gone out of Rome,
You should know that it was noon or later.
When they were fully spread out on the field,
No man who had not seen them with his own eyes
Would ever have thought or believed
That in the whole world were so many unbelievers
As those who had come on this military expedition.
For the avant-garde they had chosen
King Androine, the lord of Valgu.
He was full of prowess and great strength
And would have been a very worthy king
If he had believed in Jesus.

He and his company of men had set out
Very early to take over the land, so I have heard.
But that day they did not go that far.
They stopped four miles from Rome
By a stream beside a high, branchy wood.
They dismounted to camp in that place
And put up many a pavilion, many a tent.
Sadoine's friends and confidants,
Who were supposed to stay with him,
Remained right inside Rome with him.
He was greatly disturbed by his misfortune:
"Mohammed," said he, "what has happened to me
That Saracens will have fought Christians
Without me! Alas, now I have lived too long.
Misfortune has beaten me down.
May Mohammed save my soul,
I would rather have lost my whole kingdom
Than to have misfortune so run over me.
But since it pleases Mohammed and Cahu,
I thank them when misfortune is mine."

CXXXIX

King Sadoine had a heavy heart
When he saw that it was clear
That the others would fight without him.
To Gloriande, the gracious young girl,
Came a pagan who told her at once
That Sadoine was in the throes of sorrow.
And when she had heard this speech,
She went to King Sadoine speedily.
Very sweetly she comforted him
Like a courteous and well-taught young woman.
He thanked her kindly for it,
But I will leave them here for you a while
And we will speak of Charles the powerful
And of the French; may God's will
Give them victory over the unbelievers!

CXL

You have heard how it went,
How Carahuel took the Dane back
To Charles's army and how he returned.
Soon after he left the French,

The Pope and the clergy came there,
And Charlemagne honored and obeyed them
With his whole heart, for it was the right thing to do.
That day the Pope gave a sermon
To the Christians, and he complained to them
Of King Corsuble and those he had with him.
He implored all of them
That this be of grave concern to them, when the time came.
Many a one who heard it rendered heart-felt sighs
And wept at the request.
They were sure it would be set to rights
Quickly or each one would die in the effort.
The Pope encouraged them eloquently
On all the points that appertained.
"Lords," said he to them all, "now we will see
How each one will fare in the battle.
I myself will go into the battle
To see those whom God loves so much
That he would let them avenge his shame.
I swear to you upon my soul that whoever ends his life
Here in this place that God will call him
To be part of his fold at the final judgment
And will seat him on his right hand near him."
After this word he gave them pardon, and
Each one went away to his lodgings.
The next day, as soon as day broke,
The army moved out as one.
Each one greatly desired to go toward Rome.
The Christian army traveled so much that day
That there were not four miles between the two armies.
In Corsuble's army the news spread
That Charlemagne was already so close to them.
Many a Saracen praised Mohammed for it.

CXLI

On a beautiful plain beside a prairie
Charles's army camped by a stream.
There, those for whom we ask God's blessing
Put up many a pavilion and raised many a tent.
When they heard the news
That the pagans had come outside
Rome, the lordly city, each one thanked God;
For their hurry was such that they would have attacked Rome

Immediately, without a moment's hesitation,
If the pagans had not come out.
Among the people of Charles of the bold face
Many a man had a glad countenance that day
And many a one was without a semblance of cowardice
Knowing that pagans were in the plain
And that their army was coming very close to them.
Charles the king, so that he delay no longer there,
Let all his barons know
That the next day, right at the break of dawn,
They would mount after mass was finished;
For he wanted battle to start quickly
With the people God hated.
There was general rejoicing at this news.
That night many things were arranged
In order to be prepared earlier in the morning.
Many a banner was attached to its shaft
And many a metal-studded coat of mail drawn from its leather bag
And many a rein reinforced with rope.
Now may Jesus the son of Mary help them,
For each one has the desire and wish
To abandon body and life
So that the religion of Mohammed be brought down
And the faith of God raised and exalted.

CXLII

The next day at dawn
In Charles's army many a knight was
Very richly armed and very well equipped for battle.
When they had heard the service of God,
They mounted at once; they stayed there no longer.
There you would have seen many an impetuous warhorse
And many a vassal nobly equipped
Who certainly seemed valiant and eager
And entirely willing to fight.
This day they took away neither tent nor pavilion
But moved out when they were ready.
Their troops were disposed
As I have earlier described to you.
They proceeded arranged in five battalions
Like people of sense and goodness,
Strength, wisdom, and assurance.
I have not yet described for you

What arms Charles of the wise heart had
Nor those of many others, but now I would like to
Tell you about some of them in detail
As was shown to me at Saint Denis, for
I inquired about the pure truth
And certainty of this story.
Because of this I was able to know its authenticity.

CXLIII

In King Charles we had a resourceful knight,
Loyal, wise, handsome, and full of prowess.
People do not know, I believe, at this time
With what arms the good king was dubbed.
For this reason I am happy to describe them to you.
He carried arms partly gold and partly azure.
Within the azure were golden fleurs de lis,
And resting on the gold was a black half eagle,
Which was extremely beautiful and went well there.
He had a horse that suited him well.
Certainly his appearance gave the impression
That he would not forget to strike blows.
He exhorted his men eloquently and rightly
To do what was appropriate to the day.
Duke Thierri went beside him.
The king put his hand upon his shoulder,
For such nobility dwelt within his heart
That he honored good people everywhere.
He drew them to himself from all countries,
And he knew so well how to merit their service
That none should complain of him.
This Lord God who sits high and sees far
Had given to Christians such a king,
And truly they would need one like him!

CXLIV

What arms Charlot, the son of Charles, had
I will describe for you, for it seems to me good to do so.
Arms like the ones I have already described to you,
That King Charles of the white moustache had,
Charlot his son carried, as was right.
But there was to distinguish them
A border gules indented around them.
Flowers and the eagle were in favor then.

Who was bearing them? A king of such renown
That in many a country people still declare
That one more loyal or valiant than he
Never put on sword or spur.
The eagle and flowers, it must be admitted,
Are today in great over-abundance.
They are the arms of many a rich baron.
Today, people do not go hunting except to catch something.
But in the old days
Their only goal was
To obtain the high pardon of God
To absolve the soul.
But these customs now are rarely followed;
It is a pity that so few make use of them.

CXLV

From Normandy Duke Richars carried
A shield of gules; it had two gold leopards.
He had a good, handsome warhorse that was dapple gray.
He never liked a man who was foolish or debauched
Or outrageous or immoral or mean.
Base mockeries never came out of his mouth.
As was right, all villainous arts
Counted as absolutely nothing in his view.
It was as if they had all been destroyed.
At his side hung Escalidars,
His sword, which he treasured more than a thousand marks.
It was not a toy.
It did not seem as if a child were giving blows.
By his deeds Porpaillart was conquered
When the French fought the Lombards.
He disordered, routed, and dispersed
The pagans on many sides.
Against swords and javelins
And maces, spears, and falchions
He wreaked great destruction many a time
On Saracens, Turks and Achopars.

CXLVI

Duke Fagon was a valiant knight
He was the duke of Tours, the well-located city
Which sits on the Loire, which is rapid and noisy.
He had blue arms with three gold crescents.

Such arms had Count Hues dou Mans
But with labels gules well placed
On them, for the two men were attached to one another;
They were extremely fond of one another.
Their heirs had such arms for a very long time,
But I do not know who stopped the practice.
I will describe which arms Anquetins the Norman
Had; I would not want to forget them,
For it is worthwhile to be reminded
Of the arms he had and of the great deeds he did
In many places against the wretched cowards.
He carried elegant, ornamented arms,
Vert with two gold leopards passant.
He was a perfect and able knight,
Of great valor indoors and in the field,
Loving honor and fearing shame.
His cousin was Richars, who was a powerful duke
To whom Normandy belonged;
For by Antequein's arms, which I have been describing,
Anyone with intelligence
Who knows heraldry would know this.

CXLVII

Hoël of Nantes was very distinguished.
He was well armed and seated on a good warhorse,
Impetuous, powerful, strong, swift, and light.
His arms were white with a vermillion quarter.
Such arms, I have heard said, had
Gawain, who is considered a perfect knight.
This Hoël of whom you have heard me speak
Knocked many a Saracen to the ground
With his sword reinforced with steel.
It delighted him to cause them harm.
Charles had him carry the standard
Of Saint Denis that Aloris the other day
Brought back with him like a coward.
Whoever saw him hold it in his hand
And nobly ride in bearing down on his stirrups
And saw his valiant, sure, and proud demeanor
Could certainly say that he desired
To approach the Saracens soon.

CXLVIII

Duke Thierri was of very great renown.
He held the largest region of Ardennes
And was the first to fortify the castle of Bullon.
He was valiant, wise, loyal and a man of prowess.
He sat on the Gascon warhorse bearing down on the stirrups.
His beautiful and richly fashioned arms
Were white with a gold lion.
The first duke of Brabant, they say,
Whose name was Godefrois à la Barbe,
Carried such arms, which were like those
Of the man I have been describing to you.
This duke's body lies, it is known for certain,
At Afflighem; there one would find him
In the abbey; in this house
There were many religious
In former times; thus it is attested.
Now I will tell you of the good vassal Guy
De Saint Omer, who was a most noble man,
For he came from the lineage of Charlemagne.
He was well armed and had a warhorse from Aragon.
What arms he had, one should describe well,
For he was valiant and wise and full of good sense.
He had gold arms with a chevron vert
With a tressure gules around it.
The cruel Saracens greatly feared him,
For he had destroyed many a one of them.
This same day of which I am telling you
He made many a one of them lie on the sand.

CXLIX

Hues de Troies was a wise knight
Much renowned for his great prowess.
He was mounted on a black and white spotted horse
That he cherished greatly, for it was such a one
As had been found good in many places.
He was equipped very nobly and handsomely
With vermillion arms semés with gold eaglets.
Oedes de Lengres, who was much praised,
Was nobly armed beside him.
They had been companions in many countries
And loved one another very much.
The Saracens greatly feared

Oedes, for in many places he had often made
Them suffer and had caused them great harm.
His shield was bendy or and azure
In twelve strips; indeed it is so.
In many places he showed his shield
To those who had abandoned God
And killed or wounded many of them.
De Pierre Lee Fouchiers the strong,
Who had proved himself on many sides
So that he certainly should be called a man of prowess,
Carried a quarterly shield
Of gold and gules bordered with azure.
I could never name you all
Those that King Charles had assembled there
Nor describe the shields of each one.
Because of that I have passed over them somewhat quickly.
Charles and his rich barons rode
In such a manner as you have heard.
Now may the king of majesty guide them!

CL

Charles of the unforgettable face rode.
His route was peopled with many a vassal
Who would not give up the part assigned
To them at dawn that day
For a great chariot full of gold.
They certainly rode like confident people,
Capable with arms and well advised about war.
Corsuble's people on this morning
Were quite soon equipped and ready,
For they had looked forward with great eagerness to this hour
When they would encounter Charles's army.
They had set out on their way straight in that direction.
Eight large battalions of the evil people
Were there, and each one was arranged
Handsomely and rightly and in proper order.
There was not a mountain, slope or valley
Where the ground was not covered with Saracens.
Both the armies had one thought:
Each one believed they would find the other
Where it had lodged the night before.
So they rode like people who desire
Shortly to come to the battle.

CLI

The armies from each side rode nobly
In such orderly fashion that nothing was lacking.
There you would have seen many a rich suit of armor
And many a banner deployed to the wind,
And many a bright helmet where the fine gold shone.
Cowards should have recovered boldness
Upon seeing the fine demeanor
Of the people of Charles to whom lovely France belongs,
For they rode with such purpose.
I will not talk long to you about this.
They traveled so much that they saw quite plainly
The Saracens coming in great numbers.
Both armies saw one another clearly,
For between them they had only a broad plain
Where there was neither ravine nor obstacle
That could prove to be a hindrance.
Charles saw it; he showed it to his people.
He took his shield; without delay he hung it around his neck.
His people laced up his helmet for him quickly,
And he seized his lance very forcefully.
The two sides prepared themselves immediately
To do battle shortly,
Handsomely and correctly and without disarray.
They drew closer to one another, seized with violent desire
To take bold action.

CLII

King Charles had very great strength
And was bold, valiant, and ferocious in battle.
Yet he was gentle and courteous and full of honor.
Placed by nature within his heart were
Faith and generosity, pity and charity.
They were rooted in humility
With flowers of fine loyalty.
He had much nobility in him.
He never loved a man whom he knew to be false.
He always pitied poor people,
Often doing for them many a great deed of friendship.
Nature had certainly bestowed good moral character upon him.
He had no vices
To be torn from him.
God had provided him with such a sense of honor

That he put all his thought into good habits.
He had acted valiantly in many a combat
Where he had killed and routed
Those who scorned the faith.
He had performed many a worthy deed of war against pagans,
Killing and conquering many a one of them.
He had exiled and disinherited many a one
And Christianity is still better off;
For in many places the heirs of those
By whom it was conquered hold their inheritance.
What should I say to you? He had so much goodness in him
That I could not have told you the half of it today.
Whoever might have seen him mounted on his horse,
His helmet on his head and his sword at his side,
In his fist his lance, and around his neck his bordered shield,
Where many a precious stone shone brightly,
Could most certainly say without hesitation
That he seemed to be a noble king.
Those whom fear had made sorrowful
Could be comforted by the sight of him.
The day was as beautiful as in summertime,
But the air was cold and very clear.
The night before had been rainy and windy.
They had all one could want for a time of combat,
For they could fight without dust.
Brightness shone from helmets, from lances.
There was such a great plenty of lances both long and short
That you would never before have seen shafts so thickly planted.
When Charles saw that the Turks were assembled on the road
And had stopped before him to fight,
He called Namles, in whom there was never any cowardice.
"Namles," said he, 'the pagans did not fear us enough
When they came out of Rome like this.
They engaged in great folly
When they left their fortress."
"Sire," said Namles, "they have committed great foolishness.
It is time that our cavalry hastened
And struck the horses with their spurs.
Let them be pushed back so violently
That they hardly consider us restrained.
They will have France; of this they have boasted.
But before they have ever hidden themselves in Rome again,
They will have bought it dearly.

May God the king of majesty save us,
Many a one of them will be tormented before night."
At this word they spurred their horses sharply and ardently.
The two sides prepared to strike.
At the attack, to tell the truth,
Many a one was thrown to the ground
Who never afterward regained health.

CLIII

At the start of the fracas, the noise was deafening.
Of the lofty and storied deeds of the French
In attacking the pagan people
The premier knight, he of highest valor, was Ogier,
He was full of vigor, desiring to fight and to conquer honor.
He went ahead of the others on the prized warhorse
That he had conquered on the field in Rome the other day
When he killed Brunamon the emir.
It was Broiefort; never did anyone see a better horse.
He went among the Turks with such great impetuousness,
The lance in his fist in a thrusting position,
That most of them were very frightened.
"Ah, God," said Charles,"by your holy sweetness
Save Ogier, for in him I have put my love."
Then Charles, who seemed master of such a labor,
Spurred his horse the way an emperor does,
With him Namles, who was full of valor.
In the melee were dukes and princes and counts.
When our warriors clashed with theirs,
You would have seen many a good warhorse without its rider
Running through the grass with broken reins.
Afterward the lances were not used long.
Very soon they drew out the good, blood-stained swords.
They attacked one another violently and wrathfully.
The person was indeed bold who was not afraid in that situation.
Ogier was beside a crossroads.
In his fist was his sword, which cut like a razor.
Courtain was its name; never was there a better one.
It was all soiled with blood and sweat.
Whomever it struck was dead without return.
Pagans attacked him in front and all around.
From afar many threw their spears at him,
For they feared him more than the heron does the hawk.
They often called loudly upon Mohammed about it.

"Thwart, sire," they said, "this traitor,
Who makes our people die in pain."

CLIV

The day was beautiful; the morning, clear.
The battle was being fought in every direction.
No road was without combat.
Dangerous melees were taking place in every part.
And here, charging with great impetuousness,
Was King Danemon, who was preoccupied
With how he could most wound our people.
His lance was not yet broken.
He struck a Frenchman, the sire of Biaufort in the valley,
On the round buckler, which broke.
The cuirass was coming apart.
The shaft having passed through the body,
He fell dead from the golden saddle.
Upon seeing it, Charles, extremely displeased.
Pulled his rein toward Danemon.
He spurred the steed, cried, "Montjoie!"
And lowered the lance; he gave him such a blow
That he knocked the enemy flat on the meadow.
What was left of his cuirass did not break or weaken
And therefore saved his life from this blow.
Charles's shaft splintered.
Then the king put his hand on his sword.
Most nobly he drew it from its scabbard.
The thing had gone badly for Danemon,
But there were too many of the infidels.
You would have heard a great hue and cry for his rescue.

CLV

To the rescue of strong King Danemon
Came charging many a misccreant Saracen
Whether Charles wanted it or not,
They remounted him quickly on the Aragonese steed,
The same one from which he had fallen on the sand.
If you had seen the good vassal Namles
Charge among the pagans with great violence
And the demeanor of a lion,
You could certainly have said that he was a valiant knight.
And you would declare this reasonably,
Surely, without any mistake,

That one should certainly praise King Charles
That he loved to have such a companion beside hm.
Many, many pagans were killed,
And a great number of horses had no riders.
Ogier was near the greatest mass of the people of Pharaoh
Who hated God and loved Mohammed,
For it was certainly fitting.
He had wrought great destruction on the pagans.
As a result they fled from around him and near him
As the lamb and sheep do the wolf.

CLVI

Great was the battle even among small numbers.
You would have seen them most fiercely defend themselves
And attack and give and return blows.
While they could precipitate themselves on one another,
They spared one another no more than a hawk does a lark.
Both sides delivered blows in profusion.
You would have seen them contend so violently
That one could not have incited more violence.
Many a one was there who would have let himself be hanged
Or would have wanted to be burnt to a cinder
Before he could be surprised on any side.
For honor's sake, he wanted to make no mistake
For which he could be blamed.
If you had seen King Carahuel
Extend himself on his horse and give and take blows,
Cut helmets and bucklers and put shields asunder
And make place and occupy places around him,
You would have certainly said that he had nothing to learn
About selling his life dearly to our people
And that Corsuble had in Carahuel a son-in-law
Who wanted to act honorably, it surely seemed.
There was no need for his sword to be tender
From which there came so many fatal blows.
I can certainly make you understand
That a Christian oponnent knew how to handle himself,
That he who dared await him
Or dared attack him was bold.

CLVII

The beginning of this fight was terrible.
No one ever before saw such savage loss.

Very soon there were sown upon the sand
Many a foot, many a fist, and many an entrail.
It was a most hideous sowing to see.
There was no need to wish or predict a different outcome,
For it was settled that
One or the other of the armies would fail.
Both sides worked arduously
To do what its side valued.
And here was Charles spurring through the batallion.
He did not seem to be the king of riffraff, for
He sat on a steed whiter than a napkin,
Strong and sure and of very fine build.
He had been brought up in Cornwall.
He did not shrink from any kind of vigorous effort.
From his manner it did not seem that the battle bothered him at all.
The king did not wait for someone to attack him;
He attacked first, whatever happened.
In his fist he held a sword which cut well.
Right and left he struck often and inflicted blows
So that around him the crowd dispersed.
He delivered many a serious provocation to pagans,
Who feared him more than the quail does the hawk.
Many were thrown to the sand by his blows.
Whoever did not desire to run or attack.
Had to be ready to receive anguish.
He struck a pagan named Sardouille
Whose helmet was not worth a scale
Which falls down from a fish when one cleans it,
Nor was his hauberk worth a straw to him.
All of it broke and lost its nails and its mail.
The blow went right through the visor of his helmet.
His body was cut through almost to the entrails
It is not right that the name of the valiant be withheld
From the one who gives such blows to his enemy.

CLVIII

This battle was violent, hard, and savage.
You would have seen all kinds of people there,
From many a country, scattered all over,
Who showed that their life was dear to them.
Few people, in the plain or in the ruts,
Were not attacked or did not look for help.
No one ever saw people less cowardly

Nor who were so able and properly trained in arms.
And here was Charlot, the son of Charles of the bold face,
Charging through the brush.
In his fist was his sword, which was good and costly.
He attacked a Turk whose double cuirass
Was worth no more than a leaf of ivy to him.
Neither his helmet nor his shield helped him more than a little branch of a beech tree.
He knocked him dead into a sand pit.
At the biggest concentration of demonic people
Was Duke Namles. "Bavaria!" he cried loudly.
In his fist the sword certainly seemed warrior-like.
That day he caused many a bier to be made for these people
Who hated God and the apostle Saint Peter.

CLIX

The fracas was terrible as the source tells us.
Ogier showed well that he did not care
To dismiss his wrathful intentions
Against the people who mocked those who had faith in God
And who said that Christianity was fables and lies.
Little time passed before he struck,
And he gave them many a blow.
Quite ferociously he gripped his sword Courtain,
Which cut iron better than scissors cut cloth.
Whomever he struck well with it had no need for a doctor to put salve on the wound,
For his knowledge would not be worth a shallot there.
There was no defense for bone, spine or loins,
For it struck no buckler, be it ever so strongly put together,
Or helmet, shield, strong neckpiece, or studded cuirass
That it did not cut up and tear out its nails and disjoin it.
It is no wonder if people dreaded his blows
Nor if they tried to avoid him or get away from him.
Those from Cologne cried, "Cologne;"
Bavarians, "Bavaria," and Saxons, "Saxony;"
Flemish, "Arras," and Boulognais, "Boulogne;"
French, "Monjoie," and Burgundians, "Burgundy."
Hues de Troies threw himself amid the Turks
And struck a pagan who came from Catalonia.
His head fell to the ground, cut off from his shoulders.
It was apparent in this battle
That before the pagans had passed the forest of Soignes

Or approached the Rhine near Tremoigne
They could certainly have such great difficulty
That they would be afraid of being shamed.

CLX

The fracas was furious and the battle great.
Both sides were violent and earnest
In the way they went about weakening one another.
King Corsuble came charging into the melee,
Accompanied by many a Turk and many a Persian.
He saw his son King Danemon remounted.
His heart rejoiced, for he loved his son
More than any other father ever loved a child.
That is all one need say about it.
He came charging ferociously among our people.
He was harming both our Christians and their horses
With a javelin that he held as he went.
The Angevin Joffroi of the wise heart
Was sorrowful and sad and grieving
Upon seeing King Corsuble go along
Tormenting our people so;
Joffroi was eager to avenge it if he could.
Then he spurred his white horse
And brandished his sword like a powerful man,
Striking King Corsuble on the shining helmet.
The circlet was strong; he did not damage it,
For the blow glanced his helmet on the right side,
Striking the javelin in missing the helmet.
It cut it in two at once.
Corsuble saw it; he drew his sword immediately.
Very savagely and with a bold appearance
He struck Joffroi back on the resplendent helmet.
The blow entered deep into the helmet, but
The good hauberk saved him from death.
Numerous pagans attacked Joffroi vigorously.
Left and right and behind and in front.
They came running there to rescue Joffroi,
Those who held fiefs from him
And his friends and relatives.
Warriors came as fast from both sides as their horses would carry them,
Turks, Achopars, French and Germans;
There the Christians and the unbelievers
Exchanged many a hard and heavy blow.

If you had seen Richars the good Norman,
How he exposed himself to danger
And how he went looking for the Saracens
And rescuing Christians from harm,
You would certainly have said, "Here is a valiant man."
With Escalidar, his slicing sword, the sharp one,
He bloodied many a Saracen that day.

CLXI

The battle was hard and the clash of arms savage;
Guy de Saint Omer was fighting very well.
Everywhere there were such massacres
That no man who ever lived has seen greater ones.
Hoel de Nantes, like a bold knight,
Had thrown himself into the thickest part of the fight,
Holding tightly the standard of Saint Denis.
Behind him followed many who would have been reluctant
To do something to be criticized; not a single one of them
Would have done a single thing that would have brought criticism.
They cried out, "Montjoie!" there with loud shouts,
Which greatly frightened many a pagan.
When Charlemagne, the good, powerful king,
Saw the standard among the Arabs,
He thanked Jesus Christ for it.
"Ah, God," said he, "now it is not Aloris
Who is holding the banner of Saint Denis!"
Then he spurred the good, costly warhorse,
Which among many a good horse had been selected
And chosen as the best and most beautiful,
For he was whiter than a fleur-de-lis.
Then he brandished the sword, which had lost its shine.
He struck a pagan on the shining helmet
So violently in the front, right on the face,
That he knocked him off the horse down to the ground.
I do not know if he was killed by this blow,
But he remained on the ground completely stunned.
Many a pagan hastened to rescue him,
For he was king and lord of the Lutis.
Charles was chosen king by the Pope
And then he was certainly blessed by him,
For the Pope always went from place to place
As one who was full of faith.
He told the Christians that in Paradise

A place was nobly established for them.
"Now we will see there," said he, "those who are friends
Of the one who was put on the cross
By the perfidious Jews to save us from the enemy.
Each one of you should certainly be encouraged,
For it is my opinion that today
You will conquer those who hate him.
Each one of you must certainly rejoice
When he has chosen you to do this
Among those who remain in your country.
Many of them are now perhaps lying on their beds
Because of their miserable, faint hearts.
Many a great body is shamed by a weak heart
And many a small one is honored by a good heart."
Thus spoke the noble Pope.
All good people should obey,
Love, and serve such a Pope who
In such a place gives a sermon to his subjects.

CLXII

The Pope, who was so full of goodness,
Came to the battleground, as I have described to you,
Like one who had confidence
And right faith and fine loyalty.
With him he had a great plenty of people
Who were well armed.
They wanted to guard him,
For otherwise he would not have lasted long.
Great was the noise far and wide.
This day many a mortal blow was given there.
Namles did much and did well, in truth,
As did Joffrois d'Anjou of the valiant courage,
From Normandy Richars of the wise heart,
And Auketins in whom there was no cowardly bone;
Also Oedes of the city of Langres,
Hues de Troies of the reflective heart,
And many others that I have not named.
Duke Thierri, with the engraved sword in his fist,
Did many a great exploit this day;
He certainly showed in the blows he struck
That he had no love whatsoever for Saracens.
Duke Fagon had not forgotten
The great deeds of arms that he had performed

In many places where he had been,
For the deeds were often retold
With enthusiasm, and rightly so.

CLXIII

The combat was savage in many a place in the plain.
Many a javelin was thrown; many a lance drawn.
Never has anyone seen such very violent strife
Because each one hated and disdained cowardice,
For the fire of honor was never extinguished in him
Nor was there any restraint of prowess in his heart.
Our barons of Germany were performing well
And those of France, Anjou, and Brittany,
Burgundy, Normandy, and the people of Champagne,
Flanders and Picardy; there were none who hesitated,
And many others—may God guard and keep them—
By whom faith in him may grow and increase.
There was not a single one of our people, countryman
Or foreigner, no matter how high a personage he might be
Nor how great his prowess
Who did not need to undertake
To protect his life.
Certainly each one needed to remember
Not to let cowardice and fear surprise him,
For the multitude of pagans was so great
That they filled many a great field,
Many a coast, many a valley, many a mountain.
They desired to cause us sorrow
And certainly thought they would triumph.
Namles saw it; he crossed himself, wondering
Where such a swarm of the wretches could have come from.
He was well mounted on a Spanish warhorse;
From there to Bohemia there was no better one.
Among the Turks he loudly shouted the battle cry.
There was no need for anyone to show or signal him
The way to handle arms,
For he knew so well the right and proper work
That he never struck a man unless he hit him with a full blow
From the sword that cut iron like a wooden cudgel
So that it killed or badly wounded him.
It was fitting that his sword was tinted red,
For it was often bathed with the blood of those
Who had no respect for the law of God.

He was constantly fighting them
And causing them enormous suffering and anguish.
He struck a pagan named Malekaigne
Who was of Sartaignian extraction on his mother's side.
His helmet was not worth a chestnut to him,
Nor his hauberk a spider's web.
He knocked him down dead; it did not matter to him who lamented him.

CLXIV

Great were the noise, the shouts, and the war cries.
There was no need there for cowards or bewildered ones,
For never was a more savage fracas seen
Nor ever henceforth will be; nobody disagrees with this.
King Carahuel wasted no time.
At that point he headed toward our people,
For he had been chosen to do this.
He ran upon them on the left side.
Our people paid dearly that day
Because of the audacity that had risen in his heart.
Now I will tell you to what people he had come.
He had thrown himself into the troops of Hues,
The one from Le Mans, who was a trusted friend of Charles.
He had so many of the unbelievers with him
That by rights he certainly should have been feared.
With his well-sharpened sword he struck
Many of the blows struck that day against our people
So that many a one was flat on the ground.
Many a blow was taken and received,
Given and returned among the combatants
And many a vassal beaten down to the ground.
Hues dou Mans so conducted himself in it
That one must certainly consider him valiant.

CLXV

Oedes de Lengres with the bold face
Came charging through the melee; it did not at all seem
That he had been resting this time.
His buckler was torn up in many a place;
His helmet from Pavia was bashed in,
And his sword was tinted with blood and soiled.
Hues de Troies was in his company.
They had been companions all their lives
Since they had received knighthood.

As much as a loyal lover loves his sweetheart
The one loved the other with a love strengthened by faith.
By the prowess of the two of them many a soul
Was separated from the body among the pagan people.
The people God hated feared them greatly
In many a country and in many a region.
In his fist Hues de Troies held the sword,
Which was stained at this time.
They directed their path to the greatest crowd.
As each one shouted out the battle cry loudly,
They made a great massacre of the Saracens
So that afterwards the place was strewn
With shields, with helmets and with the wounded.
Charles saw it; he thanked the Lord God for it
And prayed fervently with all his heart that he keep them safe.

CLXVI

Mild was the weather and beautiful and clear the day
And the air cold; there was no great heat.
Many a place was brilliantly resplendent
With shields, bucklers, helmets painted with flowers,
And with banners and rich ornaments
So that the gleam appeared from afar.
There were many castanets and drums
And big bugles and horns and trumpets.
Whoever could not hear this noise was deaf.
In many a place the fracas was perilous.
Since God gave help to his own on the cross
Never were so many valiant warriors seen
Among so many people, here or elsewhere,
As were there, ours as well as theirs.
King Corsuble had brought the best
From pagan lands everywhere.
He had chosen the most valiant warriors
That he could choose, and left the worst.
He had so many valiant combatants there
That it is a great wonder he could assemble so many.
Duke Fagon of Tours did well in the battle,
He and the people that he led.
Long rests were not appropriate there,
Nor cowardice, baseness, nor fear;
But audacity, confidence, and vigor
Were fitting there and present.

Duke Thierri, in whom resided honor
And nobility and perfect valor,
Who held cities, castles and towns in the Ardennes,
Conducted himself there like one in whom fear
Did not lodge; his actions in battle indeed showed this.
The color of his sword had changed;
In the morning it was as clear as a mirror,
But it was soiled with blood and sweat.
To bear arms was his proper labor,
For he was powerful and strong as a tower.
He could withstand more blows than any bear,
And his own blows were hideous to see.
It would have been hard for any man to strike greater blows.
May God protect him by his holy kindness,
For among the Turks his violence was certainly evident:
He struck many of them who did not not revive
And afterward never moved again.
One should surely esteem in all courts
Of kings, counts, dukes, emperors
The one who so hindered Saracens.
He was one of the best of our ancestors.
He gave generously of his possessions
Oftentimes to the great and to the humble.
He gladly had jongleurs with him;
He liked good viol players and singers.
Above all he liked composers of poetry and music
And then after that the fine tellers of tales.
He never liked traitors or deceivers
Nor people he knew to be flatterers.
He was upright and a good dispenser of justice.
As best he could he destroyed traitors
And exiled thieves and robbers,
Even from all the places where he knew they had found refuge,
Even if they were part of the most important families.
With all his heart he put his love
Into serving God, who is our creator.
One could certainly say without being a liar
That this person who was so full of good ways
Should surely be councilor to the king.
If any kings believed those who thought the opposite of such people,
It would have been a great pity and calamity and sadness
That such an ugly mistreatment was kept within a royal heart.

CLXVII

This battle caused much fear,
For in so many places you would have seen massacres,
Noses and faces and fists and feet cut off
So that one could greatly marvel about it.
And you would have seen so many horses without a master,
The one dragging its lord by the stirrup,
The other fleeing ahead, the third behind,
And wounded people lying on the grass
Who could not rise or sit up.
Certainly you could reasonably have said,
If you had seen the mortal danger,
That it was indeed a thing to frighten cowards.
And here was Ogier charging into the battle,
In his fist he had the highly prized sword
That King Carahuel had given him the other day.
Many a Saracen paid dearly that day,
For the sword was of such fine steel.
Wherever he turned, the ranks trembled.
He met Androine, a powerful and proud king.
He was richly armed and on such a warhorse
That he could not have wished for a better one.
He strived hard to do us harm.
He had unhorsed many a one that day
And wounded many and made great trouble.
Ogier struck him on the pure gold helmet.
The circlets were not worth an olive branch
Nor the hauberk the sum of a half-penny.
He made the sword bathe in the brain.
Androine fell down dead on the ground across a path.
This blow frightened many Saracens
And restrained many and made them draw back.
Danemon was consumed with anger
When he saw Androine tumble down dead.

CLXVIII

When Danemon saw Androine fallen,
Lying stretched out dead on the ground,
His expression showed how much Androine meant to him.
The base unbelievers lamented him greatly.
"Oh, Androine," said they, "what a misfortune
It is to us that we have lost you!
You showed your prowess in many a place."

King Corsuble's heart was filled with anger;
He swore to Mohammed and Cahut
That he would either die on the spot or his adversary would pay dearly.
He spurred his warhorse and gripped the shield tightly to himself.
And Danemon did not hesitate.
He raised the cutting and sharpened sword
And struck a Frenchman named
Joffrois of Montagu on his pointed helmet.
His armor was not worth a straw to him;
He knocked him down dead upon the grassy meadow.
And Ogier struck King Corsuble
Such a very great blow that he beat him down
Upon the croup of the good, full-maned warhorse,
But he was not killed or wounded by this blow.
At this attack the pagans came pouring into the area;
They came to a stop around Ogier
And ran upon him most violently,
But Ogier received them in such a way
That he caused many a one of them to pay mortal tribute.
Charles and Namles came there
And many a choice vassal of prowess;
Then they redoubled the shouts and the war cries.
"Montjoie," cried Charles of the white hair.
"Bavaria," cried Namles, with strength and courage.
The Saracens were desperate for Corsusble.
They were applying themselves to his rescue with all their might.

CLXIX

In the rescue of Corsuble the king
There was now a great hubbub, great noise, and great fracas;
If so many people had not been there with him,
The death of Joffroi would have been dearly avenged.
The people of the false religion put Corsuble back on his horse.
And, if it is as I believe,
He was really glad of it, for he certainly had reason to be.
There was no need in this case to keep quiet
There where so much fighting had taken place.
You would have found there very few places
Where the dead were not lying, here four, here three.
King Danemon was extremely arrogant
And did our people much harm that day.
He struck a Frenchman named Sanses who was born in the Val Éloi.
Charles had reared him in his household,

And Sanses had served him faithfully.
Danemon sent him flying dead upon the sand.
"Ah! God," said Charles, "true king, grant
Help today to the people whom I am supposed to protect,
Who have come here with me to serve you.
May it not displease you that I remind you of this,
For I am greatly troubled when I see them killed.
I pray this of you with all my heart, sweet Sire."

CLXX

Beautiful was the day and the sun radiant.
The weather was perfectly mild.
A cool breeze was blowing.
Corsuble the powerful was back on his horse.
He hungered to do violence to our people,
And he did not neglect to do so.
He ran upon them, enraged and desiring
To do something to damage them.
King Carahuel was not sitting idly by;
He had had great battle with those of Le Mans,
And the good Hues like a valiant knight
Had defended himself against the miserable miscreants.
There were so many Turks and Persians
That he could have been losing at this point,
But he was helped by valiant comrades,
By Duke Richars and Norman barons,
So that those whom King Carahuel
Was leading had to turn from the field.
The boldest of them all was fleeing.
Then they were all routed, but Carahuel relentlessly
Came behind, pursuing like a hardy combatant.
As a bear is active and protective in defending
Her cubs against wolves, so too
Were his people toward our men.
There and elsewhere he was doing so well
In all the places where arms were at work
That one certainly must recall
That along with these qualities he was sweet and courteous and noble.
The pursuit extended up to King Corsuble.
There the pagans stopped as they came up against the Franks.
Many a one of the Franks turned against the pursuers, and
The fighting began again so heavily
That many of them were thrown down dead and bleeding.

On this renewed attack King Braimans was killed,
The one who was lord and king of the Africans.
The good Duke Namles, who held Bavaria,
Made him feel how his sword cut.
Ir grieved King Corsuble extremely
And stunned many a pagan.
Many a one often cursed Mohammed and Tervagant
About it, calling each of them cowardly
And saying they were false gods not to be believed in.

CLXXI

This battle was on a Saturday.
It was great and savage, so much more so than I am telling you.
And here came charging Grohan of Valonni,
A Persian king accompanied by such fine knights
That one could be dazzled with the sight of him.
With him were Achopars and Lutis,
Who considered him very valiant and bold.
He had mistreated many a one of our people that day,
For he had often attacked them hard
From outside the ranks and in the middle of the ranks.
His heart was very sorrowful for King Braimans,
Who lay dead upon the flowery meadow,
For they were friends and of the same lineage.
He did not neglect to avenge him.
He turned his horse right toward Ogier.
With his sword he struck him on the burnished helmet
So that he cut and broke its circlet
And split its nose-piece.
The blow broke the rivets of the helmet so
That a big piece of it fell to the ground,
But the Dane's heart was not slowed:
He struck the Saracen back with such a hard blow
That the sword bashed in the brain.
The Dane knocked him dead off his Arabian warhorse.
The pagans saw it; they were terrified by it.
Many of them shouted out to Mohammed,
Praying that he protect them from being humiliated.
They greatly feared being routed.

CLXXII

When the Saracens saw Grohan die,
Most were completely stupefied with fear.

King Corsuble knew how to recognize very quickly
Success and failure and how to find the best course of action.
He knew how to make war: I am not lying to you.
When he saw his people restrained and frightened,
He understood very well that they needed encouragement.
Then he cried to them, "Barons, strike now!
Seek no rest or leisure!
Do not be afraid of anything at all.
Let us run upon them; you will see them fleeing immediately."
After this word they charged with great violence
From all directions, impetuous and full of desire
To ravage the Christians.
King Corsuble started charging with great energy
Among our people to encourage his own men.
If you could have seen King Danemon hold
His sword in his fist and invade our flanks
You would certainly have said that he was a leader to fear.
There you would have seen many a hauberk destroyed
And many a strong helmet broken into pieces.

CLXXIII

At this charge there was incredible noise.
Charlot, the grandson of Pépin, the son of
Charles, the king with the fine heart, did very well.
The French people and those from beyond the Rhine
So conducted themselves toward the people of Apollo
That many a one met his end that day.
You should know that many lay in rows
On the fields, some face down on the ground and others flat on their backs,
Who afterward drank neither beer nor wine.
And here charging into the battle was Autekin,
Who was Duke Richars's cousin.
In his fist he held the good steel sword
With which he had wounded many a Saracen that day.
In front of Corsuble, he struck a Berber
Such a great blow on his helmet from overseas
That it was not worth the value of a Roman penny to him,
Nor the hauberk a chick's fuzz.
He knocked him down dead across a path.

CLXXIV

Great was the noise down in the meadow.
And here was Ogier, charging down a vale,

In his fist the sword with the fine blade;
The person he struck with it was not in the mood to rejoice.
He espied a Turk who was born at Compostella;
He was lord of the kingdom of Tudele.
He was holding Hues de Troies underneath his armpit
And had him bent over the saddle-bow.
Then he would have done him a bad turn;
But the Dane, who boldly rode forward,
Struck him on the helmet, which shone and sparkled;
But was not worth a hawthorn flower to him,
Nor his hauberk a scrap of wood.
He sliced through it all, right to the brain.
He knocked him down dead beside a little willow tree.
Namles saw him; he called upon our lady because of him.
His whole heart jumped within him with great joy.
"Ah! Mother of God," said he, "Virgin Maiden,
Dear beloved Lady, save this one
Who fights your sweet son's battles like this!"

CLXXV

When Ogier had thus rescued Hues,
The one from Troies, the valiant Burgundian,
Who was a doughty and upright knight,
Immediately afterward, without any pause at all,
In the thickest ranks of Pharaoh's people,
Ogier fought like a brave and noble man.
Hither and yon the pagans fled.
They feared him more than a duck does a hawk,
More than a crane does an eagle.
And here came Corsuble and Danemon charging,
In their company many a cruel Saracen.
Corsuble looked around and saw Charles,
Who did not have a great crowd of people around him.
He turned his Aragonese warhorse in that direction
And his son came toward Charles with violent force
With the ardent desire to do him harm.
Charles, who had the heart of a lion, saw them.
At once he spurred his good Gascon warhorse
And came upon them like a king of great renown.
With his steel sword he struck Corsuble
On top of his helmet in such a way
That he knocked him down onto the saddle bow.
He nearly fell onto the sand.

CLXXVI

King Danemon, with his sword raised high,
Gave King Charles such a blow
Upon his helmet that he dented it
Very deeply and knocked off its circlets.
King Corsuble struck him again
On the shield so that he cut off
More than a measured foot of it on the left.
And King Charles did not hesitate a bit;
Rather he defended himself with the steeled sword
Like a powerful king full of great ferocity.
The pagans surrounded him
And struck him many a blow.
They wounded his horse in so many places
That it fell dead beneath him on the meadow.
When the king saw that they had surrounded him
And that they had killed his good warhorse,
Adeptly he disentangled himself
From the horse like an experienced man.
He gripped his shield; he brandished his sword.
He defended himself well like a purposeful man
And one with an abundance of courage.
Like a wild boar standing its ground to fight
Among the dogs that have cornered it,
Charles of the staunch heart defended himself.
Namles saw him; he struck his horse
With the spurs and cried, "Bavaria!"
With his well-sharpened sword.
He struck so much and spurred so much
That he led his horse right next to Charles.
After him the French charged from all sides,
Eager to rescue their lord;
But there were so many of the accursed pagans
That the Christians were greatly hindered by them.
The Saracens pressed Namles with such force
That they disemboweled his horse.
It fell under him; it went forward no further.
Namles called upon Saint George.
Like a powerful man and a capable warrior
He came toward Charles, in his fist the engraved sword.
There was no possibility that the French
Would have forgotten to protect him.

CLXXVII

Charles was on foot, the good, powerful king.
He conducted himself well, like a valiant, bold man.
Beside him was Namles, who would never
Have wanted to leave his lord.
Charles had picked up off the ground a short lance
With a firm shaft and burnished iron.
Charles the noble king helped himself well with it.
There you could have seen a great press of warriors
And a great assault by the Persians and the Lutis.
They defended themselves so much, of this you may be sure,
That you could be astounded by the sight.
I believe that God, our father Jesus Christ,
Was very glad that they were put in such a situation
And that his heart rejoiced
As he saw his friends defending him
So courageously among his enemies
And that he showed it to his saints in paradise.
For you should know well
That God always is joyous when he sees his subjects
Obey his commandments with a willing heart.
Charles cried, "Montjoie! Saint Denis!"
Namles, "Bavaria!" like a perfect vassal.
The good Dane heard the shouts
From where the battle was most fierce.
He abandoned that area at once.
Seeing Charles and Namles surrounded,
He brandished his sword like a knight of merit
And hit Danemon on his shining helmet.
Neither the helmet nor the hauberk of mail were worth
Two Paris pennies against the violent blows.
Danemon fell down dead on the field, which was strewn
With shields, bucklers, the wounded and the dead.
Ogier took the horse like a skillful man.
He gave it to Namles, and he, as an able man,
One who was capable of all good deeds,
Took it at once to Charlemagne of the proud face,
And, using the stirrup, the king jumped up on it.
Then he spurred it into the Arabians.
With the lance that he had, of which the iron was well made,
He struck a pagan such a blow in the middle of the chest
That he fell on the ground completely dazed.
The pagans saw it; many a one was frightened by it.

They called upon Mohammed to help them.
When Corsuble saw that Danemon his son
Lay on the ground and that he was dead,
His heart was broken.

CLXXVIII

When Charles had knocked down the pagan,
At once he seized the good, long-maned warhorse.
He held it out to Namles by the reins.
And he, who was certainly in need of it, took it.
He did not wait long to mount it;
On the contrary, he mounted it like a man of great strength and courage.
Then he spurred it and gripped the shield,
Intending to harm the enemy.
With his sword of steel he struck a Turk with such force
That he beat him down upon the grassy meadow.
The French came running from all directions
To the rescue of Charles the white-haired,
But they would have come much too late
If the Dane had not helped him.
There the pagans increased from many sides.
There was great noise and hue and cry in that place.
Many a blow was given there and many given back,
Many Saracens wounded and many fallen.
Many were desperately troubled
That they had seen Danemon their lord
Lying stretched out dead on the ground.
Many were grieving and furious about it
And many had lost that hope
That they had had in the morning when they moved
From where they had spent the night before.
The cowardly unbelievers feared greatly
That they would have to give up the fight
That day and be killed and conquered.

CLXXIX

Because of Danemon the pagans were distraught
On many sides and terribly frightened,
And their attacks were much weakened because of his death
And the blows from most were much slowed down.
But one thing I tell you in truth:
There was one who did not have his heart sad or frightened.
Carahuel attacked our people at once

Like a courageous warrior.
If all the others had so helped themselves
As he did, in truth I swear to you
The French could well have been destroyed
If it pleased God to consent to it.
Ogier never turned that day
Toward Carahuel, nor he toward him either;
For they were great friends with one another.
And here into the battle came charging Thierri,
In his right hand the polished steel sword
Which had distributed many a great blow that day
Upon the people who were enemies of God.
Before him he saw King Charles.
He turned the Arabian warhorse in that direction.
"Sire," he said to him, "I assure you
That the Saracens are nearly conquered,
For it surely seems to me that they are diminished in number
In many parts of their army and greatly thinned out."
"The mother of God, "said Charles, "be thanked for it,
For never in my life, so help me God,
Have I seen so many valiant pagans in a single day
As I have seen in this battle today.
Their people have received ours very harshly
And have often attacked them.
Let us charge out to them." Said the duke, "I agree."
At this word they spurred together without delay.
Each one came shouting out the rallying cry loudly
Into the very spot where the pagans were most numerous.
With Corsuble had gathered
Turks, Achopars, Persians, and Amoravis,
Of which many were so trained
That they would have preferred to be dead and dishonored
Than to have left the field without him.

CLXXX

King Corsuble had a valiant knight,
Accomplished and courageous, sure and knowledgeable
In all points of arms and clear-sighted:
King Danemon, who had so much prowess in him that
Those who knew him thought he was very valiant.
King Corsuble saw him lying on the ground dead and bloody.
Within his heart he lamented his loss greatly,
But he did not reveal his grief.

Instead he went among his people, encouraging them
And confidently and constantly prodding them
So that they were more eager to strike.
"Lords," said he, "let us not delay.
Let each of us behave so as to defend his life
Against those who are challenging us here.
Remember that you used to pray
To Mohammed that you would live long enough
To be able to confront Charles, the powerful king,
And that with him would be Angevins and Normans,
English, Picards, Flemish and Germans,
Those from Hainaut and Brabant
And Burgundians and Bretons speaking unintelligibly
And all those attached to him.
We have found what you were wishing for.
See them about you here; do not look further for them.
Today henceforth the valiant fighters will appear,
For in times of need those appear at once
Who love honor and fear shame."
At this word Corsuble spurred his impetuous horse;
Right through the middle of our men he came charging hard.
He struck a Frenchman on the shining helmet,
Giving him such a blow with his sharp steel sword
That the brains spilled out onto the ground.
After him the pagans came spurring.
The Christians and the unbelievers
Struck many a savage and heavy blow there.

CLXXXI

At this charge, I don't want to lie to you,
The pagans made many a Christian die.
If you had been there and it had been possible for you
To have seen the battle,
You certainly could have heard in many places
Many steel swords resound on helmets.
You should know that whoever had to fall there
Would want to get up again.
If you could have seen the good Dane charge impetuously
Among the pagan horde and hold his own,
Give and distribute rude blows
And make the Saracens around him flee,
You would surely say that he inspired fear;
Where he fought he made the ranks tremble.

Charles saw him; he began to rejoice.
He could not keep from raising his hand
And blessing him with the sword:
"God," said he, "Sire, if it be thy will,
Protect from death today this one
Whom I see attack the Saracens like this."
And here came Corsuble charging into the battle,
Shouting his battle cry to encourage his troops.
Charles saw him and started to turn toward him,
Making the horse feel the spurs.
Corsuble turned toward him with great wrath,
For he desired to do him harm.
They exchanged such blows with one another
That sparks flew out from their helmets.

CLXXXII

The battle was violent in many places on the meadow.
The two kings were together in the melee
Giving one another many a blow.
The good king Charles raised Joyeuse up to strike,
Spurred his warhorse, and shouted, "Montjoie!"
He gave King Corsuble such a blow
That he cut the circlet from the strong helmet.
The sword fell with such force
That the strong helmet cuirass was ruptured and unnailed,
And the sword cut into the brain.
Charles knocked him down dead from the golden saddle.
His troops assembled around him there,
Eager and desiring to rescue him,
But they soon perceived that his life was gone.
His death brought forth loud cries;
Many greatly mourned for his life.
"Ah, King," said they, "of very great renown,
In whom valor and prowess abounded,
Whoever has killed you has ended the battle."
Many Saracen troops gathered there.
Many a one of them was there who felt and thought
That he would much rather have risked his life
Than have the Christians deprive them of
The great love that King Corsuble
Had often shown them in his country.
The battle stopped around him,
Where that day many a sword blow had been struck,

Many a helmet broken, many a nailed cuirass opened
And many a buckler cut into pieces.
Many a soul had been separated from its body
And many a vassal made to lie with mouth gaping.
So many dead and wounded men lay there
That in many areas the field was empty
Of the living and was piled up with the dead.
The troops of Charles of the valiant demeanor
Helped one another well there, like honorable people.
With this charge they pushed the pagan people back
Further than the bolt of a crossbow would fly,
By which the pagans saw truly that it was not their day.
They were defeated; the thing was done.
Many a one of them turned their faces away,
Fleeing with reins abandoned
Back to the side from which they had moved that morning.

CLXXXIII

The Saracens were chagrinned when they saw
That they were pushed back by force
And they were abandoning the place and the spot
Where their lord Corsuble lay dead.
Many loved him so much
That they were in great sorrow because of his death
And despised their lives for lack of his love
So that dying was of little concern to them.
Their grief was quite apparent in their behavior,
For they exposed their bodies so much
That it seemed that they coveted death.
They fought on the battlefield like savage wild boars
And allowed themselves to be killed and to fall upon their lord's body.
But a great number, you should know, defended themselves
So that our people paid dearly for their lives.
In fighting they mourned their lord,
And they encouraged one another to avenge him.
Many conducted themselves there in such a manner,
And numerous others feared to die
So that in their hearts they were content to flee,
Not daring to stay any longer on the field.
When our people saw that the Saracens
Were starting to flee and that they were turning their backs,
They praised God and his mother and the saints.

They strove with all their might to chase them hard
And to kill them when they could.

CLXXXIV

The Saracens were in sorrow and in fear
When they lost the flower of the pagan kings.
As good or a better king was not known
At that time among the pagan people, and
Many were badly shaken by it.
Certainly they should have felt grief and fury,
For before in their time they had not had a lord
Who had so many good qualites or so much kindness
Or generosity or such very great valor
As had Corsuble, or so much honor.
They called him the valiant, generous king.
Since they knew that he was dead without return,
Dispirited, they met defeat everywhere.
King Carahuel, who had so much vigor,
Had in his heart for King Corsuble so much sadness
And sorrow that his grief could not have been greater, and
He sought no delay to avenge him.
He had made many a turn that day among our people,
For which many a lady thenceforward would shed many a tear,
For he had made many a one lie on the grass
Who would not afterward enter into the land of the French.
As he sat solidly on the magnificent warhorse,
The French attacked him in front and on all sides.
With his steel sword sharp as a razor
And soiled with blood and sweat,
He defended himself like a charging warrior.

CLXXXV

The pagans, pursued vigorously,
Waited for neither cousin nor relative.
Many a one was delivered there to great torment.
In this pursuit, know in addition
That Carahuel fought fiercely
And as if he were confident and full of audacity.
He often made a good riposte to our people,
Executed exactly right and on purpose.
If all the others had helped themselves in such a way
As he did in this pursuit,
Certainly before evening the Christians

Could have been sorrowful of heart
If they had not had the protection of God.
This battle had lasted a long time,
For it had begun in the early morning
And already it was near nightfall.
I want to describe the pursuit for you as succinctly
As I can, and as briefly.
Up to Rome, you should certainly know
That the pursuit continued without ceasing.
Many of them remained behind actually,
Whether dead or taken prisoner, whether wounded or bleeding.
If I wanted to tell you everything about how
Each one did, it would be for nothing;
I would never finish.
For that reason I pass over it as lightly as I can
And still do it justice.

CLXXXVI

This battle lasted a long time.
Such was the pursuit that I have recounted to you.
The Saracens and Christians entered
Into Rome, the admirable city,
All intermingled pell mell.
King Carahuel, who was very powerful,
Was outside Rome near an old ditch.
In his fist he held the good, steeled sword
With which he had given many a great blow that day
To our people, by which many were dead and wounded
And were lying there on their backs and face down.
With him he had a great number of his people,
Who were more willing to die
Than to leave without him.
Upon them were many of our troops
Who were eager to do them harm.
Duke Richars of the virtuous heart was there
And Auketin of firm courage,
Who had broken and torn off the circlets of many a helmet that day
And broken many a shield and dismantled it into quarters.
King Carahuel, truly you should know,
Conducted himself there like a man full of valor
In whom was prowess and confidence.
Wielding the engraved steel sword,
He struck Autekin on his golden helmet

So that he broke its strong circlet.
The strong hauberk stopped the blow.
If it had not, it would have bashed in his head and killed him,
For he struck him with such great violence,
With such force and such power,
That he threw him from the horse to the ground.
And Autekin, who had so much goodness,
Whose boldness was proven for certain,
Leapt back to his feet like a man full of ability.
He looked at Carahuel savagely,
Gripped his shield, raised his sword
And struck King Carahuel with such force
That he badly wounded the king's left arm.
There was not enough of his shield left
That it could have protected him from the blow,
For the Christians had cut it all up.
The pagans surrounded Autekin,
Throwing many a blow at him with their lances;
And he, like a valiant man, exposed his body
Among them, like a man with a purpose
And in whom was proven boldness.
Duke Richars had not forgotten to rescue him;
He had remembered it well;
Nor had the people of his kingdom forgotten.
Many of them had made a great effort
To mount him behind them on their horses,
But there were so many of the wretched infidels
Who had assembled themselves in that place
That the Christians were greatly hindered by it.
Duke Richars, who was deeply loyal,
Had recovered the horse left behind
When Carahuel had knocked
The good Norman Auketin, the renowned, to the ground.
In spite of the pagans he had brought it back to him,
And Autekin mounted it there with great eagerness.

CLXXXVII

At the rescue of Auketin the Norman,
Many a savage and heavy blow had been distributed.
There you would have seen lying on the ground
Many a dead man, many wounded, many bleeding,
And many a horse fleeing across the fields
And many who went with their bowels trailing out.

And right at this moment, here Thierri came charging,
He of the Ardennes with the able courage.
He came in front of Charles, who
Was chasing pagans hither and yon.
Following after Thierri came those of the Ardennes,
Among whom was many a valiant knight.
In this battle, he went right into the thickest part of it,
As a powerful man would.
On the other side came spurring
The Hesbignon warriors and those of Brabant,
Loudly shouting the battle cry.
The Saracens were greatly disconcerted
When they saw so many Christians coming upon them.
Many a Turk and many a Persian were killed there.
The Saracens saw that the Christians were thinning them out as they came
And that the Christians were growing more and more numerous.
Then they saw very well that they would have no defense.
They turned in flight, no longer hesitating.
And Carahuel, with the sharp sword in his fist,
Stayed, indeed I assure you,
Like a lion defending its life.
Of his people certain ones remained with him,
Who showed well by what they did to defend him
That they had no desire to leave him.

CLXXXVIII

King Carahuel performed exceedingly well
Wielding the polished steel sword.
Whoever saw him attack
And strike and fight around him
Could attest that he was a warrior of very accomplished prowess.
Those who had no desire to spare him
Strove mightily to harm him.
They wounded his warhorse in so many places,
Making it lose so much blood
That beneath him it fell dead on the grass.
And he, like a warrior vassal of prowess,
Once dismounted, quickly started fighting with the lance.
Within his heart he greatly desired
To sell his life to our people so dearly
That after his death he could be accused of nothing unbecoming.
Whoever saw him handle his sword
Masterfully and execute his blows

Would not have said that he had a cowardly heart.
But his defense was not worth a penny to him.
He was struck so much in front and behind
That by force he was obliged to kneel.
Many started to leap upon him.
They held him so tightly, you should know without a doubt,
That he could not get back up.
His people saw him; they were in great pain
When they saw that their lord, whom they held so dear,
Was in this disturbing situation;
And they themselves had so much fighting to contend with
That they did not know where to look for the next attack.
You may be sure that they were filled with fear.
Nevertheless, their only desire was not to abandon him;
They would have preferred to be killed and cut all to pieces.
Right at this moment, here Ogier came charging.
He was returning from chasing pagans,
Of whom he had made many empty their saddles.
He saw Carahuel, for whom he had been looking.
When he found him, he thanked God,
For he certainly believed he needed help.

CLXXXIX

King Carahuel was seized firmly
When he was upon his knees in a great crowd of people,
And nevertheless the whole time the noble king
Defended himself as much as possible against his enemies
Like a bold warrior of prowess.
Ogier, who did not delay, saw him
And hastened to rescue him.
He spurred the warhorse and rode right up beside him.
Ogier warded off the blows of the others toward Carahuel
And said to him like a nobleman:
"Give yourself up as captured," said he, "handsome sweet friend.
Your side is beaten on the field.
No evil will come to you; by my faith I swear to you.
I am Ogier, who does not want to see that
You are blamed for anything."
Carahuel heard him; he turned his face toward him.
"Ogier," said he, "this God to whom I am subject
Does not want me to escape alive
Since Corsuble my lord has been killed.
I would prefer to die than to be so vilely dishonored

As to leave the field without him."
When Ogier heard him, he rejoiced
That he heard such words from him in such a place.
What shall I say to you? Carahuel was seized from all sides
As by force they retained and took him.
But however much I tell you, of this be certain,
That he was protected from death by Ogier.
He had Carahuel mount on a conquered horse,
Of which there was many a one, black, sorrel, white and gray,
Fleeing across the fields, here five, there ten.

CLXXXX

Ogier was glad when he had Carahuel,
Who was king of Orcanie, in his company.
When he saw that he was still alive,
He thanked God and his mother and his saints.
Our Christians had taken and seized
Many of the pagan people in this attack
That Carahuel had made this time;
And so many of them lay dead on the prairie
That they were strewn all over the place.
Of this there will be no more words said.
From all parts the pagan people
Were either dead or captured or had fled the field
Where the battle had begun.
King Carahuel's face looked defeated.
He remembered Gloriande, his sweetheart,
And was greatly afraid that she was hurt or gone astray
Or that the Christians had mistreated her.
He looked at Ogier; most gently he implored him
That he help Gloriande, for God's sake,
And reminded him of the great courtesy
And of the fine qualities that graced her.
"Truly," said Ogier, "she has well deserved
My love, for which I am at her command.
I will do all I can to protect her."
And Carahuel thanked him kindly for it.
They entered Rome, the lordly city,
And headed straight for the tents
Where Carahuel had left Gloriande.
When they arrived, they did not find her at all,
Nor a tent pitched nor an alcove set up.
Nor had there been a tent so attached

Nor so firmly implanted in the ground
That it had not already fallen down.
Now I will tell you where the beauty had gone.
When she had heard the news of the calamity
That those of their country were defeated
And killed and captured, she had left there.
Sad and angry, she had gone away
With her maidens, many of whom were in anguish,
To Sadoine, whose thigh was broken.
She had had Sadoine of Syria carried
Into the room within a gate of the ancient city
Very close to her lodging.
There his people, who were well armed and ready to do battle,
Had assembled with him
They had barred and bolted the gate
And fortified and reinforced it with big planks.
Our people had already attacked the gate,
Having rushed upon it most violently.

CLXXXXI

King Carahuel was sad and angry
When he saw the pavilions and tents on the ground
Where he had left the one with so much beauty.
It was pitiful to see him.
Then he lamented the situation, as you can now hear.
"Ah, Gloriande," said he, "considerate heart,
Where nothing dwelt except kindness,
Great sorrow and grief attend this moment
When you are delivered to such people,
By which you are brought to shame.
Ah! Why was such a noble person born
Who by rights should have been honored
And today is so dishonored!
Alas! Why have I escaped from the field alive!
By Mohammed to whom I have given myself,
It burdens me that I remain alive."
Carahuel was in such grief
That he bent his face down to the saddlebow,
For he was almost on the point of fainting;
But Ogier sustained and protected him
And gently raised him up
And very appropriately and properly comforted him.
"Sire," said he, "do not be disconsolate,

I beg of you, if you love me at all,
For we shall have Gloriande again, believe me.
I pray you to hasten to look for her,
For I will go wherever you want
And will do whatever you ask me to."
Said Carahuel, "I am grateful to you and thank you five hundred times!
For you speak loyally and rightly."

CLXXXXII

When Carahuel heard the Dane,
Who in such a situation comforted him so
And engaged himself body and soul
To do whatever he asked,
In his heart he esteemed him very greatly.
At once he thought he would go to Sadoine
Because he certainly thought he would need his help;
If he had not already needed help, he would need it soon.
He was much pained that he had delayed so much
But he had thought so much about Gloriande's calamity,
More than about anything else; and it touched him much more,
As love dictated and as was right.
And it was such that he never fought it,
And nevertheless he loved his companion
Loyally; many times he had proved it.
Carahuel headed straight for the place
Where he had left his companion Sadoine
The day that he had left Rome.
When Ogier and he had come straight there,
They encountered the assault which soon grew more violent,
And Carahuel immediately saw
That Sadoine had been removed from his spot
And carried right to safety
Within that gate, just as he imagined it,
When his people knew how the battle had gone
And that calamity was descending upon them.
King Carahuel looked up
And noticed swords and bucklers of Sadoine's people
Which pleased him greatly;
For he certainly hoped that Ogier would help them.
He saw a maiden who stuck her head
Out of the windows; all at once he hoped
That Gloriande would be there; then he pointed
And showed the maiden to the Dane:

"Ogier," said he, "I have often heard said
That a true friend never fails you in time of need.
In that tower is the beauty in whom
Only good abides, and nothing else ever will.
If the assault continues, she will be dead.
If the gate is taken by force, they will kill her
With the others, of whom not a single one will escape."
"Indeed," said Ogier, "if I can help it, it will not happen.
Never, God willing, will such a calamity occur."
He spurred his warhorse; he stayed there no longer.
He threw himself into the most ferocious part of the assault.
Courteously, he begged the assailants
To draw back; and each one did,
For none dared to refuse his order.
He did and said and commanded so much of them
That the assault ceased on all sides.

CLXXXIII

In such a way as you have heard me describe
The Dane brought this assault to an end.
The French started assembling around him.
They abandoned the assault and let it be;
For, whatever their feelings might be, they wanted to refuse
Nothing that he wished to do or command.
For they loved him greatly as they should have.
You have heard repeated many a time
That what one loves one must by rights fear.
And nevertheless they wanted to ask him
If he pleased, to show them
Why he made them stop the assault.
"Truly," said Ogier, "I do not seek to hide it from you:
For Carahuel's sake, whom one should certainly honor.
Within that gate that you see here
Is Gloriande, his beloved of the fair face.
They have well deserved that I protect
Them from grief and ward off evils
If I can do it yet again.
For this reason I wish and implore and command you
That you stay in this very spot
Until I come back from where I must go
To protect and defend them from death
If anyone appears who wants to harm them.
I want to go tell King Charles

Why I have had you stop here."
The Christians began to praise Ogier greatly
When they heard him speak of such a thing.
"Sire," said they, "worry no more about it.
We will do all that you wish."
Ogier showered his thanks upon them.

CLXXXXIV

Ogier fervently desired
To show friendship to King Carahuel.
He wanted to demonstrate that he had not forgotten
The good deeds Carahuel had done for him
When King Corsuble had him in prison.
He turned all his thoughts
To protecting Gloriande and him
So that they would not be harmed by the Christians.
He saw the situation correctly,
For you know very well that for a long time it has been customary
That when an army enters by force into
Either a castle, a town or a city,
All whom they encounter are killed and put to death.
One sees few or none there who have pity.
Ogier took King Carahuel apart.
"Sire," said he, "do you know what I have been thinking?
It would be a good idea for you to talk
To those who are at this fortification
And with whom you will be in safety
Until I have found King Charles,
For you will see that I will return
Just as soon as I have told him what I intend to."
Said Carahuel, "I agree fully and willingly."
Within the gate of venerable antiquity
Was Gloriande, as I have recounted.
She had peeked out between the crenellations
And seen Carahuel and Ogier the renowned
Who had drawn apart.
Ogier looked around for Broiefort,
And the Saracens around him showed Broiefort to him.
King Carahuel looked up
And saw the elegant young girl.
He recognized her well and called out to her,
Asking that the gate be unlocked and opened to him.
When the pagans heard him, they moved away at once

And unbarred the entrance
And received Carahuel the wise
And those of his people who had remained with him.
There were only twenty of them when they were all counted.
Of all his people no more of them had escaped,
For all were either dead or wounded
Or in fear had fled from the place.
Upon leaving, Ogier assured him
That they would be well protected by those outside
And that he would come back soon, without a doubt.
And Carahuel thanked him profusely.
Then the pagans shut the master gate again
And led Carahuel to Sadoine.
There they found her who had
A heart of perfect loyalty.
It was Gloriande, who was so beautiful.
She had wept copiously,
For she had been told about her father
And about her brother who had been killed,
Because of which she had fainted often.
When she saw Carahuel with his apparel as it was,
So torn up and ruined
And saw his helmet with its circlets ripped off,
Lying in shreds upon his shoulders,
And his hauberk broken and torn apart,
She praised him in her heart even more than she had before.
But her heart was so afflicted with sorrow
That she couldn't say a word.
The Saracens removed Carahuel's armor
And treated and bandaged his arm
Where Autekin the Norman had wounded it.

CLXXXXV

Within the gate of ancient times
That at Rome is called the Main Gate
Was Carahuel, whose heart was full of honor.
He saw Gloriande of the lovely complexion.
He saw well that she could not have been
More sorrowful and sad than she was.
Carahuel was greatly touched by her grief,
For he loved her with a very loyal love.
He comforted her like a man full of valor.
"My beauty," said he, "dry your tears.

Since it pleases our savior
That the pagan people suffer great calamity,
Let us thank him for it; I see nothing else to do.
You are mistaken
If you ever fear
That you will somehow be dishonored,
For the Dane knows that you are in this tower.
He will help you promptly.
I praise him to the sovereign creator;
For if it had not been for him, I would not have returned.
I would, you should know, have been killed in the battle.
We did well the other day, you and I,
To show him honor and gentleness.
He has been worth so much today to the French people
That many must certainly declare
That in him they have a warrior vassal
And a very sure and bold fighter."

CLXXXXVI

In such a manner as I have told you
Carahuel comforted Gloriande,
Like one in whom courtesy resides.
King Sadoine kept his head bowed down.
This day in which they had experienced
So much loss touched his heart greatly,
For nearby lay their people dead or killed.
There was not a pagan within the square gate
Who did not feel great grief in his heart.
King Carahuel told Sadoine about
The combat, and recounted everything
About the battle, how it had gone
And how it began and ended.
"Ogier routed our people,"
Said Carahuel, "that is a fact.
The Christian people should certainly be honored,
For they are so valorous; their prowess is so perfect
That no people could be found
Who could ever conquer their country."
Said the pagans, "They are people of steel.
Their prowess made us pay too dearly."
Thus these defeated people spoke.
Of this no more will be said.

I will speak of Ogier, who had not forgotten
The work which he had undertaken.

CLXXXXVII

When the Dane left Carahuel
In the way that you have heard,
As quickly as he could he went straight to Charles,
He and his people, who did not delay.
He found his Uncle Namles of the bold heart.
Charles's heart was overjoyed
And so was Namles's when they saw Ogier,
For they had not seen him since
The enemies had turned their backs
Because the Dane had so pursued
The Saracens all around and in the midst of them
That he had killed and humiliated many of them.
He certainly looked like a man who had been attacked,
For all over the armor he wore were
The marks of blows as if they were flowers sown and blooming.
Said the French, "By Saint Remi,
Today this one has certainly deserved
That Charles always consider him a friend."
The good Dane made his way on toward Charles.
"Sire," said he, "I implore your aid on behalf of Carahuel
And of his sweetheart Gloriande as well."
Then Ogier recounted the situation
Just as it was; he told no lies about it,
How they and Sadoine also were
Sheltered together within a gate.
Charles was very glad when he heard about it.
"Ogier," said he, "I assure you in good faith
That, if I can do it, they will certainly be protected,
For Carahuel has done so much for me
That he certainly should be recompensed at this time."
Said Ogier, "Sire, I thank you with all my heart.
But please, sweet Sire, dispatch someone
At once to take them into your care.
It is not far away; as a matter of fact, it is very near here."
"Ogier," said Charles, "certainly, I grant it."

CLXXXXVIII

Good King Charles did not want to hesitate
To complete what Ogier had requested.

In his heart he greatly praised Ogier
That in Carahuel's need Ogier knew how to recompense
What he, King Carahuel, had done by protecting him
And honoring him in his tents at Rome
When King Corsuble wanted to have him killed.
Of this I no longer want to say a word.
Charles had his trumpeters sound their horns
To have his people assembled around him,
For he wanted to lodge in that place
And stay there all the next day.
And Monday he wanted to enter Rome,
Bring the Pope back into the city
And put him back on his holy throne.
The sun was almost setting.
"Namles," said Charles, "you must go,
You and Ogier, and I pray you to hurry,
To save Gloriande and Carahuel
And every one of those, I don't want to omit a one,
That they would like to take with them."
"Sire," said Namles, "I would not think of refusing it,
For they are worth so much that one should certainly strive
To do what should please them."
From there Namles, who was very valiant, set out
With as many people as it pleased him to take.
Why should I draw the matter out any longer?
Duke Namles came to talk to Carahuel.
Near the gate he called to him,
And Carahuel stuck his head
Out of the window; then he saw Ogier
Beside his Uncle Namles, whom one should love
Like one who has no malice.
Immediately Namles pointed out to him
That there was no need to be afraid,
For he came on behalf of Charles to assure him
And all those he wished to protect that
Never would he be imprisoned in the army
Without King Charles delivering him
And that he need do no more than command
And what he wished would be done.
There would be no one who would oppose him.
And Carahuel thanked him for it.

CIC

When Namles had thus spoken to Carahuel
In the way I have briefly told you,
Duke Namles then looked around to see how
He could get the thing done safely.
He had a great many of his people stay there,
Who, whatever their feelings, you should know truly,
Would have refused none of his commands.
Namles entreated them with his whole heart
To guard this gate carefully
So that those within would have no trouble
From those outside nor any danger.
And they promised that all would be thus.
When Namles had done these things,
He said to Ogier, "Handsome nephew, let us go."
Said Ogier, "Uncle, do not be angered in the least.
Understand that I will not move one foot from here.
I will stay here, rest assured,
For I know well that those who are here
Will be more inclined to stay here
With a better will if I am present."
Namles saw clearly that it would not be otherwise
Than in this way despite anyone's entreaties
Nor did he want to forbid him to do
What he was doing from courtesy
So loyally; so he approved it fervently.
Then he told him that he agreed
That he might stay there, and when Ogier heard him,
He thanked his uncle for it profusely.
Namles left there at once
And went to Charles without delay.
Then he recounted how Ogier
Stayed and why and in what way.
"Ah, God," said Charles, "true, omnipotent king,
What perfect, fine and true wisdom now!
Has anyone ever seen a young man
Who had such inspired ideas?"
What can I tell you? Every last one joined
In praising Ogier for staying.
You will not hear any more said about this.
There were a variety of lodgings that night.
There were many people within Rome and outside Rome
Who were not very comfortable.

If I wanted to tell you how well
Those people were lodged that night,
I could certainly spend too long at it.
Many were happy there, and many were sad.
The French amassed a lot of gold and silver.
There were many jewels and precious objects,
For the Saracens had come
So nobly and so very richly provided for
That I would not know how to give any account of it.

CC

This night that I have mentioned to you
Was in the time of the mild season,
In the summertime when the birds sing
And when the woods and meadows and thickets are green.
The weather was so pleasant that night
That there was little one would wish to improve upon.
Charles's people were indeed happy
That God had given them the gift
Of destroying the pagans.
They praised God and his holy name for it.
In Rome were plenty of goods
That the wretched Saracens had put there.
There is no need to describe them in great detail.
Charles and his barons and all the others
Had a great quantity of provisions,
For there was a rich abundance
In the city; and all around and about
Was a great killing of Saracens,
So that they fled from house to house
And many of them were detained in prison.

CCI

In such a manner as you have heard
Was Charles situated that night.
He had many people in many places
Of whom not a one was without arms.
The next day, at dawn,
Charles and his noble barons got up.
Many of his people had already gone to the tents
Where King Corsuble had been lodged
The night before the day that he had fought
Our people, in the way that you know:

The battle has been described to you.
Of this there will be no more discourse.
The French gained so much from all sides
That the poorest had all he could take.
And of the booty that was conquered there
Charles kept nothing that was worth more than two peeled eggs.
All was received and delivered to those
Who had endured the difficulties of battle
And had often risked their lives
Against the people who had abandoned God.
Because Charles, the good king, was such
As you have heard me describe him here,
His people cherished and loved him,
And the pagans feared and dreaded him.
Such a king certainly should be honored,
In whom dwelt intelligence, generosity and goodness,
Honor, prowess, faith and loyalty.
One could surely say, for it is the truth,
That no king was born after him who was better,
That he was the first of the French
And no king was as illustrious as he.
He must surely be justly proclaimed the rightful king
Who was full and overflowing with all goodness.
That day the king rose early in the morning,
Heard mass, and then called
Duke Namles, who was his close friend.
"Namles," said he, "do you know what you will do?
Have Ogier, your good nephew come here;
I am deprived too much of seeing him.
I recommend that you go there yourself.
Bring King Carahuel with him.
Whoever could have him turn
To the law of God and become Christian
Would make all Christianity better for it.
"Sire," said Namles, "I will do your will about this."
He mounted at once; he did not delay.
Duke Thierri, who held the rights to the Ardennes
By inheritance, mounted with him.

CCII

Thierri and Namles the wise
Went together at the same time to Ogier the valiant.
When he saw them, he came toward them immediately.

They dismounted at once, going to him.
"Truly," said Therri, "Namles, here comes
The most valiant young man I have ever seen in my life.
His blows are not at all those of a child.
They are much more like the blows of a giant
Who overwhelms all he strikes.
Some of those who were in the heavy battle
Yesterday could surely bear witness to that."
Namles heard it and smiled, for
Those words were very pleasing to his heart.
And here was Ogier, who came right up in front of him.
He greeted Duke Thierri at once
And then his Uncle Namles, the powerful duke.
Thierri put his arms around him;
With his arm around him, he led him to the gate
Where the Saracens and the Persians were,
Many of whom were very mournful
About the great calamities which had befallen them.
They went together toward the gate talking.
Ogier did not show by his demeanor
That pride or arrogance were in him
Nor was he haughty about anything
Regarding the prowess he had shown in the great battle.
He trailed behind Duke Thierri,
And Duke Thierri always pulled him along.
Because Ogier was behaving so humbly toward him,
He esteemed Ogier highly
And praised him often in his heart;
He entertained these feelings all the way to the gate.

CCIII

When Namles saw his nephew
So well-mannered and wise from courtesy,
It pleased him greatly; then he asked him
How he had passed the time that night.
Said Ogier, "Sire, we have had plenty
From what was found in the city.
Uncle," said he, "the pagans have mistreated
My good warhorse Broiefort the strong.
They have injured him badly in several places.
So my heart is a little grieved about it,
For I do not believe that in Christendom
Or in pagan lands or in any other realm

One could ever again find such a horse.
I believe he knows what the one who sits on him
Is thinking, for so readily does he follow the rider's will."
Thierri and Namles listened to him
Tell that the horse's condition made him so sad.
One of them hit the other laughing,
But of this there will be no more said.
So those who were in charge of him protected him
And afterwards the Saracens were done great harm.
Namles called those of the gate.
Many pagans were already assembled there
At the windows bordered in white marble.
Namles himself told them and indicated to them
That they were to tell Carahuel at once
That King Charles had ordered that he come to his tent.
And they did it; they did not delay.
They told Carahuel all that was said,
And he, like one who has formed a plan in his heart,
Came out of the gate; he stayed there no longer.
It did not seem that he had rested
In the battle where he had been.
His face was pale and livid and swollen,
And it was sliced up and cut open in places.
By his appearance it seemed
That his heart was tormented and full of great suffering.
Thierri and Namles and the Dane
Went toward him; they greeted one another.
Namles addressed Carahuel
And told him that those
Lodged within the gate were completely safe, that
There was no reason to be fearful about this.
King Carahuel thanked them profusely for it.
What can I tell you? Soon the horses
Were ready; they mounted; they turned away from there.
They took King Carahuel to Charles.
Charles honored him as a noble king.
He embraced Ogier.

CCIV

King Charles had a fine and just heart.
He was very grateful to the good Dane
Because he saw him accompanying
King Carahuel and with such heartfelt care

Doing all he could to help him.
It was indeed something that Charles should esteem in Ogier.
If you could have seen Carahuel trail behind
King Charles and entreat him at the proper moment
And wisely humble himself toward him,
You could indeed reasonably have said
That he had nothing but wisdom within him.
Charles told Namles the Bavarian
To command that they have the area emptied,
That no one remain there except the knights.
Thus was it done immediately, without delay.
The Pope, whose name was Desiier,
Came at this time, for Charles of the proud face
Had had him come; and he came there
Without delay, for he could not do otherwise.
Charles himself spoke first of all
To Carahuel, the noble warrior,
About the matter which concerned him.
He knew full well all the points to treat
Which were appropriate to such a thing.
Certainly he told him, if he wanted to be baptized
And believe in God, who governs all,
That he should not hesitate about it;
For he would have him be heir to a great deal of land.
In France there would not be a duke, count or prince
Who would not serve him if he had need of it.
And his soul would have the highest reward
Of Paradise, so great that it cannot be imagined.
If he wanted to engage himself to do this,
Nothing could give him greater pleasure.
Said Carahuel, "Sire, I do not want to lie.
You are offering me an entire gold mark,
But I do not value a penny of it.
I greatly desire to answer you,
For there is no point in drawing it out.
May Mohammed wish to draw my soul to him
When it is separated from my body,
For I would rather allow all my limbs to be cut off
Or be hanged on a gibbet or burnt or drowned
Than to renounce his religion."
When Charles heard him, he lowered his head.
He suffered greatly from this,
For he loved Carahuel with his whole heart.

CCV

When Charlemagne heard Carahuel
Say that he would not abandon his religion
Or believe in another god than Mohammed,
In his heart he suffered very badly.
The Pope himself spoke of it to Carahuel
And used all his understanding to persuade him.
All the difficult points were reasoned out.
He preached to him of the great power of God,
And so did Duke Namles and many others who were there.
The good Dane begged him with hands joined in supplication.
Each one of the princes tried to persuade him,
And each one promised him that he would love him
And that they would thus serve him as he wished.
Each one would deploy body and possessions for him.
King Carahuel looked at the barons
And saw the love that each one showed him.
In his heart he praised them mightily.
He thanked them graciously and appropriately and profusely for it,
But his heart would not change for anything at all.
On the contrary, he told them that he would remain Saracen
All his life and would die Saracen.
No further word was spoken, for his mind was made up.
The French heard him; it pained them greatly.
It weighed upon every one of them.
Charles saw well that he would get no further with it,
But the king would never renege on
His promises because of this; rather, he would fulfill them.
"King Carahuel," said he, "listen to this.
Since thus it is that what has been proposed
Will never move your heart,
It weighs upon me; but you shall be recompensed
For the great good that you have already done Ogier
When Danemon intended to kill him.
I give you a boon; it is that I will give back to you
All your prisoners; not a single one will be left behind
In all the places they are found.
Here is Ogier, who will go with you.
A great number of people will lead you
Throughout the whole army, here and there.
Whatever you wish will be done with the prisoners."
Carahuel did not refuse this gift.
In thanking the king, he bowed.

Then he took his leave, staying there no longer.
He rested very little that day,
For he rode with Ogier throughout the army.
At his wish Ogier delivered each one of
All the prisoners to him; he held back none of them
And reassembled all of them together in the place
Where he had left Gloriande and Sadoine.
Carahuel searched the field of death so thoroughly
That he found King Corsuble and Danemon
And had them brought back with him,
But he hid this information from Gloriande.
The good Dane accompanied him so closely that
He did not stray from him a full foot
But went with him absolutely everywhere.

CCVI

In such a way as you have heard me describe
King Charles delivered to Carahuel
All the prisoners that he could find in his army.
He had them all reassemble in the place
Where it pleased Carahuel to command.
When Carahuel had them reassembled as he wished,
Then he began to thank Ogier profusely
Because he had seen him do all he could for his welfare
And strive with all his heart
To do something to help him.
"Ogier," said he, "I must certainly praise
You, in whose heart dwells nothing bitter,
For you have kept death
From me and many others that you see around me
And from Gloriande, my beloved of the radiant face.
You have protected her from dishonor
From which she could have by no means escaped
If it had not been for you, for which I must love you very much.
But now if you can arrange with Charles
That by grace he would want to grant me so much
That I could return to my country
With the prisoners that he has released to me,
You would certainly have met all my needs."
"Indeed," said Ogier, "I must refuse
Nothing that I know would give you satisfaction.
I will go relate this matter to Charles.
I believe he will certainly want to agree to it.

Now you go rest a little
Within this gate and know without a doubt
That I intend to return to you right away."
Why would I draw out this affair for you?
Ogier went to Charles to recount this thing
Fully and precisely, without forgetting anything
That one should reasonably add,
And Charles said that he certainly wanted to consent to it.

CCVII

When the Dane heard the words
That Charles of the courageous heart said,
He then remounted; he waited no longer.
He made his way straight toward the gate
Where the Saracens had gathered
And reassembled as you have heard.
King Carahuel espied the Dane
And came to the gate without delay,
And the Dane immediately dismounted.
Then he said with a joyful look,
"Charles," said he, "sends me back to you here,
And on his behalf in truth I tell you
That at your will and pleasure you may leave here;
He thus informs you."
When the pagans heard it, it greatly pleased them.
Said Carahuel, "So help me God,
A more courteous king than Charles never lived.
He has a heart filled with loyalty.
Never in my life will I put on a hauberk
Or helmet or headpiece, or at my side a polished sword
To do him harm, I swear it by Mohammed.
When he does this that I have not deserved,
With all my power he will be repaid as much."

CCVIII

When Ogier heard what Carahuel vowed
To Mohammed, his God in whom he believed,
That never would he harm Charles, that
Never against him would he arm himself,
His opinion was that the sentiments were sincere;
And he thought that he would certainly tell it
To King Charles as soon as he saw him.
Then he thought that he would leave

That place, for reason counseled it,
And he would leave the pagans to arrange themselves;
There was no need to guard them any longer,
For the whole army knew
That King Charles guaranteed the safety of all of them
That Carahuel had in his company.
To Carahuel he said that he would go away
To Charles and that he would make known
His will to whomever he wanted,
For he would make every effort
To do whatever would be to his advantage.
And Carahuel said that it certainly seemed
That what he said was true.
Upon his departure, he thanked him mightily
For having striven so much on his behalf
And undertaken to fulfill his needs so wholeheartedly.
"Indeed," said Ogier, "I am certainly right to do this."

CCIX

In such a manner as you have heard
The Dane parted from Carahuel.
He went straight to Charles's tent.
Namles, his uncle, the wise, was there.
Thierri of the Ardennes, who was renowned as a valiant man
Because in him dwelt
Prowess and loyalty,
Hues dou Mans and Joffrois the praised
Were there also and many others with them.
When Ogier entered this tent,
The barons rose toward him, and
Charlemagne took him by the hand.
"Ogier," said he, "sit down beside me.
Although you are young, you are such
That you should by rights be honored."
"Indeed," said Theirri, "he should be loved by all."
When the Dane heard these words,
He was embarrassed and blushed,
Keeping his eyes lowered toward the ground.
Charles saw well that he was disconcerted
By being praised so much in front of him.
Then the king spoke of something else.
"Ogier," said he, "say, what can you tell me
Of Carahuel? How are his wishes being carried out?

Has he reassembled all his prisoners?"
"Yes, indeed, sire, and he has taken
A vow that you would little expect:
It is that he will never take up arms against you,
Nor will he ever harm you in any way."
"Ogier," said Charles,"so help me God,
According to what has been proven to me
I must certainly believe that it is true.
Never in my whole life have I seen a Saracen
That I wanted more to be a Christian
Than he, believe me.
For he is valiant and wise, loyal, and thoughtful
And courteous and well-educated."
Thus spoke King Charles the renowned.
He gazed often and long at the Dane.
He could not get enough of looking at him.
When he had finished heaping praise upon the Dane
And each one had told what he desired to do,
How his affairs would be completely accomplished,
Then he got up and each one rose.
King Charles agreed to this,
That the next day early in the morning
He would have the Pope come; he would be led to Rome
And seated again and put on his throne.
I will stop here with this part of the story.
After supper, before the day had ended
Or the sun completely set,
Each one of the princes returned to his place.
Many a one of them was so tired
That they simply had to rest.
With the king remained Thierri and Namles
And the Dane, who was his close friend.
The night was very clear and mild and pleasant
And the air pure and temperate.
When day had broken the next day,
Charles, the good king, arose.
His custom was to rise early in the morning
And to hear mass as soon as possible.

CCX

The next day, when it was daylight,
Charles, the rightly esteemed king, arose.
When he was ready, he heard mass.

After mass the Pope and all the clergy
Were sent for as planned.
And they came there, those who could easily come;
Not a single one stayed behind.
Each one was in rags and barefoot.
The Pope thanked God greatly
For helping him so much
That on the high throne from which he had been chased away,
This seat which had been granted Saint Peter by God,
He would this day be put back and seated once again.
His vestments were wet with tears
So that it was a pity to behold.
Everyone bore witness that this Pope
Was a valiant man, you should know truly.
Charles came toward him with proper decorum.
Humbling himself greatly before him him at the proper moment,
He said, "Sire, you are very welcome here."
Said the Pope, "Charles, good day.
You have awakened early this morning."
"Sire," said Charles, "I would be so happy
If I saw that you were back on the throne
Of holy church of which you are the head."
Said the Pope, "It is certainly clear that is what you want
Since you have worked so hard for it."

CCXI

On Monday right after the day passed
Following the Saturday that the tumult had taken place
And the battle as I have described to you,
The Pope, whom the Saracens had
Cast out of Rome, re-entered the admirable city,
As I have recounted to you.
That day there were deep sighs
And tears of joy in many places.
Charles walked with the Pope beside him.
The good king Charles, in whom was nothing but goodness,
Was barefoot and dressed in rags, in truth.
On this occasion all his princes were on the road
Right after him, arranged two by two
Along with the barons who were of his realm.
So loudly sang the bishops, monks and abbots
And the clergy, of whom there were plenty,
That there was no heart, no matter how hardened,

That would not have gladly listened
And should not have felt joy and pity because of it.
Right by the Gate of Saint Peter they entered
Rome, arranged in such a manner
As I have told you here.
They went straight to the church of Saint Peter,
And before the church they all stopped.
They kneeled and leaned over on their elbows
And prayed there a long time.
As soon as they got up,
They entered the church, tarrying no longer.
They found the place dirty and laid waste,
For those who had lodged in it for a long time
Cared little about protecting it.
As best they could they tidied up the place
And returned it to cleanliness and order.
The good King Charles of the valiant heart
Led the Pope by the hand
To the throne of Saint Peter the honored.
There he seated and positioned him;
And then he, in very great friendship,
Kissed his foot for the sake of humility;
And the Pope bowed toward him.

CCXII

When Charlemagne, the good, powerful king,
Had placed the Pope back on his throne,
He greatly rejoiced in his heart.
When the Pope had been seated for a while
In this chair that I have described to you,
At a certain moment, he arose.
Immediately, he put on the arms of God.
Then he blessed the place again.
And when it was back to what it was before,
Immediately afterwards—there was no long delay—
The noble Pope sang the mass.
The king of paradise was honored and served
With a glad heart there that day.
When the service was over and done,
Then the king of Saint Denis came forward
To the Pope; he asked leave of him
Most humbly like a wise man of mature reflection,
And the Pope looked him directly in the face.

"Charles," said he, "May God, who was put on the cross
To cast his good friends out of hell,
Reward you on the Day of Judgment
For having undertaken
To harm his enemies."
Then the courageous emperor and his barons
Departed when they had taken leave.

CCXIII

The good King Charles turned away from there.
The Pope did not accompany him
Because the good king would not allow him to.
But when they parted, he sweetly kissed him
And then Charlot, as was appropriate;
And then afterward he commended them to God.
He embraced Duke Namles warmly
And also did not forget Thierri of the Ardennes
Nor the Norman Richars, for he loved him very much.
As for many other barons who were there,
The Pope did what reason dictated.
He hugged and embraced the good Dane,
And then he promised
That never would there be a day when he would fail
To do whatever he could for him as long as he lived.
Graciously and appropriately Ogier thanked him.
As they were going down the road of departure,
The Pope blessed them and prayed with all his heart
To the Lord God, who formed the whole world,
That he protect them as he has the power to do.
Soon afterward he returned to his place,
But by no means would he find it
In the condition he left it when he went away.
Each one of his clerics went back to his own place,
And each one as best he could put it back in order.
There was not a single one, believe me,
Who did not praise God that so much of it was re-established.

CCXIV

When Charlemagne and his barons,
Who held him very dear, came out of the church,
The squires had prepared
The horses and what they needed.
Whichever horses had lost their shoes had them replaced.

They mounted then, not wanting to delay.
Charles, the good king with the proud face,
Went to the Capitol, of course;
For he wanted to take lodging in the place
And stay there and have his people rest.
Why should I draw the matter out for you?
Communally, duke and count and prince,
Both one and the other, sergeant and knight,
All came to lodge within Rome.
The Pope, who was such a fine person,
Had his people sent throughout Rome
To have the churches restored.
The destruction that those devils' henchmen had done
Touched his heart so much
That nothing could have caused him more grief.
About this I do not want to say more, for
I want to shorten the matter for you.
The pagans had a great desire
To return to their lands.
Already they had had ships equipped
On which they would sail straight to Cornet,
And they had almost all their baggage loaded.
King Carahuel had made known to Ogier
That he wanted to depart,
And Ogier came there—he did not wait to be asked twice—
With his uncle, Namles, the good Bavarian.
Duke Thierri, the loyal-hearted of the Ardennes,
And many others that I will not name for you
Came there to protect their possessions,
To guard them from danger
And to accompany them.
King Carahuel, in whom was only wisdom,
Knew how to thank them very appropriately and abundantly.
What can I tell you that you do not know already?
They left the gateway; they did not care to delay.

CCXV

The pagans went out of the gateway together.
King Sadoine's people carried him
On a litter with as much dignity
As they could and with the utmost gentleness.
King Carahuel came first
And the elegant maiden Gloriande.

Ogier came to them at once
And Dukes Namles and Thierri also.
They greeted her, and she wisely
Returned her greeting properly to each of them.
It certainly seemed from her demeanor
That in her heart she had sorrow and torment;
But as she was wise and of good intelligence,
She carried this burden as she should.
Very gently Ogier took her by the hand.
"Ogier," she said, "you have worked on our behalf
With great loyalty and with much generosity,
But we have paid too dearly for
Your great prowess and your great strength.
And nevertheless, so help me Mohammed,
I do not hate you, know this in truth.
It did not work out very well for us.
In fact, it went very badly; but it would have been
Much worse if you had not been there, I know very well."
Said Ogier, "My beauty, to make amends
I would cross the sea to save you
If I could be of any value at all to you;
For in you I find love so abundant
That I praise God omnipotent for it.
I want to be yours so entirely
As to fulfill your every wish as it is
In my power; know this very well."
When Gloriande heard these words,
Sighing, she answered most humbly:
"Sire," said she, "I return to you one hundred thanks."
They came quickly to the Tiber
And entered the ships without long delay.
In taking leave, they did not lose time in discussion.

CCXVI

When Carahuel had gathered his people
At his pleasure and at his command,
He came toward Namles, and gently he implored him
If he pleased, to tell Charles
That he very much appreciated the great courtesy
He had shown him at that time and at other times.
And he asked that he greet on his behalf the noble barons
Who were so perfectly courteous and well-mannered
And who escorted him in such companionship

When he set out to leave Charles's territory.
"By this lord to whom I am subject,
That is Mohammed, to whom I owe all my faith,
I never before in my life saw people
Who were so filled and adorned with all good qualities
Nor so courteous nor so well educated
As Christians are; I will not lie about it.
And they have a lord in whose heart dwells
High prowess fortified with wisdom.
The pagan people have observed this many times.
I would have renounced my faith for love of him
If I had not feared my soul would perish from it."
When Namles heard these words,
He agreed to do it;
And Carahuel thanked him for it graciously.
Then he took leave of the knights
Who were in ranks at the port.
He took leave of Ogier; then he delayed no more.
At the parting, each of the two wept.
He entered the ship where his beloved had entered.
That was Gloriande, the blond, the elegant,
Who was very sad and grief-stricken.
Immediately afterward they raised their sail.
Each one of the ships was ready to go.
Why should I lengthen the matter for you?
Their work was accomplished in such a way
That on the third day their navy arrived
Right at Cornet, an estimable city.
It is a port of ancient origins.
Each one of the ships was unloaded there.

CCXVII

Persians, Saracens and Slavs
Had arrived right at Cornet, a port near the sea.
You should know I have heard said
That Cornet is forty miles from Rome at an accurate count.
They did not want to stay there long.
Immediately they had great ships equipped, and
When they had had their baggage carried onto them,
They boarded them without delay.
On a Saturday, right after daybreak
They raised sail; the weather was beautiful and clear
And the wind so favorable it could not have been better.

Carahuel had the sailors informed and commanded
That he wanted to arrive
Right at the land of Corsuble the baron,
Right at a certain port, Tripoli, I have heard it called.
He would have him and his son buried there.
He had them enshrouded in deerskin
And had them well embalmed.
Why should I prolong the story?
I do not seek to describe their voyage to you.
They arrived at the port which
I mentioned, you may be sure.
Up to this point, Carahuel had concealed
From Gloriande, who was so lovable,
That he had had her father brought back;
But then the first thing he did was to explain to her
What he had done to honor her father
And to preserve her serenity, which he had wanted to guard.
Then Gloriande began to cry
And in her extreme distress to sigh deeply.
For her grief was entirely brought back.
But I will put aside speaking of her grief for now.
If you had seen Corsuble mourned for
Throughout the city and had seen the pagan people
Tear their hair and rip their garments,
You would certainly have said, if you had heard them cry out,
That you had never before seen such great grief displayed.

CCXVIII

Saracens and Persians had arrived
In the kingdom of Syria the great.
They landed at Tripoli.
It is a port to which many merchants
Have returned,
And they are happily settled in that area.
The people of the land were sad
For their lord whom they loved so much
As people should love a valiant lord.
The news spread throughout the land.
Many there had a heavy heart for their lord
And went about greatly lamenting him.
"Ah! Alas!" said they, "where will we turn?
Dead are largesse and honor without arrogance."
They swore to Mohammed, in whom they believed,

That all the kings who held lands in
Pagan domains were not equal to him,
That compared to him, their honor
Was not worth the price of a glove.
For him their hearts were suffering greatly.
But I will speak no further of their grief at this time.
King Carahuel, who had a wise heart,
Had sent for relatives of Corsuble and those
Who were his vassals
From far and wide.
Why should I lengthen the matter for you?
When they had come, he had the
Bodies buried immediately, as was appropriate to do.
Both of them lie still
Right at Tripoli; several have attested to this.

CCXIX

When the pagans had buried King Corsuble
And Danemon as I have recounted to you,
King Carahuel, who had a considerate heart,
And Gloriande, who was so beautiful,
Tarried awhile there in that place.
When they had been there long enough,
They went away to the city of Sour.
All the barons throughout the land,
From far and wide, were asked to come to that place.
And when they were assembled there,
They each and every one rendered homage and fealty
To Gloriande the elegant one;
For no heir of Corsuble other than
She remained; because of this, she held the inheritance.
When all those of the kingdom had paid their respects to her,
As they should have, as I have recounted to you,
And they had sojourned there a little while,
Then all the barons suggested to her
That she take as her husband Carahuel the illustrious;
For thus had her father promised
When he was alive—of this there was no doubt.
Said Gloriande, "If I am able, I shall be happy to fulfill this request,
For in Carahuel one has a king so well proven
To be of great prowess, intelligence, and dependability
That if I had one hundred times more wealth than I have
I would consider that

I had placed myself well,
Body and soul, when I had given it to him."
What more can I tell you? Everyone agreed
To the marriage; not a one was opposed to it.
When the time came, they married one another.
You will not hear me speak further of them,
For more than this I do not know for certain,
Nor how it all ended was not shown to me
At Saint Denis, either by monk or abbot,
Nor would I want to add anything
Except by right of sure authority.
Some people say in truth
That henceforth he became a Christian
And believed in God, the king of majesty,
And she also; that is what many have told.
And may God grant it by his sweet friendship,
And if he ever does good to pagan people,
May it please him to take pity upon them.
For if loyalty is worth anything,
They should be crowned before God.
I say no more about them than
Has been granted thus by the one who gave his body in great pain for us.
I will now speak of King Charles and his barons
Who were happy to be in the city of Rome.

CCXX

You have heard how Carahuel the noble
Left Rome, the well-located city,
He and his sweetheart, the charming young girl,
When they had boarded the ship and the boats
As the story has been recounting
Shortly after Carahuel had left there,
Duke Namles was returning to Charlemagne
As were Duke Thierri and Ogier the wise,
Fagons de Tours and Richars the Norman,
Joffrois d'Anjou, he and Hues dou Mans,
And many others whom I will not now be naming.
I would not know how to describe to you
How sad each one was for Carahuel
That he did not want to be obedient
To the law of God and to his holy commandments.
Many a one of them was there who was praying to God
With joined hands and weeping eyes

That Carahuel would not die an unbeliever.
Charles himself sighed many a great sigh
And was many a time grieving for him.

CCXXI

Charles the illustrious and the baronage
Whom he loved were at Rome.
And he was still so beloved of the barons
That never at any time was anyone called king
Who was esteemed or feared as much by his people.
He stayed in this land until
He had restored to their rightful owners the places
Where God should be served and praised,
For the pagans had disturbed many of them.
When all was done to the satisfaction of many,
Then King Charles departed from this country.
He was accompanied along the route for quite a way by the Pope,
By cardinals, bishops, and abbots;
For certainly the noble king should
By rights have been honored
Who was always inspired to exalt Christianity.
His heart was never tired of this.
Many a great sigh was cast after him, and
He was often commended to the Lord God
By everyone near and far.
"Ah, God," said they, "father of majesty,
Sire, guard and keep this good king for us a long time
If you truly have the power to do it,
For he carries the key to all goodness in his heart."

CCXXII

The Pope rode with the king as far as
Was reasonable and appropriate.
Then when the time came, he turned back.
Upon departing, he kissed King Charles.
Weeping, he prayed to the Lord God
That he would reward the good deeds Charles had done
And protect all those that he loved and would love.
He raised his hand, and then he blessed them,
Commending unto God all of them together.
The good King Charles humbly bowed to him.
In such a manner they parted from one another.
The Pope went back again to Rome,

And Charles's army set out for France.
They often thanked the one who made everything
That they had accomplished their purpose for coming.

CCXXIII

Charles's army returned gladly
Toward sweet France, the noble and beautiful domain.
In this kingdom at that time were such people
Who did not love fine gold or silver or any possession
Whatsoever as much as to make war often against
Those who did not love the omnipotent king.
But this custom now is badly neglected,
For great and small, everyone everywhere
Gives it up
And, really, it is a shame that people do so.
Although this state of affairs has lasted too long,
When it pleases God, it will be otherwise, and
May it please him that it be shortly.
God clearly shows great love
To those whom he has given the will and ability
To undertake his service openly.
So each one should do this with haste,
For one cannot come to it too soon.
Of this I do not wish to speak further.
He who will do good, you may know with certainty,
Will have the reward for it, but
For evil he will also have his payment.
I would delay you too long
If I told you how
Each member of Charles's army came to his home.
They traveled so much and so speedily that
They reached Paris and there they stayed.
They were received and welcomed in a grand manner,
For they had succeeded nobly.

CCXXIV

The noble barons had returned to their country
From the land where they had conquered the high pardon
God has given as a gift to every one of those
Who has dared to take back from others
Possessions which they have unjustly acquired
Through false motives.
If the one who took it falsely does not give it back,

—Why should I hide it?—The knight has taken his journey for nothing.
It would have been better for him to stay at home
Than to tire himself without a reward.
In a few words, I would like to give a little sermon.
He who does not make up for his evil deed
At once and in timely fashion in his lifetime
Can later consider himself a fool.
You have heard of the noble King Charles,
Who was valiant and wise and loyal and a worthy man.
He behaved that way in many a place; that has been attested to.
For this, God made of him his rightful champion
To tear down the false religion of Mohammed
And to exalt his law and his renown;
For he did not want anything to do with the other religion.
His counselors were not lower class boys
Nor people of any base extraction.
As counselors he had Duke Namles,
Duke Thierri, and the good Duke Fagon,
Joffrois d'Anjou and his nephew Hues,
Who held all Le Mans and its surrounding territory,
Duke Richars and the vassal Gui
From Saint Omer, who was a very vailant man,
Hues de Troies and from Langres Oedes.
By such people as I mention to you
Must the king hear and know his royal duties.
If he wants to be of value and of renown,
He must accept nothing from base, deceiving traitors;
For from base people one has bad advice.
One should believe nothing beyond a kernel of truth
In what they say; one should believe only the upright.

CCXXV

Charles of the wise heart was at Paris
With his barons, who were very good men.
They had returned to their country in joy and in health
From the good expedition they had taken,
Of which good must forevermore be spoken;
For they had proven themselves so valiantly
That Christianity is even today the better for it
And always will be; let there be no doubt about it.
The good King Charles's heart was so ruled
By courtesy and thoughtful good sense
That he always had treasured within his heart

To do good; he would not have forgotten it
In one hundred thousand years if he had lived so long.
This appeared clearly when they had returned
From their expedition, as I have described to you
For he gave away so much of his wealth in great abundance,
Lands and fiefs, gold, silver coins,
Horses, jewels, near and far,
So that everyone had some of it, strangers and close friends,
Whatever individual had a rightful claim to it.
About this I want to say briefly the truth:
Charles, the king full of honesty, did so much
That Right was deeply grateful to Largesse.
Many went back to their country
Rich with possessions, full to overflowing with lands;
For if they had stayed in their countries,
Perhaps they never would have won
The renown that many others had earned there
Which would be honored forever.
For those who had taken part
Were wise and well-advised,
For they knew they had avoided laziness.
For in idleness there is nothing but evil.
This was apparent to many who had come back.

CCXXVI

When Charlemagne, the good, powerful king,
Had distributed to the great and the small
His gifts as I have thus described to you,
Each one went back to his country.
Charles then remained a long time at Paris,
Until he had set up his laws
By which right was maintained, for always.
He intended to do so with all his heart.
With him remained Duke Namles the noble
And with him the Ardennois Thierri,
Duke Richars, and Ogier the marquis,
Hues de Troies, and from Saint Omer, Guy.
By such people was Charles served
And his country administered.
It is no wonder if he rose in esteem
When his army was strengthened with such people.
He clearly showed that he was Ogier's friend,
For he gave him abundantly of his possessions

And gave him a great deal of land in the Beauvaisis.
Of this there will be no more said now.
When Charles had completely accomplished his gift-giving,
Had everywhere done and given much
So that he could not rightly be accused
Of any wrongdoing in it,
The desire came to him to go to Aix.
So he did; he did not seek to tarry any longer.
The first day he went to Saint Denis,
And he took two days to go from there to Senlis,
Going only five or six leagues a day.
In this way he reached Cambresis.
Many in the countryside rejoiced with all their hearts
That he had come and were glad and exuberant.
He stayed right at Cambrai fifteen days.

CCXXVII

Charles the rightful king was at Cambrai.
Now I will tell you why he sojourned there.
It was that he wanted to know
How the land was governed.
Within his power he righted wrongs.
The king acted thus throughout his kingdom;
He desired to do right to everyone.
Whenever it concerned the wrongdoer,
He gave him his just deserts according to his deed
So that each one feared to do wrong.
Where the king stopped to sojourn,
Each one came running from all around.
There Ogier first learned that Mahaut was dead,
To whom he had made so much love
In his prison when he could.
Charles saw clearly by his demeanor
That in his heart he felt some kind of wound.
Then Charles told him that he would like to know
Why he was looking like that.
Ogier told him he would hide nothing about it from him.
He told him the whole thing just as it had happened.
And he told him of the child
That he had with Mahaut, and he said many good things
Of the chatelain, as good sense counseled him.
He certainly said that if Mahaut had lived
And that even if he had possessed as much as the king,

He would have willingly taken her as a wife,
For he had agreed with her that if he escaped,
That this is what he would do.
Charles heard it; then he told him that he esteemed him for it
Much more than before and loved him more,
For loyalty demanded he do this.
He was very grateful to the chatelain
Because Ogier had praised him so much.
Then he said he would send for him at once
And he would thank him very much for these things,
And for his love he would repay him
Anytime he needed it.
For these words Ogier greatly thanked
King Charles, for it pleased him very much
That he spoke of the chatelain in such a way.

CCXXVIII

Charles had the chatelain at Saint Omer
Sent for, and without any delay at all
He came to his command, for he should not have neglected to.
Charles welcomed him with whole-hearted joy.
For the kindness he had shown to Ogier
The king thanked him profusely,
As did Duke Namles of Bavaria also.
If you could have seen the good Dane
Humble himself toward him and bow to him just so,
You would certainly have said that he behaved estimably.
Charles began to speak to the chatelain
And said, "Hues, I ask that you
Love Ogier as much as you can.
For in him there is, I can certainly attest to it,
A loyal, wise and upright man.
And know well that he told me the other day
That even if he had my kingdom to govern
Or much more, that he would have taken your daughter
As a wife to exalt his honor;
But she is dead, may God have mercy on her soul!"
Said Ogier, "Sire, may God protect me
From danger in my greatest need,
It is just as I have heard you say."
The chatelain began to weep
When he heard Ogier so affirm
What Charles of the proud face had said.

Said the king, "Hues, do not be troubled,
For I will make your grandson a knight
When he reaches an age that he can bear arms;
And I will make him heir to a great deal of land,
So help me God; do not give it another thought."
The chatelain went to kneel
Before Charles and began to kiss
His foot, without having to be told to do it.
Charles himself started to raise him back up,
For no man ever saw a more courteous
King or prince nor any less pompous.

CCXXIX

The good king Charles gave much heartfelt honor
To the chatelain, for it was right to do so;
For he was valiant and had been a man of prowess for a long time
And was perfectly loyal for as long as he lived.
And King Charles always loved such people.
The good Duke Namles thanked the chatelain
Most fervently for the good qualities that Ogier, his nephew,
Whom he kept in his prison, found in him
When King Charles delivered him to be guarded.
And he told him that he would repay him
If the time for it came, that he would not forget him.
He would put himself and his possessions, he said,
Entirely at his disposal, for never would he fail him
All his life, as long as he should live,
In any way that he could be of value to him.
Duke Thierri told him as much
And so did many other barons who were there.
Because Ogier had praised him highly,
Each one presented himself to serve him.
The chatelain looked at the barons
And did not forget to thank them fittingly.
When the moment came, he asked leave of the king.
The noble king gave him great gifts and riches,
Both to him and all those that he had brought with him.
At the departure Duke Namles kissed him.
Ogier went with him as far as Arras.
From that place he turned back.
At the departure each one wept.
Ogier begged that he take care of
Baudouin his son, and when

The chatelain heard this, he sighed deeply,
For he remembered his daughter Mahaut.
He told Ogier that about this he was never to concern himself
Because with all his heart he would care for him.
Ogier bowed in thanking him for it;
Then he left; he went on back to Cambrai.
In this country King Charles sojourned
As much as pleased him; afterward he left,
Taking the road right toward Aix;
He crossed Hainaut, Brabant, and Hesbaye
And the water of the Meuse on the bridge at Maestricht.
The king did not stop until he reached Aix.
The whole countryside showed great joy,
Each one thanking God that he had come.

CCXXX

Charles was at Aix, where he had often been;
For the king always loved this place.
All his life he held it very dear.
I have forgotten to tell you a little something
That I should not have left unsaid,
But I will very soon have set it to rights.
Before those were all reassembled at Paris
Who had been on the glorious expedition,
The queen of Hungary had sent word
To King Charles that Gaufroi in fact
Had acted toward her
So that all her relatives and friends
Should always be grateful to him.
For the Coumains had fought her people;
They had entered her country by force,
And they could have destroyed a great part of it;
But the Dane had guarded the country
And defended it against them, and had protected it
So that they had not lost the worth of a peeled egg,
And so many Coumains were killed
That they had not recovered for a very long time.
And as to how his messengers were dealt with
When their beards were cut to humiliate them,
Charles first learned there for certain
That she who had insulted him was dead.
In a letter brought to him,
On his aunt's behalf it was described

How the duchess had done her mischief by treachery.
Charles and those of whom I have spoken to you
Expressed great joy at this news.
Charles many times recalled it to Ogier
And often thanked and hugged him.
And Ogier praised God for it with all his heart.
Charles had not been at Aix very long
When he sent for Gauffois to come to his kingdom
And he came there; he did not delay.
And Charles honored him greatly with all his heart
And fêted him with a good will.
Ogier had ridden out to meet his father
Two days before he would have arrived
Like one who had a wise and well-governed heart
And had excellent qualities in all respects.
His father looked at him with a glad heart
Because he knew the selflessness of his deeds,
And how King Charles had knighted him
And for his love had pardoned his misdeed.

CCXXXI

In such a manner as I have told you
Gauffrois came from his country to Charlemagne, and
The king honored and welcomed him.
Charles, the king of Saint Denis, showed well
That he loved him and his son.
Duke Namles and many others expressed great joy;
None were slow to do so.
Before the king had left that place,
The noble queen of Hungary and
One of her sons named Henri came
To see Charles; she was eager to do it.
Henri, not yet sixteen years old,
Was tall and well-built for his age,
Very handsome and courteous and well brought up.
Charles the powerful was very joyous;
He was happy and glad that they had come.

CCXXXII

The good King Charles, who was so admirable,
Expressed whole-hearted joy that his aunt had come.
When the queen saw Charles of the proud face
That she loved so much and held so dear,

She began to weep from sheer joy:
"Sire," said she, "I must certainly thank God
When I see you returned safe and sound
From where so many warriors of prowess had gathered
Who do not believe in God, the just father.
You have certainly destroyed their great pride
And confounded and abased their arrogance
Which the holy church surely needed."
"Aunt," said Charles, "you should know without any doubt
That God has done it to exalt his honor."
Then Charles went to embrace his aunt;
His nephew Henri, to whom there was nothing
More to teach, knelt before him.
The noble king asked him to get up
And then went and hugged him and kissed him.
Now I will tell you about Namles the Bavarian,
He whose sense profited many people.
He was of the opinion that one could
Well arrange such a marriage as should
Be prized between Ogier's sister and Henri.
He went at once to King Charles to speak to him about it.
As soon as Charles heard the thing spoken of,
He greatly desired that it would happen.
The king himself went to talk to his aunt about it.
He and Duke Namles did not want to delay.
Constance said there was no need to deliberate about it;
Since it pleased the king, certainly she should grant
That her son have the daughter of such a prince
As was Gauffrois, that one could not wish
For a better knight than he was.

CCXXXIII

When Charles heard his aunt speak
In such a manner as you have heard me describe,
He saw well that she would want to agree to all
That it would please him to command.
Then the king began to suggest
That she and Gauffrois should marry
And that certainly the two marriages could be done together
And that it would be a thing that one should surely praise,
Both one and the other, in order to set things aright.
He began at once to elaborate on this to his aunt,
And the queen began to think a little.

Sighing, she said that she did not want to refuse
Anything that he wanted to arrange.
"Dame," said Namles, "may God save me,
No one could find a more loyal prince
Than is Gauffrois, anywhere in the world, beyond any seas.
And his peers in prowess are few and far between."
"Namles," she said, "it certainly seems so to me."
King Charles had Gauffrois sent for,
Him and Ogier; and without delay they
Came to the king; they did not want to linger.
Graciously and appropriately they greeted him.
Charles and Namles went to take them
Into a room to counsel them
About what was easy for them.
Charles began to describe to them the idea
About the marriages that he wanted to arrange.
Said Gauffrois, "Sire, I should not disagree about it;
Rather I will be thankful to you for the rest of my days.
I agree to both marriages."
Why should I prolong the story?
Among them they agreed so quickly
That before they departed from one another there
What Gauffrois wanted more than anything was to marry Constance.

CCXXXIV

When Charles had made the arrangement
Of the marriages exactly as he desired,
He told Gauffrois to announce publicly
That he was having his daughter come there at once.
Said Gauffrois, "Sire, at your command."
"Indeed," said Ogier, "I will go, in fact,
And bring her back, if I can, shortly."
"Certainly," said Charles, "and I agree to it completely.
You always have the desire to do
What is appropriate, without any prompting."
At this word Ogier took leave of the king
And of Constance, the elegant queen,
And of his father and his uncle also.
If I spoke to you now at length
About their plans and arrangements,
It would take much too long.
For that reason I will pass lightly on beyond that.
Of Ogier's part I will speak as briefly

And shortly as possible.
He arrived quickly in Denmark, where
His sister was delighted to see him
And hugged and kissed him often.
The people looked upon him as a great marvel
Because of his prowess, of which the renown
Extended further than had ever been for a man of his youth.
They thanked God the father omnipotent
That he had proven himself in such a way.
His friends and relatives, of whom he had
Many in many places, expressed great joy over him.
To his sister he explained courteously
His purpose for coming and how it came to be,
And the young girl answered
As a woman of understanding should respond,
In whom sense has taken up residence.
They did so well in completely arranging
What they had to do that nothing was lacking.

CCXXXV

When Ogier had arranged the matter
Beautifully and rightly and in perfect order,
They rode out with a great number of people
Of renown one morning,
He and his sister, Flandrine the wise.
The young woman was often commended
To the Lord God, for she was loved by all.
They did not stop until they reached Aix.
Riding out toward them more than a full league
Came Namles, who kissed her and hugged her.
Strangers and friends rode out to meet them;
Gauffrois came there as did those of his country;
Duke Thierri of cherished memory
And Duke Namles accompanied Flandrine on her right.
The palfrey on which she was mounted
Was whiter than snow on ice;
Nobly she sat on the padded saddle,
Which was very richly fashioned.
The bridle was of gold, of very fine work.
I will not describe to you at length
The rich fabric in which she was dressed.
The young woman, who was more beautiful than a fairy,
Was looked upon by all with great amazement.

She was whiter than any meadow flower
And redder than the dewy rose.
Of this there will be no further discussion.
The beauty was taken before Charles,
Who honored her greatly from his heart.
What more can I tell you? She was taken to the church
To be married, when she was appropriately dressed for it.
Her hair was blond, perfectly ornamented with gold filaments.
The young woman had put on her head
A very richly worked crown,
Which was encircled by rubies.
The occasion was so done and arranged
That Gauffrois married the queen
Who was the recognized lady of Hungary;
Henri married Flandrine, whose future was bright.
Great was the celebration of their marriage.
Nothing at all was forgotten
That was appropriate to the arrangements of a royal celebration.

CCXXXVI

The weddings were as you have heard,
And indeed you may be sure
That all were covered with honor on all sides
Since King Charles was involved in it.
He always recognized the importance of honor;
For he could never get his fill of it,
So great was his will to do it.
About this I will make no further remarks.
The king stayed at Aix as long as he pleased,
Afterward he turned from this place
And went forthwith straight to Cologne.
There Gauffrois parted from King Charles,
Constance also and Henri the wise,
Flandrine, in whom all goodness dwelt
And courtesy and perfect beauty.
Each one commended the others to God.
Of their taking leave, how it was arranged
With King Charles or how it was agreed upon,
For now I will say no more.
So perfectly was it done and taken and given
That never were any obligations overlooked.
Ogier stayed with King Charles,

For he would have separated from him unwillingly.
Here at this place is this book ended
Which is called *Ogier's Youth*.
May God will that it be finished
In such a manner that King Adan
By whom it is rhymed cannot be blamed.

CCXXXVII

You have heard of Charles the warrior
And of Namles his loyal counselor,
Of Duke Thierri of the Ardennes with the pure heart
And of many others about whom one must certainly pray
To the Lord God who has all to govern
That it please him to save their souls,
For they have shown well that they desired
To serve him when he had need of it.
Of this story I no longer seek to speak.
May God grant that another may wish to take it up,
Who can strive to bring it to completion,
For at this place it pleases me to leave it.
Subsequently, the good Dane made many an attack
In many places upon the enemy.
Here we take leave of Ogier's youth,
Which is such, as all will testify,
That one should evermore hold his deeds in high esteem
And make them known, to teach good people
The right path, whose value can never be underestimated,
For in it, one can—you should know without a doubt—
Earn honor and the love of God.
It is good to keep to the way and the path
Where one can earn the reward
Of having his soul accompany those
Who let themselves be martyred for God.
I want to send this book to Queen
Marie, whom may Jesus direct
To keep to this road without straying.
May God grant that here it ends!
Here ends Ogier's Youth.

Notes

Page 1: The first editor of *La Chevalerie*, Joseph Barrois, in 1842 attributed the work to Raimbert de Paris. However, scholars believe that the five extant manuscripts of the work were preceded by a lost work; and later editors believe that Raimbert (whose name appears on two of the manuscripts, written it is thought, on one by a later hand than Raimbert's) may have simply been reworking the story as did Adenet.

Pages 1 and 2: The courts of Brabant and Flanders maintained cordial relations (*Biographie*, 20). In 1273 Jean I, who became duke of Brabant after his father's death, married one of Gui de Dampierre's daughters (17).

Page 2: Henry discusses and reproduces many of these records in his *Biographie d'Adenet*.

Page 4: The closeness between an uncle and his nephew, his sister's son, is traditional in the *chanson de geste*. In *La Chanson de Roland*, Roland is the nephew of Charlemagne. The medieval man could be sure that his sister's son was his own blood kin.

Page 5: Of course, a highly esteemed opponent makes a victory over him that much more glorious.

Pages 10–12: Various scholars have offered information and conjectures about whether the *Danois* or "Dane" of the name Ogier le Danois indicates he was from Denmark. Adenet, of course, makes Denmark Ogier's home. The reader may smile a little at this concern for the origin of Ogier's epithet *le Danois* since we cannot establish a clear and complete correspondence between an historical person and the hero of imaginative literature. Nevertheless, researchers have followed some interesting etymological, historical and literary pathways in considering this question.

For example, citing sources, Jacques Barrois, who in 1812 published an edition of *La Chevalerie Ogier* (which, as we note in the introduction, is probably in its first part Adenet's principal source for *Enfances*) says that the father of Ogier, Geoffroy, was a "*preux*," or worthy and noble warrior, of Charlemagne and was called Geoffroy *de Deanemarche*, which Barrois says is a contraction or shortening of *Ardenemarche*. He goes on to tell us that *arden* was the equivalent of *dean*, which for the ancient Gauls and Bretons meant forest. The English, Barrois continues, translated "*deane-forest*" and "*arden-forest*" into Latin by the words *silva danica*. Therefore, he reasons, people said *deanois* or *danois* for *ardenois, ardinois*; and the forest itself was the *silva arduenna*. Going further into the origins of the word *Ardennes,* Barrois says that *ardu* comes from the Latin *arduus,* which itself comes from two Greek words which mean "difficult, painful or troublesome, steep." Therefore, the Gaulois word *dean*, modified by the Latin *arduus*, becomes *ardean*, *arduan*, etc. Barrois informs us that the *Arduenne* forest was the end-point of the Low Countries and bordered the great *Hercynienne* forest to the east. Furthermore, He states that *dan* or *dean* in Celtic had several meanings, in both adjectival and noun forms: "forest, valley, deep, steep." From these meanings he draws the conclusion that *Danois* could have meant forester. [1]

Barrois's detailed etymological discussion seems motivated by his apparently earnest belief that Ogier was indeed an historical character, his lineage traced in the *Chronique Mouskés* (iv), a rhymed thirteenth-century account of French history by Philippe Mousket, the factual accuracy of which is now not unquestioned. At any rate, Barrois is eager to establish (or re-establish, as he says) Ogier as French, not Danish (i-ii).

Rita Lejeune, after dicussing the Frankish origins of the name Ogier (the root forms, she tells us, mean rich [or noble] lance—an interesting link, coincidentally perhaps, to the characterization of the legendary figure) gives some details connecting a ninth-century Autcharius or Otgarius, the archbishop of Mayence, (she wonders if he could be a grandson of our hero) with Harold II, who called himself king of the Danes, and whom the archbishop baptized in 826. Lejeune wonders if those connections somehow initiated, by confusion or suggestion, our Ogier's epithet *le Danois*.[2]

Jacques Chocheyras observes that certain events, relationships and even names in the *Chanson de Roland* (where, as mentioned earlier, Ogier's name first appears) are strongly reminiscent of certain elements in Norman/Viking epics and that the latter may have influenced the development of the *Chanson de Roland*, of which different versions exist. [3] Patricia Harris Stäblein mentions mid-twelfth-century Norman politics as important in the larger role Ogier plays in the second part of the *Chanson de Roland* as compared to the first and points to

[1] Raimbert de Paris, *La Chevalerie Ogier de Danemarche*, ed. Jacques Barrois, vol. 1, Romans des Douze Pairs de France, VIII (Paris: Techener, 1812) 2 vols. Repr. University of Michigan Librairies Collection, ii-iii.

[2] Rita Lejeune, *Recherches sur le thème: les chansons de geste et l'histo*ire, Bibliothèque de la Faculté de Philosophie et Lettres de l'Université de Liège, Fascicule CVIII (Paris: Société d'Édition Les Belles Lettres, 1948), 91–93.

[3] Jacques Chocheyras, "Les Légendes épiques du Danemark (VIIIe-Xe siècles) et les origins de la chanson de geste," *Olifant* 18.3–4 (1993), 290–302.

the work of Joseph Duggan on the Baligant episode.[4] These kinds of commentary argue for a reference to Denmark in the *Danois* of Ogier's name.

Page 16: Henry tells us that Manuscript D was at one point in the library of Charles V, Holy Roman Emperor (*La Tradition Manuscrite*, 103). Manuscript F was written for, or at least belonged to, Gui de Dampierre's son, Jean I, Count of Namur from 1298 to 1330 (107).

The numbers in bold at the beginning of each item below refer to line numbers in the translation.

1: The first line reads in Old French as follows: "Bien doit chascuns son afaire arreer." The *chascuns* means each one or everyone. However, I have chosen to translate the word as "we" to avoid the awkwardness of gendered possessive adjectives in that line and the next.

2: In the Old French, this line reads as follows: "Aumosnes est dou bien amonester." Adenet plays here with the sounds of the words *aumosnes* (alms, charity) and *amonester* (to encourage), which have similar sounds but different meanings. The translation, "To give alms is to encourage good," loses this clever touch.

24: "King Adam" refers to the poet Adenet. Henry says his formal name would be Adam or Adan. Adenet would have been a diminuitive used by the household. Henry cites a record the clerk Makel wrote using the name *adenet* (no capital letter), which Makel then marked out to write "adan le menestrel" since he was writing a formal document (*Biographie*, 48).

40, 778, 919, 964, 1247, 4680, 4995, 5102, 5523, 5526, 5536, 6060, 7381, 7635, 8015: Used in several contexts in the poem, the name Saint-Denis refers to the abbey that became the repository of the official annals of the kings and the kingdom of France. After the seventh-century Merovingian King Dagobert bequeathed his library to the abbey and had himself buried there, Saint-Denis was considered the royal abbey and basilica. Subsequent kings, Charlemagne especially, continued rich donations to the abbey's library, school and *scriptorium*.[5] The poet claims to get his information from Saint-Denis because of its prestige as a center of knowledge (lines **40, 4680, 4995, 7635**).

The abbey also kept the standard that French kings carried into battle. The poem refers many times and with great pride and reverence to this standard (lines **659, 778, 919, 964, 1247, 5102, 5523, 5526, 5536**) and speaks twice of Char-

[4] Patricia Harris Stäblein, "Patterns of Textual Shift and the Alien Hero: Ogier the Dane in the Europeanization of the Old French Epic," *Olifant* 11.3–4 (1986), 58.

[5] Donatella Nebbiai-Dalla Guarda, *La Bibliothèque de l'abbaye de Saint-Denis en France du IXe au XVIIIe siècle* (Paris: Éditions du Centre National de la Recherche Scientifique, 1985), 17–50.

lemagne as the "king of Saint-Denis" (lines **7381** and **8015**). Once (line **6060**) Charlemagne uses Saint-Denis as a battle cry just after his customary "Montjoie!"

Most of the kings of France are buried within the abbey of Saint-Denis; their stone effigies lie atop their tombs. Saint Denis, the person, a missionary to Paris, is considered its first bishop. He was martyred in Paris in the year 258 by some of the inhabitants and was said to have carried his severed head two miles up to Montmartre.[6]

Saint-Denis is also the name given to the northern suburb of Paris where the abbey is located.

47: Henry observes that the poet claims a monk of Saint-Denis named Nicolas as his source for the story of *Buevon de Conmarchis*, that Nicolas presumably being the same person as the Nicolas de Rains of this line; but Henry cautions the reader that these assertions may not be fact. Medieval convention had the poet solemnly insist upon some authentic-sounding source.[7]

50, 1363, 2209: Saint Omer, for whom a town in northern France is named, was born about 600 into a noble family in Switzerland. After the death of his mother, he and his father entered the abbey of Luxeuil. Having distinguished himself in his studies of scripture, he was chosen by King Dagobert as bishop of Thérouanne, which was in the territory of the Morini in Neustria. With assistants from Luxeuil, Saint Omer was able to bring the Morini back to Christianity. His efforts were the third attempt to Christianize the Morini. Saint Omer built two churches and a monastery.[8]

249–250: William of Orange is the hero of *La Chanson de Guillaume*, one of the earliest *chansons de geste* (mid-twelfth century) and protagonist of a cycle of *chansons de geste*. He fought Saracens in southern France.

252: The term *targe*, translated *buckler*, recurs in many lines throughout the work. It usually refers to a small, round shield.

425, 928, 1696: Saint Richier (Riquier), who was born near Amiens at Celles, protected some Irish missionaries from people who would harm them although he himself was pagan. Having then received instruction from the missionaries, he became a priest himself. He founded a monastery at Celles after spending several years in England preaching. Renowned as a preacher, he spoke sternly to King Dagobert and other powerful people. Eventually, he resigned his position

[7] Adenet le Roi, *Beuvon de Conmarchis*, ed. Albert Henry (Bruges: Rijksuniversiteit Te Gent, 1953), 164.

as abbot of the monastery and lived as a hermit at Forest-Moütier, where he died April 26, 645.[9]

512, 576, 5045, 5088, 5513, 5584, 5862, 5948, 6355, 6385, 6393 7400, 7659, 7767, 7821: For information about Richars (Richard) of Normandy, Henry in his glossary to *Les Enfances* refers us to volume four of Joseph Bédier's *Les Légendes Épiques*, the first chapter of which is entitled (my translations) "Richard of Normandie in the *chansons de geste*." Bédier identifies Richard as "the duke of Normandy, son of William Long-Sword [Guillaume Longue-Épée], and grandson of Rollo [Rollon]" (*Les Légendes Épiques*, 4:1). Bédier says Richard appears in almost all the *chansons de geste* and that his role varies, but that he is never well-developed as a character (4:1–5). He ruled Normandy from 943–996; yet he appears in *chansons de geste* set in the time of Charlemagne, who died in 814 (4: 6–7). In volume four's first chapter, Bédier relates what is known about Richard in history and legend. Henry also refers us at the beginning of his glossary to *Enfances* to the work of E. Langlois, *Table des noms propres de toute nature compris dans les chansons de geste imprimées* [*Table of proper names of all types in the* chansons de geste *which have been printed*), Paris, 1904. A more recent source is André Moisan's multi-volume *Répertoire des noms propres de personnes et lieux cités dans les chansons de geste françaises et les oeuvres étrangères dérivées*, Librairie Droz, 1986. This work gives names of persons and places not only in the French *chansons de geste* but also in the foreign works derived from them. Please see further in the notes for a separate entry for line **5045**.

564, 616, 702: Henry tells us that traveling up through the Italian peninsula on his way back home from the crusade, Gui and his entourage stopped at Viterbe and stayed there from March 9 to April 2 of 1271. The cardinals were electing a Pope at Viterbe, and Gui took part in the intrigues that delayed the election (*Biographie*, 21). Henry also notes that in lines beginning with 698, Charles leaves Viterbe one morning and arrivies at Sutri in the evening. Gui also makes that journey in a day (44, note 2d).

698, 4430: Henry's glossary says *Sutri* is 45 kilometers north of Rome (*Enfances*, 380).

760, 3510, 3810, 4750, 5894, 6150: Henry's glossary identifies *Achopars* as "pagan people" *(Enfances*, 375).

760, 1250, 1813, 3802, 5548: Like the *Achopars*, the *Lutis* are "pagan people" according to Henry's glossary (379).

796, 1297, 2233, 3038: *Saint Vincent* (d. 303) refers to Vincent of Saragossa, who died a martyr after several bouts of torture during the persecutions of Diocletian

[9] David Hugh Farmer, *The Oxford Dictionary of Saints* (Oxford: Oxford University Press, 1978), 343.

and Maximian. A deacon, he had been trained by Valerius, the bishop of Saragossa (*Oxford. . . Saints*, 391).

814 ff.: Henry offers this information: "On the cowardice of Lombards, frequent theme of the *chansons de geste*, cf. J. Bédier, *Les Légendes Épiques,* II, 209" (*Enfances*, 344). Bédier, on pages 206 to 209 of the volume Henry cites, says that legends have Charlemagne humiliating the Lombards after defeating them and that epic characters remind them of their humiliation sneeringly. He also cites a little story in which a Lombard armed from head to toe goes to attack a slug and says that Lombard characters are usually comic in the *chansons de geste*. More recent sources elaborate on the nuances in the presentation of Lombards in the *chansons de geste*. (See the articles cited in the bibliography by R. M. Ruggieri and H. Krauss.)

834, 3095: Adenet's narrators tend to become irritated with characters they interpret as evil and will sometimes curse them, as here. This tendency is especially prevalent in *Berte aus grans piés*, in which "evil" characters play large parts.

975–976; 4820–4821; 4837, 5029, 5046, 5072, 5133, 5161: The French word *vert*, which means green, is used in English heraldry designations. *Gules* means red; *bordure*, border. Heraldic phrases often place adjectives after their nouns, as in these lines. A *bezant* was a coin-shaped gold piece, which was named for a gold coin from Constantinople or Byzantium.[10]

1045; 5160: A *quarterly shield*, another term from heraldry, is one divided into quarters (482–85).

1086, 2507, 2716: Saint Symon, who was an apostle but not the same one as Simon Peter, went on missions to Egypt and Persia, where he and Saint Jude were martyred on the same day (*Lives,* 441).

1224: The word *broigne*, translated as *cuirass*, appears here and in many other lines. Grant Uden defines it as "armour for the body, breast and back, buckled or strapped together."[11]

1250, 1813, 3258, 3802, 7979, 7985: The *Coumains* are "pagan people" according to Henry's glossary (*Enfances,* 377).

1275: Saint Clement died in 101, having been pope from 91 to about 101. He is famous for a letter sent in 96 to the church at Corinth, directing them, without their having requested his guidance, to re-instate some elders who had been deposed and to exile the younger members who had deposed them. These actions

[10] Henry Gough and James Parker, *A Glossary of Terms Used in Heraldry* (Oxford and London: James Parker & Co., 1894; Republished by Gale Research Co., 1966), 59.

[11] Grant Uden, *A Dictionary of Chivalry* (Middlesex, England: Kestrel Books, 1968), 67.

seem modeled after Roman examples of governance and set a precedent in church authority. Legend unsupported by fact has him martyred in Crimea, where he had gone to preach and was forced to labor in the mines and where he drowned after being thrown into the Black Sea with an anchor around his neck. His body and the anchor were claimed to have been recovered in the ninth century. The relics were taken to Rome and buried in the church that bears his name and that sits, according to tradition, where his house was (*The Lives of Saints*, 472–73).

1433: The Saracen messenger refers to Carahuel's troops as *pagan*, a slip in point of view by Adenet's narrator and a mistake not uncommon in *chansons de geste*.

1523: The poem shows ignorance about the religion of the Muslim opponents. Line 1523 refers to "their gods, Mohammed and Cahu." These two names continue to be linked in lines 2360, 3941, 4742, 4890, 5799. Line 2854 adds Tervagan to the list of supposed deities; line 4788 refers to the adversaries as "the people of Apollo" and line 5358 speaks of "the people of Pharaoh." *Chansons de geste* traditionally ascribe various gods to the Saracens, a term which includes all non-Christians.

1661: Appearing here and in many other lines, the word *hauberk*, according to Grant Uden, means "a long coat of mail, almost knee-length" (*A Dictionary of Chivalry*, 116).

1755–1758: Henry tells us that "Marados de Bronsal is known only by this passage. Did Adenet make up his conflict with Garin d'Anseüne, son of Ameri de Narbonne, or is he referring to a lost poem" (*Enfances,* 347)?

1813, 3802, 6130: In his glossary Henry identifies the word *Amoravis* as denoting "pagan people" (375).

1833 ff.: Charlot's conduct in this battle may be meant to suggest lack of judgment, as it surely does in his remonstrances about Ogier's single combat with Carahuel. Charlot acts as a foil to Ogier but also depicts an impulsiveness that in the second part of *La Chevalerie Ogier* leads to Charlot's rash violence against Ogier's son Baudouin.

2010, 2282: In these lines the character taps his tooth with his finger to confirm his intention, to affirm the truth of what he says; and in line 3185, Carahuel refers to his having tapped his tooth earlier to confirm his good faith. In today's usage this gesture means the listener is offering either an insult, an expression of vengeance, or a refusal.[12] However, Henry refers to a source that says schoolchildren in Gand tapped their teeth to mean what they said was true at the turn of the twentieth century (*Enfances*, 350).

---

12 Genviève Calbris, *The Semiotics of French Gestures*, trans. Owen Doyle (Bloomington: University of Indiana Press, 1990), 20, 25, 161.

2017: The poem mentions the day of the week, Sunday, when the combat on the island takes place. In several other lines, **3359, 5889, 6822, 7327, and 7328**, days of the week are also specified: Monday, Wednesday, Saturday. This practice, which of course, helps makes the event described seem factual, is reminiscent of the frequent mention of days of the week in *La Chanson de Guillaume* (see the note to lines 249–250). To cite a few examples from *Guillaume*, line 836 reads, "Lunsdi al vespre" ("Monday in the evening"); lines 1120–1121 read, "Cele bataille durad tut un lundi/ E al demain e tresqu'a mecresdi." ("This battle lasted all of a Monday / And into the next day and until Wednesday"); line 1208 reads "Joesdi al vespre" ("Tuesday in the evening").[13]

2119, 3260, 6538, 7573: Henry's glossary defines *Surie* as "Syria, Saracen kingdom of Corsuble" (*Enfances*, 381).

2120; 2121: In Henry's glossary *Nubie* is "one of Corsuble's African kingdoms" (379); *Boucidant* is "one of Corsuble's Saracen kingdoms" (376).

2156–2157: Note Charles's humorous use of litotes here.

2194, 2383, 2494: Henry says *Valcler* is an "island near Rome invented by Adenet" (*Biographie*. 44, note 2 d).

2219: "The French began to hit one another" [as athletes do in manly play].

2312: "Without danger there can be no honor in arms." Compare the line in Corneille's *Le Cid*, "À vaincre sans peril on triomphe sans gloire"[14] (Act II, scene 2, line 434). (To conquer without danger is to triumph without glory.")

2492: *Hesbaye* is a Belgian province bordering Brabant.

2562: The position described here in equestrian terms is called "two point" or "jumping position," according to Charles E. Moore, who raises thoroughbred horses in Kentucky. I am endebted to Mr. Moore and to veterinarian (and president of University of Tennessee sytems) Dr. Joseph Dipietro for answeres to questions about horse anatomy and physiology, especially as suggested by wounds to horses in *Enfances*.

2654: *Fretty argent* is a heraldry term meaning crisscrossed in silver (*A Glossary . . . Heraldry*, 276).

2985: This line, like the occasional line in subjunctive mood, is left in present tense to avoid awkwardness. The present tense also serves to heighten the suspense and drama of the moment.

---

[13] *La Chanson de Guillaume*, 2 vols., ed. Duncan McMillan, Société des Anciens Textes Français (Paris: A. et J. Picard, 1949), 1:38, 49, 53.

[14] Corneille, Pierre, *Le Cid*, eds. L. Lejealle and J. Dubois (Paris: Librairie Larousse, 1959), 49.

3223: The expression "with his right hand" here apparently means "in good faith."

3262: Henry identifies *Aumarie* as a "Saracen kingdom" (*Enfances*, 375).

4709: Adenet is speaking metaphorically and sarcastically here.

4820; 5144: The heraldry term *semé* means sown with or scattered over. Heraldry uses the prepositon *of* after *semé* (*A Glossary . . . of Heraldry*, 527).

4835; 5152: The heraldry term *bendy* in the terms *bendy or and sable* and *bendy or and azure* refers to diagonal bands across a shield. The *or* means gold and the *sable*, black.[15]

5004–5006: According to Gérard Brault, who writes extensively about heraldry in Adenet's works, Adenet invented this coat of arms for Charlemagne using the time-honored eagle symbol of the Holy Roman Empire and the French field of azure sown with gold *fleurs-de- lis.*[16] Brault says Adenet invented many of the coats of arms described in *Enfances* and that Adenet had a great influence on heraldry (147). The coat of arms he imagines for Charlemagne was hugely popular and appeared on many forms of art in the Middle Ages (144). Line 5004 in the Old French reads as follows: "Armes parties d'or et d'azur portoit," signifying by the word *parties* that the coat of arms was divided in some way (in this case, between the color gold and the color azure) (*A Glossary. . . of Heraldry*, 444–447). My translation does not reflect that *parties* is probably used here in its heraldic meaning since Adenet was so important in devising heraldry. A heraldic translation would probably word the line in a very particular way, using the word *per* after the heraldic word *party*. One who is extremely well-versed in heraldic tradition is needed to determine proper heraldic wording here. Those further interested in heraldry in *Enfances* and Adenet's contributions would profit from consulting the other works of Gérard J. Brault listed in the bibliography.

5045–5046; 5082–5083: Lines **5045–5046** read as follows in the Old French: "De Normandie portoit li dux Richars/ L'escu de gueules; s'i ot d'or dues liepars;" which I have translated as follows: "From Normandy Duke Richard carried/ A shield of gules; it had two gold leopards." *Boutell's Heraldry* tells us that a conventionally drawn lion was an early heraldic emblem and a perennially popular one, with the lion drawn, as time passed, in various positions to distinguish one coat of arms from another (64). "The early heralds considered a lion walking and looking about him to be behaving like a leopard, and they consequently blazoned him as a *lion-leopardé*, or merely as a leopard, though they always drew him as a

[15] J. P. Brooke-Little, Reviser, *Boutell's Heraldry* (London: Frederick Warne, 1983), 33.

[16] Gérard Brault, "Adenet le Roi et l'héraldique médiévale," *Olifant* 25.1–2 (2006), 144.

stylized lion without spots or other leopard-like characteristics. So it is that the lions of England were sometimes blazoned as leopards. They are now termed *lions passant guardant*" (65). Lines **5082–5083** read in the Old French as follows: "Armes portoit cointes et acesmans, /Verdes, s'ot deus liepars d'or passans." My translation reads as follows: "He carried elegant, ornamented arms,/Vert, with two gold leopards passant." The *passant* indicates these leopards were depicted as "walking, three paws on the ground" (65). The use of the word *leopards* suggests the early date of Adenet's ventures into the traditions of chivalry. The word *guardant*, by the way, means the animal was looking at the observer (66)

5064: The term *falchion* refers to a short, wide sword (*Dictionary. . .Chivarlry*, 86).

5072: A *label* is a small bar with hanging pendants attached, usually three of them. A younger son wears them to distinguish him from his older brother during their father's lifetime (*A Glossary. . .of Heraldry*, 359).

5117 ff.: Henry has a note about the arms of the first duke of Brabant, Godefroi the Bearded, saying that Adenet is flattering the house of Brabant by having them descend from Thierri d'Ardennes. Henry reports that Godefroid the Bearded, who died in 1139, was buried at the abbey of Afflighem (Haflenguien), but a fire in 1580 destroyed the tomb (*Enfances*, 361).

5132: A *chevron* is a bar across a shield. The bar often has an angle pointing toward the top, but the chevron can take several forms (*A Glossary. . .Heraldry*, 105).

5133: A *tressure* is a narrow border (*Dictionary. . .Chivalry*, 224, 332).

5471: Henry tells us in a note that the forest of *Soignes* is near Brussels *(Enfances*, 363) and in the glossary that this form is used on account of the rhyme (381).

5473: Henry's glossary identifies *Tremoigne* as "Dortmund (Westphalia)" and notes that the form of the word is used for rhyming purposes (*Enfances*, 381).

5540: Charlemagne's horse is whiter than a *fleur-de-lis,* an appealing comparison.

5640–5641: This is a typical comparison in *Enfances*: "His helmet was not worth a chestnut to him/Nor his hauberk a spider's web." See also **5783–6784.**

5557: Note the anti-Semitism reflected in the phrase "the perfidious Jews."

5586: The city of *Langres (Lengres)* is in the Champagne-Ardennes region.

5639: Henry identifies *Sartaigne* as a "pagan country" (*Enfances*, 381)

5646: "Who afterward drank neither beer nor wine." This image helps bring a realization of the person's death.

5739–5742: Note that the high praise given to Duke Thierri includes his appreciation of poets, musicians and tellers of tales—people like Adenet.

5827: The word *avenged* here is actually *bought* in the Old French. *Bought* is used in the sense of making the enemy pay by fighting on the battlefield.

6035: At this desperate point in the battle, Namles invokes Saint George, the patron saint of soldiers, who may have been a soldier himself and at any rate was martyred in Palestine about 303 in the persecution of Diocletian and Maximian. He represents the ideal of Christian chivalry and became the patron saint of England. Richard I put his crusading army under Saint George's protection. The story of Saint George and the dragon comes from a collection of saints' lives first put together about 1260 by Jacobus Voragine called *The Golden Legend*, which relates that the dragon was a scourge of the countryside and had required two sheep a day to appease him. The supply of sheep having dwindled, human victims were chosen by lot. One day, the chosen victim was the king's daughter, who dressed herself as a bride to meet her death. Saint George intervened, ran the dragon through with his sword and led him off using the princess's girdle (belt). (*Oxford. . .Saints*, 166–167).

6414: *Hesbignon warriors* were from the Belgian province of Hesbaye.

6174: The words *speaking unintelligibly* translate *Bretonnant,* which would refer to language spoken in Bretagne, where the tongue was Celtic, not French. Adenet plays with the word *Breton* in writing *Bretonnant.*

6498: In his glossary Henry identifies *Orcanie* as a "Saracen country" (*Enfances*, 380).

6724: The Old French for *Main Gate* in this line is *Porte Majour.* It is tempting to call it the *Porta Maggiore*, but the details given in the poem are too vague to make this identification positive. Some gates built by the ancient Romans had interiors with multiple floors and windows. It is apparently within such a gate that Gloriande and company take refuge.

6790: *Saint Remi,* or *Remigius,* who became bishop of Reims as a young man, is famous for having baptized Clovis, King of the Franks (481–511). Saint Remi founded bishoprics and churches in northern France and southern Flanders. He died January 13, 533 *(Oxford. . .Saints*, 341).

6841–6842: These two lines end with words that are spelled the same but have different meanings (*amer, amer*), an apparent play on words.

6978: Ogier has been depicted in other works as "a giant who overwhelms all he strikes."

7067: The Pope's name is given as *Desiier* for the rhyme. The Popes during Charlemagne's reign were Stephen IV, Adrian I and St. Leo III.

7173: The phrase *arms of God* refers to the Pope's traditional coat of arms.

7295–7296: The sense of immediacy is enhanced by this description of the weather.

7482–7489: These lines are an expression of admiration for this princess by one who respects entirely the fact that she belongs to another. They are also a classic courtly expression of rapturous feeling for a lady and willingness to do heroic deeds for her.

7799: Largesse as a lordly trait is important in medieval French literature and culture.